"HOWARD POWER*less*"

By Paul A. Luscombe

The Rise & Fall of the Howard Savings Bank

Paul A Luscombe

ISBN #: 0-9704372-1-8

Published by the
PAL Publishing Company
Chatham NJ 07928

April 2003

Printed in the United States of America

Table of Contents

Key Dates in the History of the Howard Savings Bank

Year	Event
1857	Howard Savings Bank receives charter from state of New Jersey
1929	Bank forms Trust Department
1944	John Kress suggests move from long U.S. Treasury bonds to common stocks
1961	John Kress named President and Chief Executive Officer
1967	City of Newark riots and subsequently experiences mass exodus
1974	Bruce Alexander forced to resign; Murray Forbes chosen CEO
1974	Donald McCormick hired by Howard as Vice President of planning
1977	McCormick and Leo Rogers named EVPs and directors
1979	Howard moves its administrative offices from Newark to Livingston, New Jersey
1982	McCormick elected CEO of the Howard; Rogers in no. 2 slot as president
1983	Howard sells 5,850,000 shares of IPO at $15 per share

1987	In January, Howard board votes 100% stock dividend (2 for 1 split). Later in September, stock trades at historic high 38 1/8.
10/19/87	Largest single day decline in the history of the New York Stock Exchange
12/12/89	Howard announces loan losses resulting in $65 million loss for QIV 89 and total loss for the year 1989.
1990	Donald McCormick forced to resign in January; Leo Rogers assumes post of acting CEO. Initial search produces leadership of Vice Chairman of the Board Donald Peterson. Last dividend on Howard common stock paid in February.
1991	Howard Board selects Bill Tuggle (from First Fidelity Bank) as CEO
1992	Commissioner of banking issues "Cease and Desist Order" which closes the Howard
2001	Donald Peterson dies on Flight 93 on September 11, 2001

Acknowledgments

The sudden demise of the Howard Savings Bank had always mystified me, and so in the capacity of my "second career" as an author, I set out to find the causes of this bizarre economic phenomenon. As a bond salesman who covered the bank for various Wall Street firms for over 30 years, my investigation started with the investment department. Walter Hislop, who logged over 50 years at the bank, was my first official interviewee. John Quinn and Richard Donnelly likewise contributed a great deal of insight into the operation of the bank. Quinn's annual report file was key to maintaining the continuity of the entire story. Frank Buckworth cited the experience of over 25 years with the bank. Bob Turrill was vigorous in his detailing of the student loan operation and the operation of his consumer credit department. Todd Tripucka also supplied some stories about the Howard in the mid-1980s.

Donald Kress, my college fraternity brother, gave me human interest stories about his father, as did Charley Forbes and his dad. Savings bankers from other than the Howard pitched in, and included Arlyn Rus, Fred Scheidig, Ted Doll, Charley Smith, Kevin Ward and Jim Kranz to name but a few. Sam Damiano, executive director of the New Jersey Counsel of Savings Bankers, assisted with the project.

On the commercial bank side, David Dickinson and Dick Nicholson detailed some of the operations of the First Fidelity Bank. Bill Tuggle praised the Howard bank's employees for their relentless attempt to bring the bank back to life. Jim Hanna and Denny Smith, both of Ryan Beck & Co., helped me compile background information on the period.

During the summer of 2002, I utilized two interns from Lafayette College to help me research the story. Lauren Frese, who was voted the outstanding graduate of

Lafayette for the Class of 2003, and Ryan Shaffer, who graduated magna cum laude, provided strong motivational support during this project. Emily Groves and Terel Klein, both interns from Lafayette in the Class of 2005, helped me wrap up the final details.

My limitations on mobility and hand-writing were at least neutralized by assistance from my close friends Doug Hobby, Ken Thompson, Raymond Monroe, Bob and Chuck Faig, and Vin Morris.

Cinnie and Paul Luscombe of Halsey Stuart & Co. plus Pam and Don Kress of Goodbody & Co. attending the New Jersey Bankers Convention in Atlantic City in May, 1965. Kress' father was president of the Howard from 1961–1970.

Foreword: The U.S. Economy

1979–1992
by Jeffrey J. Keating

Jeffrey Keating is an investment counselor who formed his own advisory firm in 1983. Previously, he headed the Trust Department of the First Bank & Trust Company of Boynton Beach, Florida, where he managed the trust investments of the A.P. Luscombe estate. He has an undergraduate degree from the University of Florida and did graduate studies toward an MBA at Florida Atlantic University.

The U.S. economy during thirteen wild years was transformed from an economy of low productivity, high inflation and stagnant living standards into one of the most dynamic economies of the 20th Century. As a result, the period 1979 through 1992 became one of the most exciting yet turbulent economic periods in the two hundred year history of the United States.

The period began with the U.S. economy firmly in the grip of double digit inflation. Oil prices continued to soar as OPEC exercised its muscle. Interest rates were approaching the unheralded level of 10%. Yet overall economic activity remained strong with corporate profits rising 25% in 1979 and stock prices continued to climb in spite of the economists' forecasts that a recession was just around the corner.

Paul Volcker, chairman of the Federal Reserve, drove short-term interest rates still higher in 1980 in an attempt to break inflation. Interest rates of 11% and 12% were now available on long-term US Treasury bonds. The American public was in the mood for change. As a result, a somewhat unknown actor by the name of Ronald Reagan was elected President. President Reagan ran on a platform calling for a 30% tax cut, a smaller government, increased defense spending and unabated pride in America.

Although interest rates dipped for a short period in 1980, they were still on the rise. The US dollar, which was the weakest major currency during the 1970s, began to rise and continued to rise sharply in step with interest rates. By early 1982 Paul Volcker's Fed had engineered a peak in the Fed funds rate and the Prime Rate of just over 20%.

Inflation within six months of this peak declined sharply from 12% annualized to the 4% level. Interest rates also began to decline, but the economy was already in the deepest recession since the Great Depression. Unemployment, by 1982 was above 10% for the first time in 50 years.

As a result of the high inflation years of the 1970s and the first few years of the1980s, virtually no one owned common stocks. It was widely recognized that the average share price of a company sold at a sharp discount to the replacement value of the plant and equipment represented by that share. Michael Milken, an unknown investment banker at Drexel Burnham Lambert, shortly revolutionized the corporate bond market. Milken's genius for corporate bond financing combined with the greed of corporate raiders and leveraged buy out firms quickly launched the strategy of buying the whole company, rather than just a few shares.

A great bull market for stocks began in August 1982 and within six months prices had risen 55%, even though corporate profits were still depressed from the recession. Many believed it was simply too many inflated dollars from the 1970s chasing a limited number of shares that drove stock prices higher.

In 1984, the U.S. experienced strong growth, 6.7% real GDP, low inflation of only 4.2%, declining unemployment down to 7.2% and a rising dollar, up 16%. The US dollar, in five short years, rose 76% as a result of the high real interest rates that now prevailed in the US. However, all was not right. The Reagan tax cuts combined with increased defense spending and a strong dollar had produced the twin deficits in the balance of trade and fiscal budget.

By early 1983 the overseas central banks were so concerned with the U.S. soaring trade deficit that the G-5, later to become the G-7, decided in late 1985 to lower the dollar through coordinated intervention in global currency markets, i.e., the Plaza Accord. Michael Milken and his use of debentures which became known as junk bonds to many, were in full swing, as Drexel's investment bankers criss-crossed the country putting one company after another in play, either as a merger candidate to a bigger competitor or as a candidate for a leveraged buy out.

The Federal Reserve continued to keep short-term interest rates high, usually above the rates on five and ten year bonds. This created major problems for financial institutions as their securities portfolios could not earn enough to pay depositors the interest they were receiving on certificates of deposit. However, the savings and loan industry found a solution for this investment problem as a result of loose regulatory rules. Savings and Loans became the biggest buyers of Drexel's junk bonds.

Congress began to tinker with the ballooning double-digit fiscal deficits, passing the Gramm-Rudman deficit reduction bill. The bull market for stocks continued with the Dow Jones Industrial Average passing 1600, 1700, 1800, and 1900 during 1986. Inflation was now down to 2%, partially as a result of the 50% decline in oil prices. Signs of forthcoming problems in the real estate markets were on the horizon. As a result of low farm prices, partially the result of the strong dollar, it was estimated that 60%-70% of the farm loans held by the Federal Farm Credit Bank were now in default.

The popular President Reagan pushed through the Tax Reform Act of 1986. With this legislation Reagan cut the highest marginal income tax bracket from 70% in 1982 to 28% by 1987. To help pay for this tax cut, passive losses on investments (primarily real estate related) were no longer deductible against ordinary income. This spelled the end of the tax shelter industry and looming problems for the banking industry.

The year 1987 was a roller coaster ride as the Dow Jones Industrial Average reached 2700 by August. Unfortunately, the coordinated efforts of the G-7 during 1985 and 1986 had broken down into outright squabbling between the Central Banks. The U.S. dollar was in a free fall as international investors worried about future inflation. The German Central Bank, always on the lookout for inflation, unexpectedly started to raise interest rates during the first quarter. The Federal Reserve, concerned by the falling dollar, started to match these rate increases. Between February and early October, interest rates rose 33% and once again reached the 10% level on U.S. Treasury bonds. By this time, most investment strategists felt stock prices were high. This, along with investors' belief that they could hedge their stock portfolio through the shorting of stock index futures, thus protecting themselves on the downside, precipitated the stock market crash of 1987. On that day, the Dow Jones Industrial Average fell 22%, and subsequently 37% over a period of seven weeks.

Housing starts declined 25% in the first quarter of 1988 as economists awaited the onset of the next recession which was sure to result from the stock market crash. The economy actually expanded at a moderate pace and the stock market stabilized during the year. Undoubtedly the stock market was helped by corporate share buy backs. During the period 1984 through 1988, one sixth of all the shares on the NYSE had been retired, representing cumulative corporate purchases of $500 billion.

Economic problems moved south of the border in early 1989 as a result of the looming debt defaults in Mexico and South America. The Brady Plan was instituted, whereby the U.S. Treasury and the American tax payers made direct loans to Mexico to meet debt repayments. The G-7 recognized their early shortcomings, worked together as a team to support global trade, and stabilized currency markets over the next twelve months.

The melt down of the savings and loan industry was in full swing by the summer of 1989. During the next two years nearly 1,000 financial institutions (savings and loans, mutual savings banks and commercial banks) would be closed. However painful this chapter was for the banking industry, it represented one of the final steps in the efficient re-allocation of capital, which would lead to a sharp rise in productivity over the next decade.

The U.S. stock market rose 27% in 1989. German re-unification was the highlight of 1990. However, the Iraqi invasion of Kuwait in the summer of 1990 doubled oil prices from $20 to $40 per barrel. The Federal Reserve Bank moved quickly to keep this oil shock from once again igniting inflation. The Coalition forces began bombing Iraq on January 16, 1991 and the stock market began to move higher. The U.S. economy experienced a short six month recession followed by a very gradual recovery which would become the longest business expansion in history.

Introduction:

The Power of Savings

July 30, 1938
Glen Ridge, NJ

On the day I was born (July 30, 1938), my father opened a passbook savings account for me at the Howard Savings Bank. Schooled in the economics of the Great Depression, my father impressed upon me the importance of savings as soon as I had a minimal understanding of money matters. He also encouraged me to invest in "blue chip" stocks such as Standard Oil of NJ (now Exxon-Mobil Corp) and the Ford Motor Company. It didn't matter that I was an "odd lot" buyer and literally bought shares one at a time. Any dividends from such investments were immediately deposited in the Howard Savings account. Just before entering Lafayette College in 1956, I worked 6 days a week as a dishwasher at the Normandy Inn in Normandy Beach NJ. Again, my father urged me to save 30% of my earnings before I spent my wages on the movies or adding to my record collection. Also, he restrained me from using my savings for a specific need such as a new car or an upscale phonograph. To save was a virtue, an end unto itself.

My father's name was Albert P. Luscombe, and when I was born, my parents inverted his name to produce mine, Paul Albert Luscombe. As the years went by, I always enjoyed my PAL initials. At any rate, in my early youth, I was indeed exposed to the world of banking. In 1946, when I was in 3rd grade at the Yantacaw School in Nutley NJ, I was surprised one day to see my Dad's picture on the bulletin board noting current events. It was included in a newspaper clipping telling how my father had just been elected Executive Vice President of the Peoples Bank of Belleville NJ. I distinctly remember Miss

Hill, my teacher, stressing to the class what an important job that was! I later found out that the title of executive vice president encompassed a wide range of responsibilities, including the chief lending officer, the main investment guy, and the only trust officer. Other than the Chief Executive Officer, he also was the only bank representative on the board of directors.

My father's best friends were all bank presidents. Archie Barbeta of the Bank of Nutley, Frank Steyert of the Millburn-Short Hills Bank, and Otis Beaton of the Hudson Trust Company were frequently at our house which encompassed cocktails, dinner out, and then a game of cards. Perhaps a result of the Great Depression, my father was the only one of this group who had any children. They all wanted to convey to me any advice they had about the banking industry. In many respects, I was like a "surrogate son."

Frank Steyert, who I referred to as "Uncle Frank", was probably the craftiest of them all. His specialty was founding a bank, building it as a viable business entity, and then selling it to an acquisition minded institution. He also attempted to turn around problem banks. For example, he founded the South Orange Trust Company, which he sold to Howard Savings Bank—their first move outside of Newark. He bought the Hudson County National Bank , cleaned up the debris, and resold the bank at a profit. His favorite project was founding the Millburn-Short Hills Bank , building a franchise, and subsequently selling to the Midlantic.

Oddly enough, the three bank presidents advised me not to go into banking as they anticipated the day when only a few large banks would dominate the financial landscape. They were right, but I don't think they foresaw that it would take over 50 years to materialize.

Furthermore, for many years, my parents took me to the New Jersey Bankers Convention in Atlantic City. In 1946, my mother bought me a high powered water pistol which I used to fill at the fountain of the Chalfonte-

Haddon Hall[1] and ultimately decorated the bank presidents as they were en route to meetings and such. Later in life, as a professional on Wall Street trying to do business with these gentlemen, they often reminded me of my impish deeds as a youth.

Soon, Dad was elected President of the bank. He was a bank president who firmly believed in the product his industry provided. In the case of my passbook account, he felt the Howard represented a form of infrastructure capable of generating the power of compound interest. Although I understood the math, I intuitively identified the brick and mortar of the Howard with my bank account more than with any mathematical formula. The presence of the Howard in the community, in Essex County and the State of New Jersey added to this mystique. Advertising campaigns later labeled depositors as being HOWARD POWERED!

Understanding the sophisticated nuances of how the Bank managed its investment and loan portfolios would come later in my life. At the time, I was aware that the bank did more with the money it took from its depositors than stash it in a gigantic cookie jar.

To a certain extent, my father was a "profit of doom" as he dwelled on the many bank failures that resulted from the Great Depression. He frequently cited inadequate Government bond portfolios (i.e., liquidity) as the source of these failures. He showed me photographs of bank depositors lined up around the block seeking to withdraw their funds from fragile banks during the 1930s. Given his emphasis on personal savings, I am convinced he felt the Great Depression was a segment of a long duration business cycle which would someday again wreak havoc on the economy. The virtue of savings implied accumulating a nest egg sufficient to weather any economic storm.

---

[1]Chalfonte Haddon Hall became Atlantic City's first casino in 1978 and was called The Resorts Casino Hotel.

On March 5, 1933, in the wake of the many bank failures during the Depression, President Franklin D. Roosevelt called for the infamous "Bank Holiday" whereby the nation's banks closed for four days. Effective immediately, the surprise announcement was made on a Sunday, thereby closing the flow of currency until that Friday. Bank depositors were left little or no time to plan their funds for routine activities. My father told me that the act put the banks in a bad light and was probably counterproductive. In his eyes, the "Bank Holiday" further exaggerated the faltering system and was deemed a failure. From a longer term point of view, the act did lead to the creation of the Federal Deposit Insurance Corporation. My father never spoke very highly of FDR.

When I entered Lafayette College in 1956, the school had an all-male enrollment and a fraternity system which pervaded most activities. Within days of stepping foot on campus, after making the rounds as part of the formal rush program, I selected Delta Tau Delta. Among my early advisors on the social scene at Lafayette, upperclassman Donald Kress of Verona NJ picked me to be his "little brother".[2] At the time, neither of us were aware of the other's family background—we just had a lot of fun together! We never brought up the matter of "Faith in the Banking System" or other critical subject matters. Later on in life, Don would discover that my Dad was President of the Peoples Bank in Belleville NJ while his father was President of the Howard Savings Bank.

After graduating from Lafayette in 1960 with a BA in Philosophy, I entered the Wharton Graduate School (University of Pennsylvania) in pursuit of my Masters Degree in Business Administration. During the summer break, I

---

[2]Ray Carey, then treasurer of the fraternity, was also instrumental in my selection of DTD. At the time of this writing, he was Chairman of the Board of the Boiling Springs Savings & Loan Association in Rutherford, NJ. His wife to-be (Margot Nelson) was a waitress at the Normandy Inn.

upgraded my job experience from dishwasher to that of a clerk in the municipal bond department of the First National State Bank in Newark, NJ. I quickly discovered that I loved working with bonds—in certain respects my passbook account was like a miniature bond—and before long I fashioned myself as an expert on the municipal bond market. For those who would listen, I could recite the various ratings (both Moody's and S&P) of the 21 New Jersey counties from memory. My boss was Alexander Seidler, one of the most well-respected bond professionals of the era. Tony Butera and Jack Carpenter let me observe all their activities, listen in on their telephone conversations, and were excellent teachers of the business. Karl Farnow taught me how to research municipal bond credits, and even sent me on a mission to the Department of State & Local Governments in Trenton NJ. Once I returned to Wharton in the fall, I was so pumped up about bonds that I wrote my required Masters thesis on a comparison of the municipal bond markets of California, Connecticut and New Jersey. Among the members of the MBA class of 1962, only one other candidate wrote his thesis on a fixed income subject, Preferred Stocks. All the others at Wharton wrote their theses on equity topics.

Upon graduation from Wharton, I hit the job market confident that I would find a position in the municipal bond industry. Because of my passion for writing, I initially sought a position in the bond research departments of various municipal underwriters. I also had an interview with *The Wall Street Journal,* but their only opening at the time was as an elevator operator. When Mr. Seidler learned of my interest in municipal research, he strongly advocated that I consider becoming a bond salesman instead. My father and other confidants reinforced the idea. My resume was revised accordingly. On January 3, 1963 I accepted a position with Halsey, Stuart & Co., Inc.—one of the nation's leading municipal and corporate bond underwriters for the first 75 years of the 20th Century. The Halsey Stuart name was continuously on top of the *Bond Buyer List of Managing Underwriters.*

One of the influential executives involved with the sales training program was Paul Van Doren, who recommended that I take over for the two retiring Halsey salesmen (Jim Gustat and Jay Richardson) covering the major institutions in northern New Jersey. I jumped at the opportunity to work with Mr. Van Doren (we all called him "PVD") and to have such a fertile sales territory to start my career.

My father was very supportive of my choice of employer and my entry level position on Wall Street. His main recommendation was that I construct a personal budget and continue to save a significant portion of my paycheck. He suggested that I save 30% of my take-home pay. This came right off the top before all else.

With the exception of two rather large insurance accounts, my client base was distinctly dominated by banks. Every commercial bank and every mutual savings bank located within the Federal Reserve District of NY was fair game for my cultivation. For years I would spend hours on end waiting in the lobbies of banks. For the commercial banks, I attended many of their annual stockholder meetings. After the 1980s and demutualization, I attended the MSB annual meetings as well. Although a bond specialist in the securities industry, I constantly sought to upgrade my general knowledge of the banking business.

The Halsey Stuart management urged me to focus on the existing clients of the firm, and I was delighted to learn that the Howard Savings Bank was on the list. In a matter of weeks, at age 25, I was scheduled for an appointment to meet John H. Duerk, senior investment officer of the Howard Savings Bank.

I retrieved some old textbooks from Wharton and brushed up on the subjects relating to commercial banking, trust department operations, and some general economic theory. The most important was a course entitled _The Federal Reserve System_ which was flawlessly taught by Dr. A.I. Bloomfield. As I would learn in my unfolding bond career, investors were always asking the question, "What's the Fed doing?" Paying attention to my father's dinner discussions and the lectures of Dr. Bloomfield gave me a strong foundation in this regard.

As I waited in the lobby to see Mr. Duerk, I was awestruck by being so close to the pulse of the largest savings bank in the state. I found it amazing that I would soon become a part of the process of how that little blue passbook in my desk drawer at home found its way into the securities markets.

John H. Duerk was a tough-looking man, who peered at you over his rimless glasses with a somewhat skeptical demeanor. Since I was replacing a retiring salesman (Jim Gustat) and because of his familiarity with the support activities of Paul Van Doren, it probably helped me "break the ice" with Mr. Duerk more easily than I had anticipated. Before long, Mr. Duerk became "Jack Duerk" and we enjoyed a long relationship of buyer-salesman until he retired in 1970.

I often thought of the Howard's illustrious history and its position within the industry. Throughout most of my association with the Howard Savings Bank, I always regarded it as a paradigm of strength. It was the largest in the state with its $5.2 billion in assets (1988 annual report) and ranked 7th nationally among the mutuals. Its seventy-five full service branches gave it visibility statewide. Prior to the banking laws of 1980, it had built its reputation on a "plain vanilla" business plan. The Howard, for most of its existence, took in retail deposits, paid retail rates and earned a handsome spread by investing in a diversified portfolio of high-grade securities and residential mortgages. The strong trust department added to the Howard's profile and probably gave it an edge over its New Jersey counterparts. Indeed, at this early stage in my business career, I was proud to cover the Howard for a managing underwriting firm such as Halsey Stuart & Co.[3] As an ambitious young salesman, I set out to cover *all* the commercial and savings banks in the

---

[3]Cite obituary for A.I. Bloomfield in the *New York Times*.

Arthur I. Bloomfield

A. I. Bloomfield, 84, Economist and Author

By KENNETH N. GILPIN

Arthur I. Bloomfield, an economist, author and educator, died on Oct. 6 at the Maplewood Park Place Nursing Center in Bethesda, Md., from degenerative neurologic disease, his wife, Dorothy, said. He was 84 and lived in Bethesda.

A specialist in international trade and finance, Mr. Bloomfield wrote many books on the topic, including "Capital Imports and the U.S. Balance of Payments" (1950), "Monetary Policy under the International Gold Standards, 1880-1914" and "Essays in the History of International Trade Theory" (1994).

A native of Montreal, Mr. Bloomfield received his bachelor's and master's degrees from McGill University.

After graduating from the Univer-

A specialist, he 1998 helped Koreans lay the foundation for a central bank.

sity of Chicago in 1942 with a doctorate in economics, he joined the staff of the Federal Reserve Bank of New York, where he was a senior economist and consultant until 1958.

From 1949 to 1950, while at the New York Fed, Mr. Bloomfield served as a financial adviser to the Bank of Korea, helping to create the foundation of the country's central bank in the postwar world. He later

served as a financial adviser to the Korean Ministry of Finance and the United Nations Korean Reconstruction Agency.

In 1958, Mr. Bloomfield left the New York Fed to accept a teaching post at the University of Pennsylvania.

He remained a member of the economics faculty there until he retired in 1985. During that period, he was also a visiting professor at a number of institutions, including Columbia and Princeton Universities and the University of Melbourne in Australia.

Mr. Bloomfield is survived by his wife, the former Dorothy E. Reese; a sister, Harriet Joseph of Scarsdale N.Y.; a stepson, Alan Reese of Memphis; five nephews, and four nieces

Northern corridor of New Jersey. Following Mr. Van Doren's advice, I spent a lot of time calling on the banks personally as well as attending many conferences, conventions, seminars and outings and such. Over time, I got to know Jack Duerk fairly well. When he retired in 1970, my new contact at the bank was Walter Hislop.

In contrast to Jack Duerk's "tough guy" image, Walt Hislop had a more studious or research-oriented approach. Walt had joined the bank at age 17 and retired at age 70 in 1990. He earned both his undergraduate degree (Seton Hall University) and his masters degree (Rutgers University) at night. Walter and I became members of the

Money Marketeers of NYU and we attended many of their functions together. Walter joined the Bond Club of New Jersey in 1962 and I joined in 1964. For over twenty years, Walter and I played golf as part of a continuing foursome at the BCNJ outings. The other two members of the group were Dave Dickinson and Dick Nicholson , veteran trust investment officers from the First National State Bank NJ. My friendship with Walter brought me even closer to the inner operations of the Howard bank.

When I originally set out to cover New Jersey's banks, I soon learned that the various types of banking institutions differed as to their type of ownership, their investment powers, and their regulatory environment, to mention just a few. Commercial banks were owned by their stockholders, whereas mutual savings banks and savings and loan associations were owned by their depositors. Commercial banks emphasized commercial and consumer lending while the thrifts were largely excluded from this area. S&Ls exhibited a more limited appetite for corporate bonds, and used governments and federal agencies only as a liquidity reserve. S&Ls were almost entirely invested in the mortgage arena.

Roughly two-thirds of a mutual savings bank's assets were held in the form of residential mortgages, mostly of a local variety, thereby servicing their own territory. For the balance of funds available, mutual savings banks had broad investment powers. Governments, agencies, corporates and municipals were fair game. They also could invest a limited portion of their surplus in the common stock market. Commercial banks could buy common stocks in their holding companies but not in their operating banks. Some commercial banks owned common stocks before 1933 and they were "grandfathered" on these holdings.

In the early 1980s, many mutual savings banks in New Jersey and along the East Coast of the United States began the process of converting from their depositor owned charter to one owned by shareholders, a process dubbed "demutualization". The process effectively transferred the ownership from its depositors to its shareholders in the form of an *initial public offering.* Existing depositors and members of the community served by the issuing bank had first crack at these offerings, the vast majority of which were instant successes in the marketplace. In effect, the bank went from the status of "absentee ownership" by a disconnected group of depositors to an identifiable group of entrepreneurs looking for some market appreciation on their investment. The Morris County Savings Bank and the Howard were two early entries in the New Jersey market, and their issues performed extremely well. The HWRD stock, which came to market in 1983 at $15 per share, traded as high as 38 1/4 in 1987.

But for the fourth quarter of 1988, the bank reported a loss of $65 million and the stock tumbled accordingly. Over the course of the 1980s, the bank had moved substantial funds into the risky area of commercial real estate lending. Through mid-1986, these loans paid handsome rates and were a significant contributor to the Howard's earnings.

In 1986 the Congress passed the Tax Reform Act which eliminated the deductibility of mortgage interest on second or luxury homes. Construction loans designed to finance these dwellings were suddenly in jeopardy as demand sputtered in the wake of this legislation. Permanent funding so critical to the construction loan process failed to materialize and many construction loans remained outstanding on their anticipated repayment or maturity dates. Banks holding such paper had to report such loans as "non-performing assets". As a major player in the construction loan area, the Howard saw its earnings prospects evaporate quickly and its stock price tumbled accordingly.[4]

Ron Kulik graduated from Nutley (NJ) High School with me in 1956, and was infatuated with the potential positive market action of the HWRD shares. A graduate of

---

[4]HWRD was the over-the-counter securities market symbol for the Howard Savings Bank common stock.

Montclair State University, Ron was thwarted five times as he sought to make the United States Olympic team as a race walker during the 1960s and 1970s. His best performance was a 5th place finish in the 1972 heats, but his lifelong goal of participating in the games went unfulfilled. Ron taught physical education and drivers education for 26 years at Montclair (NJ) High School. Ron became excited about the HWRD common stock in the middle of the 1980s and he bought a bundle of the HWRD stock. At one point, he held 26,000 shares. Feeling the initial reports of the Howard's weakness were temporary or an aberration, he was soon locked into the shares when the HWRD shares took such a precipitous decline. Ron lost over $80,000 of his life's savings during the episode.

For others like Ron Kulik and for members of the Howard staff, I felt a deep sense of compassion. For the over 1,000 employees who participated in the HWRD stock, they faced not only market losses but the unemployment line as well.

On a personal basis, I briefly owned the HWRD shares but sold them in mid-1987 to free up funds to participate in the Harmonia Savings Bank new issue. My intentions were to flip the Harmonia stock and reinvest in the HWRD shares. During that time-span, the negative news on the Howard intensified and I never reentered the HWRD market. As I was taught by Marshall Houx, one of my mentors at Halsey Stuart & Co, sometimes, in the game of investments, it is better to be "lucky than smart"!

Nonetheless, my Howard passbook savings account had grown substantially over the years, even after initially financing the purchase of our first home in 1967. Later, as my disciplined savings program grew into a nest egg of some significance, I seemed to experience an element of financial independence compared with my more consumption oriented peers. But the days of my blue passbook account were over. Once a powerful force in the New Jersey market-place, the Howard Savings bank quietly folded into the deposit mix of the First Fidelity Bank, never to be seen again.

The context of this book will examine the history of the Howard Savings, the reasons for its strength for the majority of its 135 year history, the problems it faced in transferring power from one CEO to another, and the causes of its sudden demise in the deregulatory climate of the 1980s.

Hopefully, the value of savings as a virtue will live on.

Part One:

"They were great people. The Howard was a great bank."

—Bruce Alexander, Retired President
Greenfield, Massachusetts
June 26, 2003

The Rise of the Howard Savings Bank

1857–1982

Chapter 1

The History of the Howard Savings Bank: The Newark Factor

"Your bank for life."

—Slogan from Howard Savings Bank
1985 Annual Report

October 2, 1992
Livingston, New Jersey

From his office atop the Howard Savings Bank complex, William Tuggle eyed the procession of stark vehicles wending its way down the road toward the bank entrance. In his brief tenure as chief executive officer of the bank, he had worked long hours hoping to fortify the surplus account of the weakened financial institution. A multitude of last-ditch efforts had produced somewhat stronger capital ratios and had given the Tuggle management team some hope that they might rescue the bank. But seeing the somber caravan approach the bank brought home the reality—his program to save the bank was probably a case of too little, too late.

Tuggle watched as the lead car of the caravan came to a halt by the fountain in the Murray Forbes Plaza, an area built in honor of the Howard CEO between 1974–1982. The cars in the caravan contained varying signs of identity. Those with license plates marked "FFB" carried representatives of the First Fidelity Bank. The other vehicles had subtle markings indicating they ware FDIC or state of New Jersey sponsored. Once in position, the cars sat with their engines idling, essentially waiting for the signal to move into the bank.

Unknown to Bill Tuggle, Steve Szabatin—the deputy commissioner of banking of the state of New Jersey—had covertly preceded the caravan by 15 to 20 minutes. He drove alone in an unmarked state vehicle, which state officials dubbed a "confidential car." The deputy drove an inconspicuous 1987 Dodge Aries K and parked somewhat out of view. As he waited for the caravan to arrive, he quickly calculated that he must have closed almost 50 banks—mostly thrifts—over a five-year span (1987–1992). Most of the operations were local franchises and resulted in little emotional involvement on his part. But today was different. Almost $5 billion in deposits was about to change hands. Potentially 800 of the bank's 1,200 employees were about to lose their jobs, either immediately or in the near future. Roughly 17,000 shareholders winced as Howard common stock traded at 37 cents per share. The deputy checked his watch. At 2:30 P.M., he was within 30 minutes of closing the Howard Savings Bank, one of the state's oldest, most popular, and certainly the largest mutual in the state. Today, he would have to work extra hard to maintain the "business as usual" demeanor expected of his position.

Because of the fortress of the Howard headquarters and the seventy branch operations around the state, the mission of closing the bank involved extensive planning and somewhat resembled a military invasion of another country. For several weeks, the state department of banking was convinced that the Howard's financial cancer was terminal and so steps were taken early on to effectuate a smooth closure.

For example, two weeks prior to Szabatin's mission, he had dispatched P. T. "Pete" Steffens, a bank examiner from his department, to the Howard site. Performing the role of a forward observer, Pete's job was to monitor the bank's activities and to watch for any "unusual" activity such as a possible run on the bank. He set up shop in the reception area adjacent to the executive offices. He was joined in his efforts by James Feeney, who performed a similar function for the Federal Deposit Insurance Corporation. Ultimately, Steffens planned to rendezvous with Szabatin. Steffens had the specific responsibility of withdrawing the Howard's charter originally granted in 1857. In effect, he was the designated executioner.

The banking department even made contingency plans in the event their deputy was somehow delayed or injured en route to the closing. A duplicate set of the documents that Szabatin would read was carried by an agent in one of the caravan vehicles.

As Szabatin moved from his vehicle toward the entrance to the bank, he was joined by another official who Szabatin surmised to be the attorney representing the FDIC. After passing through a series of glass doors, Szabatin and the attorney finally made their way toward the reception or security area. While they proceeded, their shoes caused a slight echoing sound which reverberated throughout the lobby.

Szabatin nodded to the receptionist and introduced himself. "We are here to see Mr. Tuggle."

Many vendors sought the business of the bank. But today, Friday, October 2, 1992, was not a typical day at the bank. The receptionist knew this was no Wall Street bond salesman seeking the ear of the president. She politely responded, "I will tell Mr. Tuggle that you are here and I am sure he will be right with you. Won't you take a seat?"

Relieved they needed no further introduction or explanation, Szabatin and the attorney both nodded and remained standing.

The receptionist quickly used the "hot line," connecting her desk with the president's inner office. Upon hearing Mr. Tuggle's voice, she informed him that the two officials were in the lobby.

Tuggle replied, "Hilda will be there in a second and she will show them to my office." "Hilda" Costanza was

Tuggle's executive secretary, held the title of "vice president," and had served all the Howard CEOs dating back to John Kress. Tuggle checked his watch. The time was 2:45 P.M.

When the pair arrived at Tuggle's office, they were immediately joined by Steffens, who had been working nearby in his temporary office. The mood was somber as introductions and handshakes were extended in a businesslike manner. There was no need for another layer of protocol. Tuggle offered the men seats, but they remained standing. They somehow resembled the gunmen of a firing squad.

While waiting for the discussions to start, P. T. Steffens eyed the endless array of pictures in Tuggle's office and nearby he could see even more photographs depicting the long history of the Howard Bank. The picture of Frederick Frelinghuysen, president of the bank from 1887 to 1902 and a relative of Congressmen Peter and Rod Frelinghuysen, added to his warm feelings about the Howard. As a professional in the financial industry, Steffens understood the forces that undermined the Howard. To many in the state of New Jersey, the Howard was like family. Nonetheless, he held back any outward signs of emotion.

Although admitting to a modicum of "feelings," Deputy Szabatin was more accustomed to the routine. Many banks had succumbed between 1987 and 1992. To a degree, it was just another day at the office, and he spoke methodically as if he were mouthing a recording. He read the following from a prepared text.

"I am Steve Szabatin representing the state of New Jersey Department of Banking. Joining me is P. T. Steffens, examiner of the state of New Jersey. At 3:00 P.M. today, Mr. Steffens will take back the charter granted the bank in 1857 and all the terms of the cease and desist order become effective at that time." The deputy further mentioned that the order had been signed and submitted by the commissioner of banking Jeff Connor, becoming effective October 2, 1992 at 3:00 P.M. The governor of New Jersey was James Florio.

As Tuggle digested the deputy's statements, he noticed the time again. The bank, known as the Howard Savings Bank, would be closed by executive fiat in a matter of minutes.

A veteran of over 40 years in banking in New Jersey, Bill Tuggle realized the finality of the facts just presented to him. His plans to shore up the capital position of the once proud and powerful Howard Savings Bank would go unfulfilled. Although Tuggle instinctively sensed the answers to his next questions, he innocently asked, "What happens next?"

Without hesitation or emotion, Deputy Szabatin informed Tuggle that a number of actions would soon take place.

"The state of New Jersey has issued a press release announcing the closing of all of the Howard Savings Bank offices. As of 9:00 A.M. on Monday morning, all offices of the Howard will be reopened under the name of the First Fidelity Bank and all accounts will be transferred automatically unless otherwise instructed by the depositor."

Furthermore, Szabatin mentioned that every attempt would be made to effectuate a smooth transition to the First Fidelity depositor base. The state, above all, wanted to avoid a financial panic from occurring within its borders.

The grandfather clock quietly rang out in the reception area, indicating that it was 3 P.M.

Without further ceremony, Szabatin was on the phone with the lead vehicle of the caravan positioned in front of the bank. "Time to move in," he ordered to the driver, who then relayed the order to the remaining vehicles.

Within seconds, a veritable army of FDIC agents and First Fidelity representatives were moving out to preassigned locations within the bank. Simultaneously, similar actions were taken on a smaller scale at the Howard branches throughout the state of New Jersey. For the accountants, this marked the time the bank was officially closed. In essence, it was the point in time when the Howard's assets were valued and transferred to the books of the First Fidelity Bank. All records and properties had to be frozen in time, and this FDIC-FFB hit squad was there to make sure nothing was missing.

Some of the Howard personnel had received an advance call at about 2:30 P.M. that the FDIC-FFB convoy had been spotted in the vicinity of the Holiday Inn in nearby East Hanover. For a few members of the Howard team, the convoy's actions were well anticipated. For many of the Howard staff, usually relaxed and unaccustomed to any impolite leadership from its own management team, it was quite a change to be suddenly told to stay by their desks and sit still. No brutality took place, but the swift action of the "SWAT team" shocked the Howard employees. One female member of the Howard staff was particularly helpful to the "takeover committee" of the bank. Many thought that she might have been planted by the First Fidelity management to prevent any unauthorized pilferage. Soon, boxes were handed out enabling the Howard employees to pack and remove their personal belongings. Checkpoints were set up where the contents would be inspected.

The reality began to set in. The identity of the Howard Savings Bank, once the largest in the state of New Jersey, evaporated as if it never existed.

July 4th Weekend, 1978
Jenkinson's Pavilion
Point Pleasant, New Jersey

Jenkinson's Pavilion in Point Pleasant is one of the many public beaches along the Atlantic Ocean generally referred to by locals as "the shore." "The shore" stretches for approximately 105 miles from Sandy Hook to Cape May, and is frequented by many young college students on summer weekends as an escape from the hot humid weather typical of New Jersey.

On a sunny Saturday in July of 1978, the Banner Airlines division of Columbia Air Service was readying its fleet of World War II vintage airplanes to roll out the advertisements for the day. After take-off from the Monmouth Executive Airport in Wall Township (N.J.), these *Cesna Bird-Dog C-170s* were tooled to fly at around 50 miles per hour in order to make it easy for those on the ground to read their ribbon-like messages across the sky. At 2 P.M., Banner Airlines Flight no. 1 lifted off from the main runway at the small airport. This was prime tanning time and the WWII plane was quickly positioned over Jenkinson's Pavilion carrying a banner which told the readers about the opening of a new restaurant and the entertainment on tap for Saturday and Sunday night. About ten minutes later, Banner Airlines Flight no. 2 was in the air, and its upbeat message read as follows:

"INTEREST-FREE STUDENT LOANS AT THE
HOWARD SAVINGS"

Immediately, the Howard message reached its intended captive market, gaining the Howard a lot of recognition among the young sunbathers at Jenkinson's and beyond.

The cultivation of the student loan market by the Howard Savings Bank was a major undertaking by the bank. The Howard promoted its program with a large staff which maintained contact with the principals and guidance counselors from every high school in New Jersey. Many of these same representatives set up booths at "Back to School Nights" attended by students and parents. Although the bank had long been a supplier of funds in the student loan market, the promotional program of the mid-to-late 1970s accelerated its holdings and resulted in a portfolio of approximately $300 million of these relatively small loans. The Howard was the largest issuer of these loans in the State of New Jersey (ranked 8th in size among banks nationally) which solidified its stature within the thrift industry. Above all, the program illustrated the Howard's commitment to *servicing* the needs of its clients.

Actually, the concept of a "service-oriented" bank was at the heart of the Howard's foundation dating back

121 years to May 5, 1857. In the 1850s, there apparently existed a cleavage or class distinction among existing banks in Newark, and new settlers to the area were upset with the fact that their deposits were too small to matter to these institutions. Inspired by the organizational efforts of 27 local citizens, the Howard Savings Institution was created in Newark in May of 1857. Whereas most of the existing banks in Newark shunned smaller accounts, the Howard gained instant popularity for its willingness to accept *any deposit,* no matter how small. To the competition, these accounts were viewed as "intolerable nuisances." To the upstart Howard, they opened the door and over time created a foundation of "core depositors."[1]

Newark: The First 301 Years—Religious Freedom and Manfacturing

The historical gridlock symbolized by the Middle Ages and the dominance of the Catholic Church was effectively shattered by the actions of Martin Luther in 1517 when he tacked up his Ninety-Five Theses on the door of the church in Wittenberg, Germany. In his treatises, Luther openly criticized the use of "indulgences" which allowed the church to sell remission of their punishment to apparent sinners. Luther also denied the infallibility of the Pope and the church councils. When the church sent its ace debater, John Eck, to request Luther to retract his theories, Luther refused, and his "Here I Stand" response became a rallying cry setting the Protestant Reformation in full swing. The church's excommunication of Luther aggravated the turmoil as religious sects surfaced throughout Western Europe.

Ultimately, the religious unrest led to the settlement of Newark, New Jersey in 1666 by New England Puritans

---

[1]Cunningham, John T. *Newark.* Rev. ed. 1994. New Jersey Historical Society, pp. 123–124.

in search of religious freedom. The Puritans (who eventually became the Presbyterians) had initially broken away from the Roman Catholic Church and then from the Church of England, and were basically looking for an isolated location to practice their religion. At the time, Newark provided the setting as Puritans came from England, Connecticut, and Long Island to establish residency.

As time rolled by, the natural harbor of the Passaic River nurtured economic growth and enticed immigrants from Germany and Ireland to settle in the city. The original industries were leather tanning, brewing, and chemicals. Oddly enough, despite unbelievable change over three centuries, the initial location of the 1666 settlers—the four corners including Broad and Market Streets—has continued on as the center of town.

Even as the city matured as a predominantly industrialized entity, a theoretical snapshot of Newark's skyline in the 1830s would have illustrated the continuing influence of religion. No fewer than twelve church spires pervaded the city's landscape. Prominent among the church buildings were the Old First where the Puritans worshipped and the Trinity Cathedral at Military Park, the worshipping locale of the Episcopalians. Other religious denominations coexisted in the Newark setting, as Methodists and Baptists brought their faithful to the area. Immersion of the Baptists in the Passaic River was a startling practice to the other sects. The Methodists were also conspicuous with their loud singing and "fire and brimstone" sermons.

In 1844, the presidential election pitted Democrats James K. Polk and vice presidential candidate George M. Dallas against the Whig party nominee Henry Clay and his running mate Ted Frelinghuysen, who was then the Mayor of Newark. Clay, who had orchestrated the Missouri Compromise in 1820, was defeated in his fourth bid for the nation's highest office, probably as a result of his negative stance on accepting the Republic of Texas into statehood. Frelinghuysen proved to be an effective campaigner and was the first of a long line of the family name to be influential in Newark and New Jersey politics. Frederick Frelinghuysen was the third president of the Howard Savings Bank and held office from 1887–1902 and is credited with introducing the use of the telephone at the bank. In the 20th century, Peter H. B. Frelinghuysen served for over 25 years in the United States Congress and also sat on the Howard Savings Bank board during that period. In November 2002, Rodney Frelinghuysen was reelected to Congress in a generally strong showing by the Republican Party.

In 1856, James Buchanan was the first and only bachelor elected to be president of the United States. Buchanan's administration was torn by the issue of slavery and the resultant forces leading to the Civil War. When Abraham Lincoln was elected president in 1860, the state of South Carolina quickly seceded from the United States. The responsibility of immediately holding the country together belonged to Buchanan but was soon transferred to Lincoln. During the same period, wild speculation in western land and railroads brought on an economic panic. Many banks, railroads, and factories failed. Thousands of unemployed workers stood in line looking for free food. Amid all this turmoil, the Howard Savings Bank started doing business on May 5, 1857 and survived for 135 years.

The original founders of the Howard Savings Institution were inspired by the philanthropic deeds of John Howard (1726–1790). Howard spent most of his life investigating prisons and jails in England and in other countries. In a time when crime was more loosely defined and debtors' prisons were commonplace, John Howard sought to have the prison system not only in England but throughout the continent become more humane. John Howard constantly fought uphill battles against local authorities, but in 1774 his message broke through when he published a pamphlet entitled "State of the Prisons" which led to two reform acts within the British Parliament. The first act abolished jailer's fees, which an accused debtor had to pay even if proven innocent. The second act established a system of sanitation inspection inside the nation's prisons.

His efforts were relentless, but constantly exposed him to the illnesses that ran rampant throughout the prison systems of the time. At age 64, while investigating the "scandalous state" of Russian military hospitals, he died of "camp fever" at Kherson in southern Russia.[2]

In the 1850s, Newark was the acknowledged commercial center of the northern New Jersey economy. Newark benefited from the growth in Irish and German immigrants and its population expanded from 19,732 in 1836 to 347,469 in 1910. In its embryonic stages the savings bank industry catered to the new citizens of America. The Emigrant Savings Bank of NY was an obvious name seeking the small savings accounts of the newcomers to New York City. The Dime Savings Bank was another bank structured to encourage the small saver. Representing the "earthier" segment of New York City real estate was the Bowery Savings Bank, which was one of the city's largest. The simplicity of the passbook account and the availability of mortgage money were probably the two main attractions to foreigners just getting a start in life in this country. Many banks included "Mechanics" or "Seaman" in their titles in order to identify with the small investor or saver.

In 1839, the Provident Savings Bank became the first mutual savings bank to be chartered in New Jersey. The word "mutual" was devised to emphasize that the mutual savings banks had no shareholders. At the outset, mutual savings institutions were not necessarily "entrepreneurial" in their business psychology, but rather were established to provide services more or less overlooked by the commercial banking sector. The following quotation from the book outlining the history of the Provident and entitled *An American Success Story 1839–1989* stressed the

---

[2]*Britannia*—a British Internet Magazine—1998 article entitled "John Howard" by Brenda Ralph Lewis.

original purpose of the mutual. In some respects, it can be referred to as the "Mutual Savings Bank's Credo."

"Because a mutual savings bank has no shareholders, it pays most of its earnings to its depositors as interest on their savings. The absence of stockholders also means that those who serve on its board of managers may not profit personally from the bank's investments or operations, and must set policies that best serve the interests of the savings bank depositors."

Oddly enough, the Provident remained a mutual savings bank until 2003, the year this book was published. The initial public offering (IPO) for the Provident was highly successful as the Chairman and CEO Paul Pantozzi rang the New York Stock Exchange opening bell on January 15, 2003, when the stock first traded at 15 1/2 or 55% over its issue price of $10 per share. The financing raised nearly $615 million from depositors and was handled by Sandler O'Neal, specialists in mutual conversions.[3]

Eleven years after the Provident received its charter from the state of New Jersey, the founders of the Hudson City Savings Bank started a bank in the town of Hudson. Within three years, Hudson merged with the nearby towns of Bergen and Jersey to form New Jersey's second largest city—Jersey City. Hudson City Savings received its state charter in 1868. Jersey City was like a melting pot, experiencing an initial wave of Irish and German immigrants early in the nineteenth century and later on a second wave of Italians, Russians, Poles, and Hungarians.

Many familiar industrial names got their start or opened operations in New Jersey in the mid-to-late 1800s; Campbell Soup Company, Johnson & Johnson, Lenox China Co., Westinghouse Electric, and Tiffany's jewelry highlighted the list. As the century drew to a close, the Howard showed footings of around $3 million and the

---

[3]See conclusion of Chapter 9.

Hudson City $1 million. In 1899, beer and ale from Newark breweries represented $8 million in revenues.[4]

Throughout the nineteenth century and spilling over into the early 1900s, Newark's natural harbor location and the man-made Morris canal provided a supportive backdrop for strong manufacturing growth.

The needs of World War I increased the demands on these plants, and Newark's population bulged to 442,327 in 1930. With the bulk of New Jersey's population growth coming in the northern sector of the state, the Howard Savings Bank was well situated—relative to its peers—to take advantage of this trend. Banks in New Jersey were not permitted to branch outside the county of their home-office location. The Howard was where the action was!

The lag in branch banking legislation spawned a splintered banking structure which sustained close to 400 separately chartered commercial banks, almost 200 savings and loan associations, and 20 mutual savings banks. Up until the change in branch banking legislation, the various forms of banking somewhat peacefully coexisted.

Mid-Twentieth Century Newark: The Glory Years

In the mid-1950s, Newark, New Jersey was indeed a flourishing community. Distinguished by its Grecian pillared façade, the home office of the Howard Savings Institution at 768 Broad Street presented an imposing structure to the local community. Inside, the banking floor featured three-story high ceilings. There were twenty-five teller windows, most of which were earmarked for servicing passbook accounts. Seldom did a depositor have to wait on line to transact business with a Howard teller. Other stations handled Christmas clubs, student accounts, and activity referred from other branches.

---

[4]Hudson City Savings Bank. *"Historical Events: New Jersey, the Nation, and Hudson City Savings Bank.*

SELECTED CENSUS POPULATION FIGURES
FOR NEWARK, NEW JERSEY: 1830–2000

Census	Population
1850	38,914
1860	72,056
1870	105,239
1890	181,830
1900	246,676
1910	347,469
1920	414,524
1930	442,327
1950	438,736
1960	405,220
1970	381,930
1980	329,248
1990	275,221
2000	273,546

The National Newark & Essex Banking Company (NNE, the predecessor bank to the Midlantic National Bank) was the state's second largest commercial bank and featured a thirty-six-story towering brick structure situated immediately to the north of the Howard. The two institutions shared directors, a practice referred to as "interlocking directors." As such, Robert Cowan of the NNE sat on the Board of the Howard, while John Kress of the Howard was a member of NNE's board. The Essex Club, an exclusive luncheon club for high-ranking executives in the area, was located on the top floor of the NNE building, while Huyler's restaurant catered to middle management on the ground floor. The United States Savings Bank, with its conspicuous white façade, was on the south side of the Howard. U.S. Savings was noted for its jovial leader CEO Bill Lickleider, who joined the bank after a successful career as a bond salesman at Halsey Stuart & Co. He was known as "Three Martini Bill" and after his mid-day libation, he would often wiggle his ears for his party.

The First National State Bank of New Jersey was the state's largest commercial bank. In 1964, the bank moved its headquarters from 810 Broad to its brand new offices at 550 Broad. The Fidelity Union Trust Company ranked third in the state and was the only major bank on the west side of Broad Street. Newark was also the headquarters for the Prudential Insurance Company of America and the Mutual Benefit Life Insurance Company. Incidentally, First National State Bank and Mutual Benefit shared interlocking directors. In 1954, Mutual Benefit announced that it would construct its new home office in Newark opposite Washington Park. With the Prudential and Mutual Benefit leading the way, Newark ranked first as the city with the most insurance assets "in force" in the 1950s and 1960s. For the record, Newark ranked ahead of New York City and Hartford by this measure. Blue Cross & Blue Shield of New Jersey added to the city's presence in the health insurance industry.

Virtually all of Wall Street's major brokerage firms were represented in Newark during the period. Also, several regional dealers and small specialist firms thrived in the city, the largest of which was John J. Ryan & Co. (later renamed to Ryan Beck & Co), a specialist in bank stocks and New Jersey municipal bonds. Hanauer Stern and JB Hanauer were two firms which exclusively featured municipal bonds. Adams and Hinckley was regarded as the market maker for the stocks in many of New Jersey's smaller commercial banks. Among the general brokerage firms located in Newark were:

Merrill Lynch
Dean Witter & Co.
Reynolds Securities Inc.
Hornblower & Weeks-Hemphil-Noyes
Bache & Co.
Shearson Hayden Stone & Co.
Kidder Peabody & Co.
Clarke Dodge & Co.

Blyth Eastman Dillon
EF Hutton
Goodbody & Co.
Tucker Anthony & R. L. Day
Paine Webber Jackson & Curtis
Bevill Bressler & Shulman
Loeb Rhodes & Co.
Drexel Burnham & Co.
Spencer Trask & Co.
Smith Barney Harris Upham
Thompson & McKinnon-Auchencloss & Kohlmeyer

As a result of Newark's extensive commerce activity and its role as county seat of Essex County, large legal firms ran their businesses from offices located in the various office buildings around the city. In addition to United States Congressman Peter Frelinghuysen, who ran his local operation in Newark, McCarter & English, and former Governor Meyner were just a few of the many prominent legal names with their main offices in Newark. Late in the period, Jack Kraft founded the Newark-based legal firm of Kraft & Hughes which, as a bond attorney, almost immediately took business away from the believed invincible Hawkins Delafield & Wood firm from New York City.

The state's largest electrical utility—Public Service Electric & Gas Company—had its headquarters in Newark as did the state's major telephone company—New Jersey Bell Telephone. A modicum of corporate headquarters included Walter Kidde & Co. (actually nearby Belleville) and Englehard Industries.

Shoppers from the surrounding suburbs came to visit Newark and take advantage of the exclusive department stores such as Bambergers, Orbach's and Haynes, and to a lesser extent Kresge's. For the economy-minded shopper, there was always S. Klein on the Square. A collection of prominent restaurants awaited these out-of-town visitors and commuters. The Brothers Restaurant, The

Renaissance, and The Roost were all frequented by local businessmen for lunch and dinner. From the exterior, Don's 21 Diner presented an unimpressive façade, but inside the restaurant you enjoyed a marvelous view of the Ironbound section of Newark and volumes of good food. Hobby's Deli on Washington and Branford was the working man's favorite.

The Ironbound section of Newark was a residential area on the eastern side of town, between the transportation hubs and New York City. The area featured neatly kept houses with immaculately manicured lawns and a myriad of restaurant styles including Portugese and Spanish influences. Restaurants Don Pepe and Spain always seemed to be packed. The aroma of garlic was indigenous to the area.

Cultural uplifts were provided by the Newark Museum and the state symphony. The museum was renowned for not only supplying the artifacts and remnants of history but also providing dynamic displays of how these inanimate objects became part of our civilization and culture.

The State Symphony Hall was located at 1020 Broad Street and was originally named the Mosque Theatre. Over the years, a broad variety of entertainment was provided, including a basketball game featuring the Harlem Globetrotters against their regular traveling opponent, the Hawaii 50th Staters. A highlight day in the Mosque's history was when Judy Garland appeared on May 2, 1961 before an overflow crowd of 3,600 fans. The Rolling Stones appeared on the Mosque stage in November 1965 as a part of the rock group's fall American tour.

Around the middle of the twentieth century, the adult entertainment business thrived in Newark. The Empire Burlesque Theater located on Washington Street and Branford was the epicenter for the stripper activities of Lili St. Cyr and Evelyn West and her "Treasure Chest." The Empire featured not only the scantily clad ladies, but also comedy acts and a chorus line of a dozen dancers. At the intermission, local vendors sold miniature books (then called "big-little books"), which, when you flipped the pages, gave a personalized version of the animated stripper in action. In the late 1930s, New York City Mayor Fiorella LaGuardia closed the striptease shows there, and the Empire Theater (as well as the Hudson Theater of Union City) quickly filled the void. The charge for admission generally ran about 30 cents.

By 1957, the burlesque industry succumbed in part to "other forms of entertainment" and the Empire Theater closed. A year later, the building was torn down and leveled into a parking lot for out-of-town shoppers.[5]

Students attending Newark College of Engineering, Rutgers University at Newark, and the Seton Hall Law School added to the city's vitality. Seton Hall's School of Nursing and Seton Hall's Business School featured night classes in Newark. The prestigious prep school of Newark Academy moved its campus to Livingston, New Jersey, in the late 1950s.[6]

For most of the century, the city supported two daily newspapers. The morning publication was the *Newark Star Ledger* and its counterpart was *The Newark Evening News*. Going the way of most evening papers, the *News'* last publication was on January 23, 1973, following a lengthy strike.

The Newark Bears were a minor league affiliate of the New York Yankees which shared the local Ruppert Stadium with the Newark Eagles, a Negro league team. A consistent winner throughout their history, the Bears set the AAA all-time win-loss record for a single season when in 1973 they compiled a 109-43 record. The Eagles won the 1946 World Championship. Hall of Famer Yogi Berra played for the Bears in the 1940s, and Larry Doby (the first African-American to play in the American League), Monte Irvin, and Donald Newcombe played for the Eagles.

---

[5]Bodian, Nat. "Burlesque at the Empire Theater," from *Old Newark Memories.*

[6]Roman, Harry. "The Newark Museum—Home to Me," from *Old Newark Memories.*

The influx of weekday commuters and shoppers to Newark created an endless flow of pedestrian traffic on the city's streets. The trains stopping at Penn Station and Broad Street Station were probably the most efficient way to access Newark from longer distances, whereas those coming from New York City or Jersey City connected via the Port Authority of New York and New Jersey (popularly called PATH) trains. Several bus companies and the city subway system added to the alternatives. Rush-hour traffic notwithstanding, commuters electing to drive to Newark on their own connected readily to the New Jersey Turnpike or the Garden State Parkway.

For years, my father frequented Newark in order to get his regularly scheduled haircut at the barber shop located in the rear of the NNE building.

For many years, Newark has been served by the infamous highways of Route 22 and Route 1-9. Decidedly obsolete by the time of their completion, the two highways were major arteries for the trucking companies. In the mid-1950s, as one drove along these highway relics, a horrible odor emanated from the garbage dumps located in the area known pejoratively as "the Swamp." The label known as the "Newark Meadows" (and later the "Meadowlands") seemed to catch on once the developers and investment bankers realized the profit potential of the area. Part of "the Swamp's" problem stemmed from a persistent outflow of pollution from the smokestacks attendant to the chemical companies and oil refineries. A large portion was also attributable to the pig farmers of Secaucus, the most notable of whom was eternal presidential candidate Henry Krajewski. Running as an independent, Krajewski twice was defeated (in 1952 and 1956) by President Eisenhower, despite his program of "Free Beer, No Taxes and Isolationism." He ran his campaign from his personally owned tavern in Secaucus. Ironically, Krajewski died on election day, but his memory lingers on as a part of the lore of the Meadowlands area.

In the 1950s and 1960s, before the construction of the multiple facilities of the New Jersey Sports & Exhibition

Authority, the region featured the state's largest drive-in movie theater and a multifaceted golf layout including a driving range, plus a par three and a miniature golf course. Nearby, docked on the Passaic River, was a floating tavern (named The Barge) which catered to college students using altered IDs and other young adults. Huge volcanic outcrops near Exit 16 on the New Jersey Turnpike provided the advertising medium for just about all the nation's fraternities whose Greek letters were painted on the dark-colored rocks. Sustained by the ever-creative ingenuity of local college students, the eyesore of the painted rocks survived until a conscientious effort by the area's development leaders removed the Greek letters in 2001.

Although Newark International Airport functioned as a major transportation facility for the entire New York and New Jersey metropolitan area, a large percentage of the passengers probably never set foot in downtown Newark. As you enter Newark Airport, you drive by the Budweiser brewery. Only Bud remains from a litany of local beers once manufactured in the area. P. Ballentine & Sons, Rhinegold, Schaeffer and Pabst were all part of the local New Jersey economy of the 1950s-1960s.

Up until 1969, the restrictive branch banking laws of the state of New Jersey precluded the Howard Savings Institution and other Newark-based banks from operating outside the boundaries of Essex County. In the 1967 annual report, the Howard listed the various offices and their relative deposit size.

The Howard Savings Bank had Newark totally surrounded!

In the late 1960s, Essex County had a total population of just under one million residents living within a 126-square-mile area. Representing the service area of the Howard circa 1970, the twenty-two constituent communities and some of their demographics are listed in Table 1.

BRANCH LOCATION	DEPOSITS
Head Office (768 Broad St.)	$351.0 million
South Orange	79.2
Vailsburg	67.3
Wessex	60.9
Bloomfield Avenue	40.3
Weequahic	40.2
University	33.5
Irvington	30.8
Stuyvesant Village	28.2
Springfield Avenue	24.3
Total	$762.3 million

The Newark Riots: The Summer of 1967

The smoldering unrest of the city of Newark was a major concern to the members of the New Jersey National Guard as it prepared to move out to its summer camp destination in July 1967. As a 1st Lieutenant in the New Jersey National Guard with the designation of a "riot control platoon leader," I was especially sensitive to any potential misconduct by the local citizenry. With our unit from the West Orange Armory slated to rendezvous with its counterpart at the Roseville Armory near downtown Newark, the two units would form a joint convoy headed for the New Jersey Turnpike, and then ultimately for Fort Picket in Blackstone, Virginia, where, as reservists, we would fulfill our two weeks summer camp requirement. The main concern of the Guard leadership was the use and control of live ammunition. Aggravated by the oppressive July humidity and 90 degree temperature, racial tensions were running extremely high in Newark, New Jersey. Looting and protesting in the predominantly black downtown area had been occurring all week.

The officers of the Guard did not alter their plans and the convoy proceeded as scheduled. Once the connection with the Roseville unit had been made, our multi-vehicle caravan snaked its way through the back streets of

TABLE 1 POPULATION AND AREA COMPARISONS OF ESSEX COUNTY—1970

Community	Population 1970	Square Miles
Belleville (Twp.)	37,629	3.3
Bloomfield (Twp.)	52,059	5.3
Caldwell (Borough)	8,677	1.2
Cedar Grove (Twp.)	15,582	4.5
East Orange (City)	75,471	3.9
Essex Fells (Borough)	2,541	1.4
Fairfield (Twp.)	4,990	10.1
Glen Ridge (Twp.)	8,518	1.7
Irvington (Twp.)	59,743	2.9
Livingston (Twp.)	30,127	13.9
Maplewood (Twp.)	24,932	3.9
Millburn/Short Hills (Twp.)	21,086	9.4
Montclair (Twp.)	44,043	6.3
Newark (City)	329,248	23.8
North Caldwell (Twp.)	6,733	3.0
Nutley (Twp.)	31,913	3.4
Orange (City)	32,566	2.2
Roseland (Borough)	4,453	3.6
South Orange (Village)	16,915	2.9
Verona (Twp.)	15.061	2.8
West Caldwell (Twp.)	11,913	5.0
West Orange (Twp.)	43,710	12.1
Total Population	932,526	126.2 sq miles

Newark's South Ward and soon headed in the direction of Exit 13 of the New Jersey Turnpike. Oddly enough, the groups of protesters limited their activity to merely staring out windows, or jeering and gesturing as the Guard units progressed through the city. Before long, our units were on the turnpike and off for the long trip south.

As if part of an overall plan, the riots erupted in Newark two nights later. Governor Richard Hughes of

New Jersey hastily pieced together a force of 100 National Guardsmen from units who were not at summer camp in Virginia. These units eventually quelled the riots, but not without cost. President Lyndon B. Johnson offered federal assistance following the slaying of a policeman in Plainfield, New Jersey. Rooftop snipers using stolen weapons caused most of the damage, as they focused on hospitals and firehouses. All in all, twenty-five people (twenty-four citizens and one guardsman) perished in the riots and an estimated $10–$15 million in property damage was inflicted on the city of Newark. The coverage by the national TV news services and other media outlets was quite explicit in illustrating the desperate conditions of center-city Newark.

The citizens of Newark who incited the riots were attempting to bring their deplorable living conditions to the attention of the nation's population. The unemployment rate, especially among young black males, was considerably higher than the national average. Housing, in many cases, implied more than one family living in one unit of a project. Luxuries which we take for granted (such as air-conditioning) were too costly for the Newark constituency. Understaffing of the local police force was a major problem. Overcrowding of the public schools, despite efforts to pass unqualified students on to the next level, continued to agitate Newark's youth. When interviewed, the local citizens complained of the *filth* of their living conditions.

As listed in the U.S. Bureau of the Census, the racial composition of Newark between the years 1950 and 1990 had changed dramatically.

Newark was not an isolated case of urban blight. Urban centers such as Camden and Trenton had experienced similar problems. Plainfield, a quasi urban-suburban community, also was the site of some serious rioting during the summer of 1967.

As our Guard units returned from Camp Picket, Virginia, we bivouacked in Thoroughfare, New Jersey, a tiny

Year	Blacks (%)	Whites (%)
1950	74,965 (17.1%)	363,149 (82.9%)
1960	138,035 (34.1)	265,889 (65.6)
1970	207,458 (54.3)	168,382 (44.1)
1980	191,745 (58.2)	101,417 (30.8)
1990	160,885 (58.5)	78,771 (28.6)

municipality near Camden. In a quickly drawn up summit meeting between President Lyndon B. Johnson and President Aleksei Kosygin of the USSR, Glassboro State College was selected as the "neutral location" for the talks and suddenly there was the New Jersey National Guard unit acting as a security force for LBJ and Kosygin.

At long last, when our Guard units returned from our summer exercises, we were placed on alert for the balance of the year in the event of further outbursts. For over a year, I left my military gear in my closet, organized and ready to go if called. Fortunately, it never happened.

Likewise, across the nation, the black community took to the streets to emphasize its collective state of desperation. Hartford, Detroit, Los Angeles and many others were scenes of death and destruction.

For Newark, New Jersey, shortly after celebrating the 300th year anniversary since its founding in 1666, the summer of 1967 represented the low point of its otherwise long and illustrious history. By 1970, Newark was ranked by the Federal Bureau of Investigation as the "most crime-ridden city in the United States."

Following the riots of 1967, a noticeable change in the commuting habits of Newark's work force started to take place. Many workers altered work schedules so that they started earlier in the day, preferring to post at 7:00 A.M. and leaving at 3:00 P.M. Regardless, few workers stayed at their desks beyond 5:00 P.M. and many disappeared even earlier than that. The word was unanimous—Newark was no place to be after dark. As Wall Street and other markets rapidly expanded their global activity, the phenomenon of the 24-hour trading session became more of a reality. While Newark contracted the amount of hours worked in a day, the rest of the world was expanding. For the first time in its economic history, Newark was suddenly out of step.

The New Jersey Association of Certified Public Accountants, the local chapter of the American Bar Association, and the Bond Club of New Jersey were just three of the several professional societies which centered their activities and/or made their headquarters in downtown Newark. The Bond Club's membership composition and activities seem to mirror the cyclical patterns of Newark. Since its origin in 1921, the BCNJ held its periodic board meetings at Hornblower & Weeks after the close of the markets on Thursday afternoons. Then the board would adjourn to nearby Brothers Restaurant and socialize throughout the evening. For many years, the BCNJ held its annual Christmas Party at the Downtown Club atop the Bambergers Department Store. In 1967, Anthony V. Butera from the First National State of NJ municipal bond department was president of the BCNJ. At the time, a majority of the board members also worked for securities firms located in Newark.

Many of the Howard staff were members of the Bond Club, including President John Kress, Jack Duerk, Walter Hislop, George Hughes, Wallace Scanlon and later on John Quinn, Rich Donnelly, and Leanne Plunkett. Most smaller institutions in the state had at least one representative member and those of the Howard's size registered multiple memberships. Usually, seven or eight of New Jersey's largest mutual savings banks were represented on the club's rolls. At its peak in 1977–78, the Bond Club membership numbered 325. I joined the Bond Club along with my Lafayette College "big brother" Donald Kress in 1964, and the president of the club at that time was John Unkles, senior partner in charge of the East Orange brokerage firm of Nugent & Igoe (subsequently acquired by Tucker Anthony). Unkles later on was selected for the Howard Savings Bank board in 1980 and served until the very end.

Since 1924, the Bond Club of New Jersey has held a golf tournament for its members. Each year, the club awards the Edwin F. Kezer Trophy to the player registering the low net score for the day. John W. Kress, later on selected president of the Howard Savings Bank, won the trophy in 1946. John J. Roe, president of the Hudson City Savings, took the event in 1939. Also, the club sponsors an annual tennis tourney for its members, and the all-time champion in this event is Jim Kranz, vice president and chief investment officer of Hudson City. Jim has 13 titles to his credit since joining the club in 1974.

At the most recent BCNJ function held at Rock Spring Country Club in West Orange, New Jersey (May 19, 2003), Don Kress shot a 102 in the golf tourney to finish second low net in his flight and, more importantly, held the winning ticket worth $5,000 in the organization's annual fund raising raffle. Howard alumni Rich Donnelly (who won the tourney in 2001) and Walter Hislop also participated in the outing.

I have always valued my membership in the Bond Club of New Jersey. The organization provided a setting where competitors and clients could become friends and enjoy social and sporting events together. My father and others from the Great Depression era had made work sound like such a grind. The BCNJ broke down many barriers and we all seemed to help one another. I served as president of the BCNJ during 1977–78, sponsored the amendment permitting women to join the organization, and continue on as a member of the board of governors to the present date.

Within a few years of the Newark riots, the Bond Club shifted its board meetings and the Christmas party to the Rock Spring Country Club in West Orange, New Jersey. At the same time, Wall Street firms relocated most of their Newark operations to scattered suburban locations. Almost overnight, Newark's representation on the BCNJ board disappeared.

The Bond Club was a mere microcosm of the larger trend taking place. Institutions, retailers, brokerage firms, and securities dealers began to move waves of their personnel to more desirable suburban areas. The National Newark & Essex Bank dropped "Newark" from its corporate name and became the Midlantic Banks. Spearheaded by the personal appearances of CEO Bob Van Buren, the bank flooded the advertising circuit with its new nickname, "The Hungry Bankers."

Midlantic constructed an operations complex in West Orange while First Fidelity built their new center near Princeton. When the dust finally settled, the Prudential was the only major institution to truly keep the bulk of its operations in Newark.

The New Jersey Association of Mutual Savings Banks (NJAMSB)

The New Jersey Association of Mutual Savings Banks was a vital part of the operation of the 20 member banks for most of the twentieth century.

Almost all of the presidents and their respected senior management teams attended the annual convention traditionally held in June at the Monmouth Hotel in Spring Lake. Directors and junior officers were also invited. Anyone who was anyone in the New Jersey savings world was at the event. Over the years, a mutual trust evolved among the members. Outsiders such as bond salesmen and other vendors attended by invitation only.[7]

The NJAMSB was perceived by its members to be an elite group which held a special status within the arena of New Jersey banking. Standing committees of the officers below the top level spread this unity even deeper. For

---

[7]For most of the 1970s, my wife and I were privileged to attend many of these functions as the guest of the Orange Savings Bank.

example, the committee on investments included all the major banks' investment officers, who frequently met to exchange ideas. Sophisticated methods for hedging portfolios, for example, were compared and thus made available to even the smaller members of the association.

The association's members actively participated in the National Association's School of Savings Banking originally located at Brown University in Providence, Rhode Island. The junior officers of the various banks spent two weeks a year for three years at the campus. The courses were challenging and included written theses for credit. Ironically, the various officers of the New Jersey Association of MSBs all learned their banking fundamentals from the same source. Their future competition was their current roommate. Some years later, the location of the savings bank school was shifted to Fairfield University in Connecticut.

The ultimate career highlight of a New Jersey savings bank executive was to be elected president of the association. Like many organizations, the group had three officers who worked his (or her) way through the "chairs" to be president. To be in the queue, you first were the secretary of the group, next vice president and then president. Originally terms of office ran for two years, but were changed to one-year posts in 1972. The highlight of the year's convention was the moving up of the veep to be president, with his acceptance speech and outlook for the banking climate in the near-to-longer-term future.

Following the speech, almost everyone moved en masse to the golf course for the NJAMSB annual tournament. The evening was for cocktails, dinner, and dancing.

A great deal of prestige was associated with being president of the NJAMSB. As New Jersey's ambassador of the industry, the position entailed extensive traveling to the other state and annual conventions. All past presidents back to the origin of the association were listed in the program for the annual convention at Spring Lake. The group tried to rotate every bank president into the top

FORMER CHAIRMEN OF THE NEW JERSEY ASSOCIATION OF MUTUAL SAVINGS BANKS 1952–1992

Years in Office	*Name*	*Bank*
1952–54	Howard D. Biddulph	Bloomfield Savings Bank
1954–56	Ernest R. Hansen	Perth Amboy Savings Bank
1956–58	William E. Thomas	Provident Savings Bank
1958–60	Frederick H. Hoffman	Harmonia Savings Bank
1960–62	Norman P. McGrory	Howard Savings Institution
1962–64	Austin P. Hutchinson	Plainfield Savings Bank
1964–66	Edmund J. Sauer, Jr.	Orange Savings Bank
1966–68	William B. Lickleider	United States Savings Bank
1968–69	Edwin W. Baier	New Brunswick Savings Bank
1969–70	H. Wemdall Phillips	Morris County Savings Bank
1970–72	Kenneth L. Birchby	Hudson City Savings Bank
1972–73	James W. Allen	Savings Bank of Central Jersey
1973–74	Harold J. Paterson	Morris County Savings Bank
1974–75	James K. Feely	Bloomfield Savings Bank
1975–76	Kenneth F. X. Albers	Provident Savings Bank
1976–77	James J. Pinto	Washington Savings Bank
1977–78	Murray Forbes	Howard Savings Bank
1978–79	Arlyn D. Rus	Raritan Savings Bank

1979–80	Donald C. Sims	Union County Savings Bank
1980–81	Bernhard J. Martin	Montclair Savings Bank
1981–82	Rudolph P. Novotny	United States Savings Bank
1982–83	Andrew J. Egner	Orange Savings Bank
1983–84	Beatrice D'Agosgtino	New Jersey Savings Bank
1984–85	Walter D. Tombs	Harmonia Savings Bank
1985–86	Donald F. McCormick	Howard Savings Bank
1986–87	C. William Kuhlthau, III	New Brunswick Savings Bank
1987–88	Thomas F. Grahill	Rahway Savings Institution
1988–89	Joseph P. Gemmell	Bankers Savings Bank
1989–90	Wendell T. Breithaupt	Trenton Savings Fund Society
1990–90	Thomas H. von Arsdale	Savings Bank of Central Jersey
1990–92	Leonard Gudelski	Hudson City Savings Bank

slot without repeating the same bank twice, although this was not a strict rule. The association was a source of pride, a prime example of fairness and a conduit for sharing information. The NJAMSBs activities were so vast that the group required a full time, paid executive secretary.

New Jersey commercial banks and the New Jersey savings and loan associations had their own separate trade groups. However, their memberships were so large that they didn't have the opportunity to enjoy the bonding experienced by the mutual savings organization. Outsiders who knew most of their contacts by their name tags flocked to their conventions. The annual turnover of personnel at the larger events was high compared to that of the mutuals.

To a certain degree, the status of a mutual savings bank may have led to a sense of invincibility, even a sense of complacency. For the first eighty years of the twentieth century, a nucleus of roughly twenty banks evolved with but one merger taking place (i.e., Fifth Ward Savings was acquired by Hudson City in 1969). Unlike the commercial bank sector where new banks were constantly being formed and mergers were a regular diet, the group of New Jersey mutual savings banks offered the retail banking client an element of stability. While roughly 71 new commercial banks were started between 1969 and 1985, there were no new savings banks created between the end of World War II and 1992. Many commercial bank depositors were agitated by the constant name change of their local bank, finding themselves continually shredding old check books as they took down new check books to reflect a merger and subsequent name change of their bank.

But the Reagan proposals brought about several changes for the mutuals, the commercials, and the entire spectrum of banking in the United States. After the dust settled from the consolidation phase of the latter twentieth century, only four remain as viable independent banks which somewhat resemble their original structure. The demutualization process enriched many of the MSB executives but also led to many of the banks merging into oblivion.

(See the following table describing the changes in the individual banks of New Jersey over the last fifty years.)

The only new mutual savings bank to be started in the period was the Watchung Hills Bank for Savings. Headquartered in Warren, New Jersey, and led by former president of the New Jersey association, Jim Allen, the bank merged into the World Savings Bank around 1995. Bobby Thompson, whose 1951 three-run home run snagged the National League pennant away from the Brooklyn Dodgers, was among those named to the board of directors.

The following numbers illustrate the relative importance of the various types of banking institutions within the state of New Jersey.

TABLE 2 CHANGES IMPACTING THE SURVIVAL OF NEW JERSEY MUTUAL SAVINGS BANKS

Surviving Banks as of June 2003

Hudson City Savings Bank
*Provident Savings Bank
Rahway Savings Institution
Union County Savings Bank

Non-Surviving Banks:	*Acquiring Institution*
Bloomfield Savings Bank	Provident SB
Elizabeth Savings Bank	Chase
Fifth Ward Savings Bank	Hudson City SB
Harmonia Savings Bank	Sovereign Bank (PA)
Hoboken Bank (then Washington SB)	HUBCO
Howard Savings Bank	Closed by state of New Jersey, deposits assumed by First Fidelity Bank
Morris County Savings Bank	First Fidelity Bancorp
Montclair Savings Bank	Collective Federal S&L
New Brunswick Savings Bank	National State Bank (Elizabeth)
Orange Savings Bank	Hudson City Savings
Perth Amboy Savings Bank	Bankers National (then Sovereign)
Plainfield Savings (then Starpointe)	Dime Savings NY
Raritan Savings Bank	United National Bank (NJ)
Somerville Savings (then NJ Savings, then Bancorp NJ)	United Jersey Banks (then Fleet)
Trenton Savings Fund	Sovereign Bank (PA)
United States Savings Bank	Assumed by the Hudson City Savings Bank

*Provident completed its IPO and effectively "demutualized" in January 2003, leaving just two MSBs in the state without equity ownership.

Type of Financial Institution	NJ Deposits	Percent of Total
Commercial Banks	$50,004,491	49.9%
Mutual Savings Banks	13,821,341	13.8
Savings & Loan Associations	36,356,068	36.3
Total	$100,181,900	100%*

Source: Ryan Beck Banking Manual for 1986.

General Operations of the Howard Savings Bank

Sources of Funds: From 1857 to 1978, the Howard Savings Bank essentially built a solid banking franchise based on retail banking. For most of the period, the centerpiece of its growth and profitability was the passbook account. By and large, the passbook accounts collectively built a core deposit base, a form of raw material which sustained the Howard bank throughout its existence. Savers were mostly driven by the convenience factor rather than by any minor interest rate differentials at competing banks. Savers loved the way passbook accounts rolled up the compound interest. Unlike certificates of deposit which carried a specific maturity date, passbook accounts could last forever or could be withdrawn in whole or part "on demand." When the depositor presented his passbook, the bank had to pay on the spot. Despite this on demand characteristic, passbook accounts tended to remain on the books for a sustained period of time. Most mutuals in effect could count on passbook accounts as a stable long-term source of funds which were pegged off short-term market interest rates. The Howard built its passbook account with its advertising slogan "Be Howard Powered."

The comfortable status of the passbook account was shaken by the credit crunch of 1966 and subsequent tight money conditions that prevailed in 1969 and 1973. The term "disintermediation" seemed to originate in the 1966 environment and entailed heavy depositor shifts from the savings bank industry to other forms of investment carrying higher rates of return. Given the interest rate ceilings established under the guidelines of Regulation Q, the savings banks were unable to offer competitive rates with those readily available in the marketplace. However, the severity of the cycles was manageable albeit painful to many of the banks. The inconvenience of moving deposits from bank to bank may have been limited by the constraints on branch banking. This would change in the next round of interest rate volatility.

Competition for the passbook account was largely provided by the brokerage industry. During the 1970s, Merril Lynch and Dean Witter developed a rival to the passbook in the form of the "command account" or the "active asset account." As the broker-sponsored accounts grew in popularity, they did so at the expense of passbook accounts by siphoning off new money rather than causing a wholesale shift in deposits. The phenomenon of "disintermediation" continued to impact the thrifts during the surge in oil prices in 1973–74 and the attendant rise in short-term interest rates. The process whereby money flowed from the mutuals to the brokers gathered momentum from the mid 1980s on. Savings banks which served the most sophisticated clients were the hardest hit. The Washington Savings Bank, which had 40% of its deposit base in passbook accounts in the hands of elderly savers wasn't affected. Ted Doll, EVP and investment officer of the Washington in the late 1980s, succinctly described his bank's situation: "I had a great customer base of low cost, loyal money in the hands of senior citizens. But with eight branches, where was I going?" It was only a matter of time before the Washington's strategic advantage would become obsolete. The Washington soon thereafter sold out to the Hudson United Bancorporation. Likewise, the slow pace of branch banking at the Bloomfield Savings apparently led to its merger with the Provident Saving in 1983.

With only three branches in their system, the Bloomfield was behind the curve and merging with the expansionist Provident was deemed the appropriate solution.

In 1969, in Trenton, New Jersey, the NJAMSB lobbyists and the likes of Ken Birchby finally witnessed the passage of the legislation enabling the New Jersey thrifts the opportunity to branch outside of their home office county. The Howard effectively kept pace with the industry. By 1983, the Howard listed fifty-four banking offices statewide with thirty-four branches located in the northern part of the state. Newer banking offices were concentrated at the rapidly growing New Jersey shore area. Hudson City Savings, on the other hand, forged its growth in Bergen County.

The negative spread environment of the early 1980s drained many of the banks with respect to their capital and surplus positions. The FDIC mandated that the member banks focus on strengthening these accounts. When the capital markets opened up the window which encouraged more equity financing, many savings banks rushed to issue common stock as a source of capital funds. Referred to as the "demutualization process," the equity issues raised the necessary capital but brought vast changes to the operations of those savings banks opting to pursue this vehicle of raising capital. Prior to the issuance of IPOs, mutual savings banks were not required to publicly issue income statements. The twenty New Jersey savings banks customarily had copies of their balance sheets on display in the lobby, but annual dips in earnings (which appear on income statements) were not necessarily revealed. Suddenly, as players in the stock market, the banks had to report earnings variations to their stockholders. Extensive footnoting detailed the actual classes of loans and investments. Earnings, after all, were tied to an equity's market price as represented by the price earnings ratio. Banks soon learned that equity investors want their shares to grow a certain amount every year.

There is an art (recently alluded to as "tweaking") to managing earnings from year to year, but the savings bank industry had yet to be baptized in this practice. Undoubtedly, a proclivity to "reach out" and take down some extra earnings was a temptation to these new issuers of common stock. Particularly when the factors of a negative yield curve were adversely impacting spreads, the banks were forced to deviate from their historical franchise to an area of higher rate of returns. Otherwise, they feared a drastic decline in the price of their stock in the equity arena.

It is interesting to note that none of the four surviving MSBs in New Jersey issued stock in the 1980s, and the Hudson City Savings waited until 1999 to issue stock. As noted, the Provident completed its IPO in January 2003.

The Depository Institutions Deregulatory Act of 1977 essentially removed all interest rate ceilings previously associated with Regulation Q and allowed the banks to issue CDs and other instruments at whatever level the market would tolerate. When the market for short-term federal funds rose to 22% in 1981, many of the savings banks issued six-month CDs indexed to the funds level. One of the New Jersey savings banks allowed its depositors a penalty-free transfer from outstanding CDs to these high-yielding six-month accounts. The bank virtually wiped out its surplus account overnight and was forced to merge out of business.

Uses of Funds: The composition of the asset side of the bank was relatively one dimensional in the early stages of the mutual savings bank industry. Mortgages, primarily residential mortgages, represented the main ingredient of the bank's "cookie jar" of investments or its uses of funds. The balance of the bank's investments was held as a liquidity reserve, usually cash in the form of hard currency.

In the early 1900s, as the money and capital markets developed in the United States, the liquidity reserve found more sophisticated outlets such as federal funds, commercial paper, bankers acceptances, and treasury bills to mention just a few.

The dominant position of mortgages in the mutual savings bank asset structure remained relatively constant throughout the twentieth century and for the most part represented two-thirds or more of any given bank's holdings. Part of this percentage was necessitated by the requirements of the bank's charter, and part was induced by preferential tax treatment for mortgages and mortgage-related investments. In effect, the savings bank industry was mandated to make mortgages. The Howard Savings Bank and its other New Jersey peers essentially kept themselves close to or at the 65% bar throughout its pre-1980 history.

The development of the federal agency securities market facilitated the bank's ability to achieve an acceptable 65% holding of this asset classification. Certain agency securities were viewed as "qualifying assets" and counted as fulfilling the bank's obligation to the mortgage market. The main issuers of these securities were:

Federal National Mortgage Association (a.k.a. Fannie Mae)

Federal Home Loan Banks

Federal Home Loan Mortgage Association (a.k.a. Freddie Mac)

Government National Mortgage Association (a.k.a. Ginnie Mae)

At the risk of oversimplification, the acknowledged key to a bank's profitability, indeed its survival, is its ability to earn a positive spread on its assets versus its cost of funds while simultaneously matching the two categories on a maturity basis. Asset-liability matching implies buying short-term investments when sources are predominantly short, buying long-term investments when sources of funds are mostly longer in duration. For the bulk of the mutual savings banks' 200-year existence, they tended to feel comfortable with the acknowledged imperfect match-up of passbook accounts with mortgages even though the passbooks were payable on demand and the mortgages had a 30-year maturity.[8]

Actually, the callable nature of the mortgage instrument added to its complexity in any match-up analysis. Homeowners taking down a mortgage at relatively high rates can refinance these debts at any time in the event that interest rates fall at a later date. Conversely, in a rising interest rate climate, mortgage borrowers allow their original mortgage rates to remain in effect, tending to savor the fruits of a low-cost loan, and their loans lengthen as a result. In summary, the classic mortgage instrument shortens in a bullish interest rate climate, and lengthens in a bearish background. These patterns are exaggerated in the more financially sophisticated areas of the United States. John Quinn, the latter-day investment chief at the Howard, referred to this phenomenon as "negative convexity."

Throughout history, interest rate volatility has been a way of life in the financial markets, and prior to the perverse cycle of the 1980s, this volatility was manageable, although producing some notable casualties. However, the 1980s brought about the highest interest rates ever posted in the United States. The extremes created havoc in the mutual savings bank industry. While the regulators were quick to change the laws concerning ceilings on rates paid by the banks, there was a distinct lag in the sector affecting the use of funds by the banks. Usury laws in many states limited mortgage rates to 6%, while market rates on longer high quality items such as U.S. Treasury securities and even municipal bonds offered yields of over 14%. Mutual savings banks were also left holding 6% fixed-rate mortgages written in previous cycles. Likewise, the prolonged aberration of the inverted yield curve took

---

[8]Since the mortgages issued throughout the period under study pay off both principal and interest on a monthly basis, generally speaking they have an assumed "average life" of 12.5 years.

away the positive spread between mortgages and short-term investments. Sorely mismatched and losing money, many savings institutions fought for survival during the double-digit interest rate period of the 1980s.

Around 1970, as the imperfections associated with matching "the old fashioned way" became more obvious, mortgage bankers, savings and loan associations and mutual savings banks began to "remodel" their mortgage product. By the end of the century, the adjustable rate mortgage (ARM) had become the main use of funds within the mortgage asset category. ARMs featuring three- or five-year windows appeared more like intermediate term assets and refinancings were somewhat discouraged, as the refinance anniversary date was always just around the corner.

The remaining 35% of banks' asset structures—those assets other than mortgages—were basically split between short-term or liquidity reserve funds and those earmarked for longer term investment. With most MSBs investing approximately 10% of their assets in the short-term markets, the remaining 25% of a bank's discretionary assets could be deployed in the broad variety of investment vehicles available under the investment laws of the state of New Jersey.

The state of New Jersey established certain "legal investment laws" in 1876. The purpose of the laws was to prevent speculation in the securities markets. The major category of investments excluded was that referred to as "junk bonds" or bonds rated "BB" or lower. Given the collapse of the junk market in the late 1980s and 1990s, the New Jersey MSBs were fortunate to be excluded from this marketplace. The thrift institutions in California and elsewhere in the Western part of the United States were not so lucky, and thus witnessed several major failures directly attributable to junk bond trading.

The junk market aside, mutuals could invest in corporate bonds carrying a combined minimum of a 6-B rating (i.e., Baa by Moodys and BBB by Standard & Poors). As a practical matter, most of the banks invested in bonds carrying at least an "A" by both services. Prior to 1970, most MSBs bought longer corporates because of the lack of supply in the shorter area. The development of the intermediate corporate bond market began with Cleveland Electric Illuminating Co. selling 10 year corporates in 1970. The sector has grown dramatically ever since, and has seen a strong participation on the part of savings bankers. Corporate bonds are also used selectively by the commercial bank investment portfolio. Municipal bonds were eligible investments for savings banks, and many banks sought the bonds to fulfill certain "community development act" requirements. However, most savings banks mitigated their tax liability by keeping the mortgage component of their balance sheets running at about 65%. The savings banks could also benefit from the higher gross income level afforded by the mortgage area. Municipal bonds carrying lower coupon rates failed to help the savings bank sector cover its operating expenses. Mortgages kept the doors open and the bank saved some taxes as well. Commercial banks looking at a 48% tax on their portfolio investments found municipals to be very attractive, depending on their relationship with the U.S. Treasury market. Preferred stock also provided some tax relief for mutuals as well as some larger commercial banks which invested under the guise of a "bank holding company."

Likewise, the commercial bank holding company was permitted to invest in common stocks. Most of the stocks held by the commercial banks tended to be used as a ploy to facilitate merger activity. Savings banks bought and traded common stocks as a means of investment with the hope of growing their surplus account. Many commercial banks and mutual savings banks took huge profits when their original investment in the form of restricted stock in the Federal Home Loan Banks became a publicly traded security. As the restrictions governing the trading of this security were phased out in the late 1980s and early 1990s, this windfall profit may have helped many banks survive the period.

From 1956 through almost the entire decade of the 1960s, mutual savings banks posted a passbook rate of about 3%. Mortgages, Ginnie Maes, agencies, and corporates all varied but over time created a hypothetical rate of 6% for the entire industry. State usury laws also sustained the 6% rate on investments. The comfortable investment process for the banks at the time was captured by the famous "3-6-3" characterization of the mutual savings bank president. In this example, as graphically illustrated in Michael Lewis' *Liar's Poker*, the typical president would get his daily deposit increases by 1 P.M. (cost = 3%), invest the proceeds by 2 P.M. (yield 6%), and be on the first tee at the local country club by 3 P.M. Given the advances in computer technology, the contemporary bank president could have been on the tee by 9 A.M!

Many bank presidents, including my father, used their interest in golf to promote business. On many occasions, when I called my father's bank, I would receive the response that he was out of the office on a "real estate inspection."

Among the larger New Jersey savings banks, dedicated investment officers handled the deployment of funds for their respective institutions. Most were members of the Bond Club of New Jersey and included Kevin Ward and Linda Niro at the Provident, Tony Grippaldi at Montclair, Tony Callabrese at Hoboken (later renamed Washington Savings), Al Chamberlain and Joan Thompson of the Harmonia, and Jim Kranz at the Hudson City. Actually, the investment officers enjoyed a fair degree of "autonomy" and extended their investment activities beyond the laying off of 3% money. Fred Scheidig of the Savings Bank of Central Jersey and Charley Smith of the Raritan were both very active in trading their portfolios on a daily basis, taking advantage of interest rate swings, hedging in the financial futures market, and thereby enhancing the surplus accounts of their respective banks. Whenever the tandem of Fred and Charley got together, few if any of the rest of the group could get a word in edgewise.

Because of its sheer size, the Howard Savings Bank handled its investments differently. Handling the deployment of funds was a fully staffed investment department headed by the Chief Investment Officer (CIO). The investment needs of the constantly growing trust department were also a responsibility of this department. From 1960, the department was dominated by Jack Duerk, Walter Hislop, George Hughes, and Ed McClellan.

John Quinn joined the Howard investment department after working at Mutual Benefit Life Insurance Company in their credit research area of the bond department. In 1976, John was named vice president in charge of the investment department (Hughes retained the position of chief investment officer). Quinn was subsequently named chairman of the investment committee for the NJAMSB in 1981. Unlike the smaller MSBs, Quinn had a team of specialists who covered dedicated areas of the money and capital markets. For example, Richard Murphy was mainly responsible for short-term investments such as federal funds and the like. Leanne Plunkett and Rich Donnelly worked out longer on the curve. Donnelly also was the main liaison with the trust department investment needs.

While Fred and Charley of the SBCJ and Raritan constantly "turned over" their respective portfolios, John Quinn and his staff actively managed the assets in a more deliberate fashion. Under Quinn's direction, the bank annually swapped its portfolio to upgrade coupon income and improve credit quality while achieving certain tax benefits. The Howard rarely if ever swapped its portfolio to purely take advantage of minor or temporary aberrations in the marketplace. This fundamentally conservative investment style added to the mystique of the Howard Savings Bank as a super solid financial institution. Whereas the "Fred and Charley" banks examined and employed many new portfolio techniques, the Howard was the classic example of a "plain vanilla" investment philosophy.

In the wake of its IPO, a sudden and drastic change swept the Howard's deployment of new money flowing into the bank "cookie jar." Indeed, the use of the funds generated from the proceeds of the new issue of Howard Savings Bank common stock deviated from the past uses of funds when the bank existed as a mutual. Some would classify it as a *mis*use of funds, and took the form of investment in real estate development projects. Virtually overnight, the bank emerged as a size player in this marketplace. Instead of extending the process of adding to the gradual accumulation of its diversified mortgage portfolio, the bank totally reversed its posture and opted to buy real estate investment projects averaging $25 million in size, and one particular loan participation entailing a $110 million project in Garden City, Long Island. Prior to demutualizing, the Howard had focused its entire mortgage effort within the twenty-one counties of New Jersey. Now, in a sudden thrust, they were involved with projects outside their service area and included forays into Washington, D.C., North Carolina, Pennsylvania, and elsewhere. The Howard lending activity carried all the way to California, where it must have bought some of the mortgages unwanted by the broad list of savings and loan associations within the huge state. The Howard's timing couldn't have been worse, as it acted when the nation was on the brink of recession and the housing market was in a tailspin from the Tax Law of 1986.

The state of New Jersey investment laws might have restrained the Howard if the bank had bought a package of securitized loans bearing the characteristics of those directly acquired by the bank. Applying any form of "prudent investor test" would have provided some market protection for the bank. In the securities area, the investment department generally limited itself to a position of 5% of the bank's capital and surplus account, approximately $10 million per line item. Although real estate loans were not explicitly covered by the New Jersey investment laws, the Howard had at the very least violated the spirit of the law. The Howard Savings Bank under McCormick's leadership had done nothing expressly illegal.

As a practical matter, the decisions of the McCormick team were imprudent.

For 131 years of its history, the Howard Savings Bank existed as a bullet-proof institution because of its conservative policies and diversified approach to lending and investing. It was the classic example of the well-run savings bank. At its zenith, it was the largest bank of any kind in the state of New Jersey. But the unprecedented restraints of the Volcker monetary policy set up the U.S. banking industry for an inordinate number of bank failures. Once the dust settled, as Jeff Keating mentioned in the foreword to this book, over 1000 banking institutions had disappeared into oblivion. On one drastic day alone, October 10, 1991, the five largest banks in New Hampshire failed and were swiftly closed by the state's commissioner of banking. Citicorp and many other conspicuously large banks around the nation were experiencing balance sheet woes.

Why focus on the Howard Savings Bank's demise? That it was the largest mutual savings bank in New Jersey (peaking out at about $5.8 billion) should have been overshadowed by the closing of the $9 billion City Federal Savings & Loan Association of Somerset, New Jersey, almost a year earlier.

Several factors placed the Howard on a pedestal. The bank had, after all, survived several economic crises and seemed to come through the Great Depression stronger than ever. The bank was revered by its depositors and its employees. They all loved its service orientation. Once branch legislation was liberalized, it sought to locate its offices for the utmost convenience of its customers. Its rates were always competitive. It was the first and one of the few mutuals to have its own trust department. It was the widely acknowledged leader within the state, and in many respects along the East Coast, in the student loan market. The initial losses and the ultimate failure of the Howard Savings brought major headlines in the *Newark Star Ledger*. In the state of New Jersey, across the nation, there was really only one Howard Savings Bank.

But when the numbers hit the news wires in December 1989, the bank reported a massive increase ($650 million) in "non-performing assets," which included the well-publicized Garden City project and which exceeded the total accumulated surplus of the bank. Shareholders, employees, and depositors were all shocked by the news.

The banking industry, as a regulated business, by its very nature entails a certain amount of politics. When the Howard left Newark, it attempted to do so in a subtle or innocuous manner. They called the new multi-acre facility their "administrative" or "operations" center and actually delayed the introduction of the word "headquarters." The legal offices of the bank remained in Newark where it housed the "stockholder relations department." Newark's other financial institutions also tip-toed out of the center city area. Still, the bank seemed unable to muster any clout among the Trenton or Washington, D.C., politicos. For example, twice in the 1980s, the FDIC and the state of New Jersey awarded notable franchise banks (the Orange Savings and the United States Savings) to the Hudson City Savings Bank, the Howard's nearest rival for the largest bank in the state honors. In many respects, the bold management style of Donald McCormick, whose main focus was the forthcoming and self-enriching Howard initial public offering, may have been repulsive to the politicians. Indeed, McCormick's demeanor was in sharp contrast to the soft-spoken Ken Birchby of the Hudson City Savings. Later on, when the Howard was on the brink, the catalyst seemed to be the decision by fourteen members of the board of directors to cash in their deferred compensation ahead of other possible uses of the funds. Jeff Connor, then commissioner of banking in New Jersey, was livid with the board and publicly denounced their lack of confidence in the bank's ability to survive. As unsecured creditors of the bank, the directors had invaded the "corpus of funds" available to all claims against the bank.

Officers and employees who sought to remove their deferred compensation from the bank were unceremoniously denied and aggravated the growing split between the board and its operating staff. As news of the directors' activities spread, Jeff Connors readied his first draft for a "cease and desist" order pertaining to the Howard Savings Bank.[9]

---

[9]Actually, upon investigation, the move by the board created a windfall tax credit, which helped the flow of funds for the bank. This revelation did not impress the commissioner of banking.

THE PRESIDENTS OF THE HOWARD SAVINGS BANK

Since the bank was founded in 1857, there were 13 "Chief Executive Officers" of the Howard Savings Institution, which later was named the Howard Savings Bank. Up until 1961, the CEO of the bank held the title of President. After 1961, the CEO held the title of Chairman of the Board and CEO.

CEO	Term
Beach Vanderpool	1857–1884
Joseph N. Tuttle	1885–1886
Frederick Frelinghuysen	1886–1902
Eugene Vanderpool	1902–1903
Horace T. Brumley	1903–1910
Samuel S. Dennis	1910–1914
Wyant D. Vanderpool	1924–1944
William I. Maude	1944–1961
John W. Kress	1961–1970
Bruce Alexander	1970–1974
Murray Forbes	1974–1982
Donald McCormick	1982–1990
Leo Rogers	1990*
Donald Peterson	1990#
William Tuggle	1990–1992

*Acting CEO
#Vice Chairman of the Board

The following chapters are mini-biographical sketches of the six most recent CEOs and how they impacted the ultimate fate of the Howard Savings Bank.

Chapter 2

The Benevolent Reign of John W. Kress 1961–1970

"We grow our own flowers."

—*John W. Kress*

Supreme Court Justice William J. Brennan Jr. was born the son of an Irish immigrant worker who swept coal for the P. Ballentine Brewing Company in Newark, New Jersey. Brennan graduated from Barringer High School, one of at least five public high schools in Newark, as a member of the class of 1921. John W. Kress, who later in life became CEO of the Howard Savings Institution, was also a member of the Barringer class of 1921. Kress' father was a member of the Newark police force, but died when John was only four years old. Kress then was brought up by another member of the Newark police.

Brennan subsequently graduated from the Wharton School of the University of Pennsylvania and then the Harvard Law School. In 1956, Brennan was named by President Eisenhower to the Supreme Court as the first Catholic justice in the nation's history. Meanwhile, John Kress joined the Howard Savings Institution in 1921 and started a fifty-year career at the bank. He was seventeen years old and planned on pursuing his undergraduate degree at New York University at night. John Kress and William Brennan were self-made men.

☆　☆　☆

When John Kress started his career at the Howard, the executive vice president of the bank was Jason S. Quimby. Quimby was a classic example of a hands on manager who readily identified with his underlings. He admired the innocence and spirit of youth, and he was particularly interested in the activities of John Kress. His intuition told him that young John had the potential to become a business success.

One day, when Mr. Quimby's secretary had called in sick, John Kress delivered mail to Mr. Quimby's office. Normally, Kress would have left the mail with the secretary, but that day he left it directly with Mr. Quimby. The mail was neatly stacked and properly prioritized. Kress bore a great big smile as he handed over the package.

"Good morning, Mr. Quimby, sir! How are you today?" asked John Kress.

"I am fine, John and good morning to you also," replied Mr. Quimby. "I hear good things about how well you are doing in your new job."

"Thank you, sir," Kress politely responded.

"Can you type?" Quimby asked.

Kress replied, "Well, I took a typing class in high school. Can I help you with some typing today, sir?"

Mr. Quimby had a very important letter which had to be typed and in the mail by the next morning. Quimby explained his dilemma and asked Kress if he minded typing the letter for him. Kress immediately obliged.

Mr. Quimby dictated the two-page letter to Kress, who took his notes to the mail room. That afternoon, after his regular round of chores was completed, Kress worked on translating the dictation and produced a flawlessly typewritten letter for Quimby to sign. Kress checked the clock—it was almost 8 P.M.

Early the next morning, John Kress sped to Quimby's office to show him the letter. Quimby was so impressed that he fired his secretary, who had stayed home for the second day in a row. Mr. Quimby's new secretary was John W. Kress, who had just made his first upward advancement at the bank.

In keeping with the Howard's policy, Jason Quimby retired from the bank at age 65, and shortly thereafter his wife of many years passed away. The couple had one son, and as a father Jason Quimby was determined to teach his son the railroad securities business. Every night, he would bring home stacks of information about the rails including cumbersome Moody's and Standard & Poor manuals. Quimby's "overkill" educational practices backfired and his son became a Greenwich Village hippie in the process. His long hair and sloppy demeanor symbolized his rebellion. He was an unwelcome figure whenever he visited the bank to check out his trust account. For Wallace "Wally" Scanlon, trust officer and manager of young Quimby's finances, the responsibility was nothing but a headache.[1]

One last note about Jason Quimby. Mr. Quimby himself remarried. Belying his age, he sired yet another son. The Howard staff continued to be awed by Mr. Quimby.

---

[1]Scanlon, after retiring from the Howard, became a trust officer with the Chatham Trust Company, which quickly experienced a series of mergers ending in its current parent, Fleet.

Although John Kress exhibited a broad variety of talents, it became apparent early on that his interests and abilities were best suited for the trust and investment areas of the bank. While studying nights for his undergraduate degree at New York University, at age 25, he played a key role in establishing the bank's trust department. The trust department was created at the very top of the stock market in 1929. The Howard thus became the first mutual savings bank in the nation to enter the trust business. The trust area fit very well with the bank's emphasis on service and family as it focused on trust funds created by parents for the benefit of their children.

Four years later, a multitude of actual or anticipated bank failures prompted President Franklin D. Roosevelt to adopt the Bank Holiday Act of 1933. FDR used the element of surprise in an attempt to stop the run on the nation's banks. He announced the terms of the act on a Sunday that effectively closed the banks for the next four days.

After weathering the Great Depression, John Kress achieved his first title at the bank in 1941 when he was named vice president and trust officer. Upon turning age 40 in 1944, he was named to the board of managers (referred to as the board of directors in later annual reports of the Howard). He served as executive vice president of the bank from 1949 to his election as president in 1961.

From the moment John W. Kress took over the reins at the Howard Savings Institution, he emphasized how the bank's *raison d'etre* was to service its customers. He stressed how he wanted to pay the bank clients the highest rates of interest on all types of accounts the Howard offered. He also insisted on fortifying the bank's surplus account as a means of protecting all depositors. In his first year as president, he raised the dividend rate (which was effectively interest) to a then very attractive 4%. Deposits grew dramatically, both in absolute dollars and in number of accounts. Kress played the role of a generous banker whose purpose was to service his clients but not to engage in a rate war. Throughout its history, the Howard always maintained a distinct visibility in the area of student savings and student loans. Kress was a strong advocate of continuing this program, even though a cost analysis might have revealed it to be a loss leader in its own right. To Kress, the student savings program equated to image advertising and strengthened the Howard's posture as a bank stressing service over profit.

The role of the mortgage portfolio under President Kress was basically in line with its peers in the mutual savings bank sector. The following recap quantifies the Howard involvement in mortgages in 1969. Figure 2-1 shows the 1967 mortgage portfolio by county.

Size of mortgage portfolio (1967 Annual)	$582 million
Mortgages as a percentage of total assets	68%
Conventional mortgages as % total mortgages	58%
VA guaranteed	21%
FHA Insured	21%
Number of line items held in mortgages	41,684
Number of applications received in 1969	3,613
Dollar value of applications	$82 million
Acceptance ratio	70%
Geographic distribution (% located in New Jersey)	100%
County distribution of mortgage portfolio	21 (all)
Largest county concentration of mortgages	Essex (22%)

The Methods & Research Division was started in 1953 mainly to study automation. The division's first tangible efforts resulted in the establishment of *Telefile*. Initially designed to cover just savings accounts, *Telefile* became identified with the bank's vast mortgage portfolio as 30,000 mortgage loans were converted to the system. In 1969, Kress and his staff made the decision to adapt a new

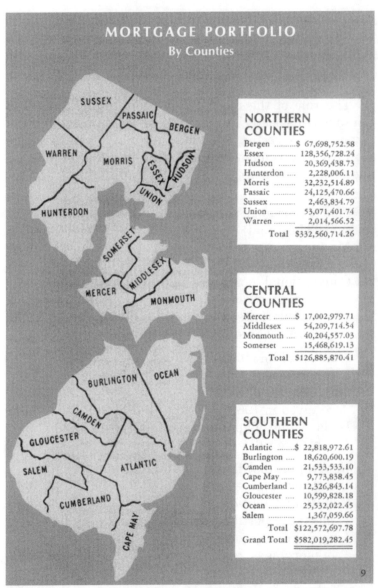

Figure 2-1 Composition of Howard Savings Bank Mortgage
Portfolio December 31, 1967
Source: Annual Report dated 1-1-68.

electronic data processing system to replace the main-frame computer it had just installed in 1961. The Kress team concentrated its efforts on the systems and procedures analysis of all of the applications to be computerized on the new National Cash Register Company's Century 200 system. The new computer center was completed and one of two Century 200 computers had been installed. Eventually, the Howard was recognized as having established the nation's first totally on-line computer system linked to teller machines. John Kress was extremely proud of the equipment relating to this computer system, and he referred to it as "his toy." Whenever visitors from the other savings banks came to his office, Kress proudly demonstrated the system's capabilities. With one animated push of the main button, he could retrieve the bank's prior end-of-the-day footings (total asset size) in a matter of seconds. The figure that beamed across Kress' desk reflected a batching of all the items posted such as deposits, withdrawals, interest, and miscellaneous other items.

During the installation of the computer system, Kress was obsessed with obtaining up-to-date information about the size of the bank and the distribution of its assets. For many years, on New Year's Eve, he would have the accounting department work until 9:00 P.M. so that he could announce the figures at the party that he and Mrs. Kress were attending. Mr. Kress loved to announce the numbers to those in attendance, usually just before the stroke of midnight. One particular New Year's Eve, the comptroller worked beyond the 9 P.M. hour and when he tried to call Mr. Kress, the phone just rang and rang. The comptroller finally gave up on the exercise. At the opening of business following New Year's Day, the comptroller questioned Kress to see if he had the right number for the party. Kress, slightly embarrassed, apologized. The crowd at the party decided to turn off all the phones at the party so as not to be "disturbed." Shortly thereafter, the computer's installation was complete and provided Mr. Kress with all the information he needed before he left the bank for the day, New Year's Eve or otherwise.

During the first half of 1966, the Howard Savings experienced a fairly significant outflow of deposits. The Kress-led management team wanted to see if the deposit trend reflected any flaws in its servicing of its customer base, and thus they ordered the marketing department to conduct two surveys to determine the cause of the money shifts. The first survey, which elicited responses from 3,413 depositors, cited the stock market as the alternative outlet for their withdrawals. Home improvements, transfer for higher returns, investment in bonds, and purchases of automobiles, TVs and appliances were also mentioned. The second survey, which drew 5,275 respondents, confirmed the same consumer patterns. While satisfied with the size of the response, Kress was most pleased by the extensive compliments for the Howard's operation. Less than 1% of those surveyed registered any dissatisfaction with the Howard's service or personnel.

The activist Kress was constantly down in the trenches in Trenton in an effort to achieve legislative gains for the Howard and the rest of the mutual savings banks in New Jersey. In particular, he pushed for improved branch banking laws. Essex County, given its population density, and the city of Newark, just recovering from the riots of 1967, acted as restraints on the Howard's growth potential. As the population of New Jersey began to move south of the Howard service territory, Kress wanted to be able to follow these accounts by opening branches in Monmouth and other southerly counties. He did not want to compromise the service of these accounts, and ultimately his efforts paid off with the statewide branch banking system we know today.

Perhaps more than any other CEO of the Howard, John Kress felt very strongly that the investment portfolio should provide a positive and dynamic role in the bank's overall performance. The investment portfolio was an active force which could help sustain greater long-term growth of the bank's deposit base. The function of the bank's investments went beyond providing liquidity in times of economic stress.

Kress was a strong advocate of the bank's common stock purchase plan, which he felt gave the mutual savings bank industry a substantial competitive edge over commercial bank counterparts. In 1944, Kress proposed to the Howard's board of managers that the bank specifically sell some of their longer government bonds and buy common stocks with the proceeds. In all simplicity, he foresaw a post World War II economy which would experience substantial long-term growth because of pent-up consumer demands but perhaps suffer through some inflationary phases. He saw an economic climate which was favorable for stocks, unfavorable for bonds, and made a policy proposal based on his convictions. The board endorsed the Kress proposal and the bank soon embarked on an aggressive equity acquisition program.

The postwar economy vindicated Kress' moves.

John Kress took great pride in showcasing the various investment holdings in the bank's annual report. While he was president, the annual report always included a multi-page listing of *all* the individual securities held by the bank. The report included the amount invested in the security and a brief description of the item. By placing the portfolio on display in the annual report, though not required nor done by many of the other mutuals, the Howard demonstrated the quality, maturity distribution, and liquidity factors inherent in its holdings. Like almost any diversified portfolio, the Howard had some weaker investments listed. Nonetheless, Kress aired the entire list out to the public. Mr. Kress had nothing to hide.

Another aspect of the annual reports issued during the Kress years was that he included an income statement along with the customary balance sheet, just another example of the Kress professionalism.

With Kress at the helm, the Howard emerged as one of the more visible buyers of new issues of railroad equipment trust certificates. In the 1969 annual report, the Howard listed holdings of approximately $20 million in equips and terminal bonds, representing about 15% of its total commitment to the corporate bond market. The Howard was active in the shorter end of these issues, and frequently could buy some of the paper cheaper than the advertised level in the marketplace.

Once, while on a visit to the bank, I bumped into Mr. Kress on the elevator. He was aware that my firm (Halsey Stuart & Co) had just underwritten an issue of Gulf Mobile & Ohio rail equips. However, we had been unable to move the first three maturities at the officially advertised level (also known as the list price). As we got off the elevator, Mr. Kress asked me, "Is there any room in the offering price of the Gulf Mobile & Ohio equips? They seem awfully tight to me!"

The expression "tight" implied the equips in question represented less than minimal value when compared to U.S. governments of comparable maturity. I was quite sure that Mr. Kress' assessment was correct and so I encouraged him to make a bid for the strip of bonds. Mr. Kress loved the thought of meddling in the arena of the investment department. I replied to Mr. Kress, "They might have an .05 of room in the bonds, and I will check as soon as I get to the office."

Upon checking, the syndicate contact Francisco "Frank" Sinatra said that they would hit a down bid on the bonds if the client took all three maturities. He circled me on the bonds, I proposed the deal, and we had a trade. Although in the final analysis we wrote the ticket with Jack Duerk, it was gratifying to have a trade sparked by a chance encounter with "the Big Guy."

Part of the Howard's interest in equips evolved from the fact that there were virtually no intermediate corporate bonds available in the new issue (i.e., current coupon) market. Utilities, telephone companies and high grade industrials were active issuers of longer dated paper (30–40 year maturities). The rail equips helped the investor to fill a maturity void while obtaining a little more yield.

The Howard also was an active buyer of utility bonds. Most of the utilities issued first mortgage bonds which were secured by a first lien on all the company's plant and equipment. As in the case of the rail equips, the pledge of collateral provided the investor with attractive protection and so they accumulated a sizable volume of these securities. Since 2000, utilities have been using other methods of issuing bonds or providing collateral through "fall away" mortgage bonds. Presumably, the original concept of mortgage bonding with utilities was an outgrowth of the Depression as well.

In general, the activity of the investment department emphasized quality and the use of intermediate maturities. The Howard's investment philosophy was viewed as being ultraconservative and representative of the overall posture of the bank.

The Howard was also an active participant in the IPO market for common stock. Using the clout of the investment department, the Howard frequently got favorable treatment on "hot issues" of common stock. But they didn't buy these issues with the intention of holding them. Nor did they buy them as temporary investments in the bank's portfolio. The individual officers of the bank bought the shares for their own personal accounts and flipped the holdings back to the street, most often registering a tidy trading profit in the process. The Howard officers set up numbered trust accounts, and Wall Street confirmed its trades to these accounts. A typical confirmation might have read:

Halsey Stuart & Co., Inc.
30 Broad Street
New York, NY 10292
January 15, 1969

You bought 100 shares of STP Corporation Common
    Stock
        Prospectus Enclosed
        When as and if issued
Order billed to: Howard Savings Institution
                For account # 987654321
                768 Broad Street,
                Newark, New Jersey 07102

As shown, in early 1969, Halsey Stuart was a part of the underwriting of the new issue of the STP Corporation. The Howard actually bought my entire allotment and subdivided the order into a lot of small numbered accounts. At the time, the Howard officers' scheme was not prohibited by any part of the securities law. However, once the practice spread and the consideration of "fairness" was evaluated, the SEC stepped in and banned the concept of privileged accounts. The extent of the profits generated to the various officers was "found money." The activity was entirely funded with their own finances, and no agreement between the bank and the participants existed whereby the bank would buy sour deals.

During the Kress administration, the Howard was restricted to branching within the county of its home office location. Although Essex County had the largest population of the twenty-one counties, further growth was impeded by the high density of the area.[2] The Howard and the other Newark banks lobbied aggressively for a change in the branch banking laws. The walls of protectionism were slow to tumble, as the smaller commercial banks in the state had their own profitable fiefdoms and an active lobbying group. As a compromise, the state initially set up three banking zones (north, middle, and south). The Howard was able to expand outside Essex County and into the northern "zone" of this plan. A decade later, the three-zone split of the state was discarded and the right to statewide banking arrived. Similar activities took place in many other states across the nation.

Kress was also an active lobbyist on behalf of the Howard and the industry in general. He vigorously campaigned against the proposed 2.5% tax on the accumulated surplus of MSBs as proposed in the state assembly and senate.

☆　☆　☆

---

[2]See Table 1-1 on constituent communities of Essex County.

John Kress was a people-oriented president. He was very sensitive to any customer or depositor complaints, and aired many on an individual basis. He relished mixing with the bank's employees. He drove a DeSoto sedan with a rumble seat and chartreuse fenders. While commuting from his home in Verona, New Jersey, he picked up many of the workers along Bloomfield Avenue as they waited for their bus ride to downtown Newark. When he and his wife took vacation trips, he often sent postcards to employees. He enjoyed playing golf with the bond traders from the Bond Club of New Jersey. He was particularly proud of the bank's softball team, which won the Greater Newark Bank and Insurance League in 1940 & 1941. Starring for the team as a part of its "murderers' row" were first baseman Walter Hislop and outfielder Jack Duerk.

He nurtured the concept of the Howard staff being like a family. He was most excited when he found out that Walter Hislop was going to marry Marie Elaine Preston from the bank's trust department. Kress sent the newlywed Hislops on a business trip to Detroit to attend a seminar on securities analysis. Mr. Kress had attended the same seminar several years prior with his wife Rose.

To emphasize the family aspect of the bank, Kress often was quoted as saying, "We grow our own flowers."

The entrance to the Montclair Golf Club was less than a mile from the Kress' home on Whalen Drive in Verona, New Jersey. The club has four challenging nine-hole courses and was the scene of the United States Amateur Championship in 1986. The Kress family greatly enjoyed the fruits of its memberhip in the Montclair Golf Club.

The employees of the Howard derived a sense of pride in their institution when John Kress was elected president of the National Association of Mutual Savings Banks. Similar vibrations occurred when he was selected president of the New Jersey Association (1944–46) and the Essex County chapter of the American Institute of Banking. In the process, John Kress achieved the stature of being a strong banker on a national level. As he guided the bank

Howard Investments Portfolio: Sample Pages
(1967 Summer Report)

Public Utility Bonds cont.   *Book Value*

Virginia Electric & Power 1st & Ref. "E" 2¾s 1975 $251,392.90
Virginia Electric & Power 1st & Ref. "Q" 4⅞s 1991   52,406.52
Washington Gas Light 1st 3½s 1976   145,893.06
Washington Gas Light 1st 6¼s 1992   150,946.50
Western Massachusetts Electric 1st "F" 5¾s 1997   306,000.00

INDUSTRIAL BONDS

Associates Investment Co. Deb 5¼s 1977 $194,625.20
Associates Investment Co. Subordinated Deb.
  5¾s 1977   71,839.53
Atlantic Richfield Deb. 5⅝s 1997   98,218.75
Beneficial Finance Deb. 4⅞s 1981   511,228.54
Beneficial Finance Deb. 5s 1977   515,559.06
Beneficial Finance Deb. 5s 1990   500,000.00
Bethlehem Steel Cons. "I" 2¾s 1970   101,259.76
Bethlehem Steel Deb. 5.40s 1992   305,000.00
Borg-Warner Deb. 5½s 1992   300,000.00
Byam Realty Secured Note "A" 5⅝s 1981   227,780.88
Carborundum Deb. 6s 1992   200,000.00
Caterpillar Tractor Deb. 5.30s 1992   500,000.00
C.I.T. Financial Deb. 5⅛s 1980   240,559.00
C.I.T. Financial Deb. 6⅜s 1986   248,750.00
Coastal States Gas Producing Deb. w/w 5½s 1980   250,000.00
Commercial Credit Subordinated Note 4½s 1977   490,300.00
Deere Deb. 5.40s 1992   299,125.00
Diamond Alkali Deb. 3⅜s 1978   350,785.73
Electronic Associates Promissory Note 5s 1978   165,000.00
Electronic Associates Promissory Note 5¾s 1973   120,000.00
Electronic Associates Promissory Note 6½s 1981   300,000.00
General Acceptance Senior Deb. 4⅞s 1985   445,725.00
General Acceptance Senior Note 5¼s 1977   750,000.00
General Acceptance Senior Deb. 6s 1980   255,885.38
General Electric Deb. 5.30s 1992   497,500.00
General Motors Acceptance Deb. 3½s 1972   500,000.00
General Motors Acceptance Deb. 4⅝s 1982   405,528.27
General Motors Acceptance Deb. 4⅞s 1987   396,000.00
Harsco Deb. 5½s 1992   299,250.00
Hooker Chemical Deb. 4⅞s 1991   322,968.75
Household Finance Deb. 4⅜ 1987   747,165.00

Household Finance Deb. 5s 1982	164,243.92
International Minerals & Chemical	
Conv. Subordinated Deb. 4s 1991	207,984.50
May Department Stores Deb. 2⅝s 1972	250,898.72
May Department Stores Deb. 3¼s 1978	250,000.00
May Stores Realty Gen'l 5s 1977	$266,906.12
National Steel 1st 3⅛s 1982	199,500.00
Sears Roebuck Acceptance Deb. 4⅝s 1972	200,203.03
Sears Roebuck Deb. 4¾s 1983	1, 388,010.48
Shell Oil Deb. 4⅝s 1986	1,020,538.60
Shell Oil Deb. 5.30s 1992	498,750.00
Sherwin-Williams Deb. 5.45s 1992	300,000.00
Standard Oil Company (New Jersey)	
Deb. 2¾s 1974	498,393.54
Standard Oil Company (New Jersey) Deb. 6s 1997	300,000.00
Sylvania Electric Products Deb. 4¾s 1980	232,965.95
Texas Oil & Gas 1st "A" 4⅞s 1985	350,000.00
Texas Oil & Gas 1st "B" 6¾s 1986	1,150,000.00
United States Steel Deb. 4½s 1986	504,554.47
Westinghouse Electric Deb. 5⅜s 1992	500,000.00

OTHER BONDS

Alberta Government Telephones Commission	
Deb. 6¼s 1992	$296,250.00
Alberta Municipal Financing Deb. 4¾s 1984	274,678.31
Bankers Trust Capital Notes 4½s 1988	483,418.02
British Columbia Hydro & Power Authority	
"AK" 6¼s 1992	296,250.00
Chase Manhattan Bank Capital Notes 4.60s 1990	499,375.00
Edmonton Deb. 4¾s 1983	298,501.37
International Bank for Reconstruction &	
Development 3¼s 1981	250,622.52
International Bank for Reconstruction &	
Development 4¼s 1979	657,451.89
International Bank for Reconstruction &	
Development 5s 1985	412,646.10
International Bank for Reconstruction &	
Development 5⅜s 1992	501,875.00
Meadow Brook National Bank Capital	
Note 4.85s 1989	500,000.00
Montreal Deb. 3½s 1968	300,000.00
Montreal Deb. 5⅜s 1980	996,000.00
Montreal Deb. 6⅜s 1992	196,940.00

Morgan Guaranty Trust Co. of New York	
Capital Notes 5s 1992	492,500.00
Newfoundland Municipal Financing	
Deb. 7s 1987	500,000.00
Ontario (Province) Deb. 3¼s 1975	241,875.00
Ontario (Province) Deb. 4¾s 1984	102,110.94
Ontario (Province) Deb. 5⅝s 1997	500,000.00

SAMPLE pages from the Howard Savings Bank investment portfolio as shown in the Annual Report of 1967. Represents a partial listing of the bank's public utility bonds, the entire list of industrial bonds, and most of the international bonds held by the bank.

Source: Howard Savings Bank Annual Report.

through a period of expansion and profitability, the bank built a reputation for being a very solid institution.

As a consequence of his expanded role on the public speaking circuit, Kress decided to hire a public relations expert to write his speeches. Leo Rogers, a Villanova graduate and a member of the Rider University faculty, was selected to be the creator of more eloquent oratory on the part of Mr. Kress and other management types at the bank.

Kress also used the bank's annual reports to recognize the achievements of its employees. He listed all promotions and titles as far down the hierarchy as assistant secretary, assistant trust officer, and assistant vice president. He congratulated those who had retired within the last year. With his regime overlapping the Vietnam War, he recognized the members of the Howard staff who were on military duty. As if to fulfill a designed objective, the profile of the Howard Savings as a family of employees strengthened during the Kress years. This cohesiveness was not an accident but a result of many deliberate programs initiated by Mr. Kress himself.

John Kress married the former Rose Louise Ruegg whom he met in church. The couple had three children in 14 months. John Jr. was born and then the identical twins (Donald and Raymond) arrived. Actually, the Kresses had hoped for a daughter after John was born, but instead wound up with three sons. Don jokingly says he was supposed to be "Rosemary." The three boys enjoyed the fruits of a college education, with John graduating from Princeton and the twins graduating from Lafayette College in Easton, Pennsylvania.

Donald Kress was the only offspring to have a career in finance, spending over 40 years working on Wall Street. His twin brother Raymond was an Episcopal priest in Ft. Myers, Florida and his older brother Jack was in the advertising business.

At the suggestion of his father, Don started his career at Goodbody & Company in the fall of 1959. Mr. Kress said of Goodbody, "They will be around forever." In reality, Goodbody was one of the first security firms to fail as a result of the operations crisis that resulted from the sudden surge in stock market volume. A series of Wednesday closings solved the problem for most firms, but Goodbody became a casualty in the late 1960s.

In his early years at Goodbody, Don covered the Howard Savings Bank for equity and fixed income products. At the time, Goodbody had a strong municipal bond department and their traders had an aggressive bid for a block of close to $400,000 principal amount of some Wharton Sewer Authority (NJ) bonds. As a result Don worked up a swap proposal whereby the Howard could sell their holding and replace it with a higher yielding yet better quality issue. Don presented the swap in full detail to Walt Hislop, who felt the trade was quite compelling. Walter then proceeded to Mr. Kress' office to explain to him what he wanted to do. Without hesitation, Mr. Kress spurted out, "Sell the bonds to Merrill Lynch." Without disclosing his source, Walt explained to his boss that he thought the bank should do the trade with the salesman originating the idea. Again Mr. Kress said, "Sell the bonds to Merrill." Finally, Walter indicated that Don and his firm Goodbody had generated the trade idea. Mr. Kress then stood his ground and told Walter that when he bought the Wharton bonds years ago, he assured the Merrill salesman that if the bonds were ever sold, Merrill would do the trade. "My word is my bond," said Mr. Kress. Walter sold the Whartons to Merril Lynch.

The custom of retrading issues with those that sold you the securities is common during new issue marketing periods. Managing underwriters frequently oversell or over-allot bonds just to satisfy all their customers, often resulting in a net short position. Clients so treated are expected to retrade their bonds with the dealer who supplied them. However, in the case of seasoned issues such as the Wharton Sewer Authority bonds, several years had passed since their issuance and Merrill's involvement should have been on an equal basis with Goodbody. But Mr. Kress wanted to keep his word. He always did.

While the Kress twins were at Lafayette, Frank Buckworth was playing football as an interior lineman for rival Lehigh University. Frank graduated from LU in 1961 with a B.A. in economics and joined the Howard Savings Bank in 1965. At the age of 25, Frank accepted a position in the trust department.

Buckworth enjoyed working for John Kress. "He was an old-line, highly respected banker" succinctly captured the former gridder's opinion of the esteemed executive.

On numerous occasions, John Kress received various honors and distinctions from a broad variety of causes and civic organizations. For example, he received the Annual Brotherhood Award from the National Conference of Christians and Jews in 1967, the Advertising Club's Outstanding Citizen of New Jersey award for 1967, and the Americanism Award from the Anti-Defamation League in 1969. He was bestowed with honorary degrees from Bloomfield College (1967) and Monmouth College (1970).

While the Howard presented an outward image of corporate unity and harmony, the bank had its share of internal discomforts and rivalries. Early on, as John Kress sought to climb the executive ladder, he had to combat several other equally ambitious officers of the bank. Kress' CEO was William Maude who delighted in the competitive struggle for the top positions. It was integral to his own business philosophy that such contests strengthened the character of the surviving executive. Jonas Swenson gave John Kress a run for the top position. When the board named Kress executive vice president and Swenson senior vice president, the combination of Maude-Kress-Swenson was isolated on the staffing chart for being the only three executives with senior titles. Swenson performed well, but ultimately succumbed to a brain aneurism and died on the job. Subsequently, Kress moved up to the CEO slot when Maude retired. Kress solidified his leadership position as he progressed through his nine-year reign.

As John Kress approached age 65, the mandatory retirement age for all Howard CEOs, the issue of his successor became the major project for the board of managers. For all his strengths, Kress was very uncomfortable working under the chairmanship of his predecessor William Maude. Maude seemed jealous of Kress' achievements as well as his popularity. Even in the role of a lame duck chairman, Maude seemed to work to neutralize some of Kress' power. Throughout the Kress years, Maude maintained a makeshift office at the bank, essentially utilizing the board room, which contained no phones.

Maude's best friend in the Howard hierarchy was Norman McGrory, whose titles included that of executive vice president and director. Kress and McGrory acted as the only two active officers of the bank who were also on its board. The rest of the eighteen directors came from various segments of the corporate world, the legal fraternity, academia, and even the realm of politics. The era permitted interlocking directorates, and as previously mentioned Robert G. Cowen, chairman of the National Newark & Essex Banking Corporation, sat on the Howard Board while John Kress enjoyed the same privilege as director of the NNE. Congressman Peter H. B. Frelinghuysen from the fifth district (NJ) served the Howard board for many years.

Educators included Dr. Robert W. Van Houten, president of the Newark College of Engineering and Dr.

Mason Gross, president of Rutgers–The State University, giving the bank strong representation from the nation's academic world.

Corporation CEOs, some active and some retired, included the following board members:

Name of Director	*Corporate Affiliation*
Hubert O'Brien	Rockwin Corporation
Donald C. Luce	Public Service E&G
William C. Cochran	The Reinsurance Corp. of NY
Lloyd Christianson	Electronic Associates Inc.
Robert Krementz (VP)	Krementz & Co.
Albert G. Mumma (also retired Rear Admiral USN)	Worthington Corporation
Richard R. Wiss	J. Wiss & Sons
Orville E. Beal	Prudential Insurance Co.
Fred B. Sullivan	Walter Kidde & Co.

Attorneys included John Farrell and Everett Scherer. Bernard J. Grad was a prominent architect.

Whereas the members of this board were normally in agreement on most policy matters, they were far from united concerning the matter of Mr. Kress' retirement. A candidate seeking the CEO slot had to receive at least two-thirds of the votes from the members of the board. Historically, the job had been more of a "rubber stamp" since an incumbent EVP moved up to be president of the bank upon the timely retirement of the existing president. But John Kress sought to block the advancement of Norm McGrory.

Although Kress liked McGrory personally, he was not especially impressed with McGrory professionally, and relegated his assignments to mostly giving benedictions at banquets. To those who monitored such developments, it seemed only natural that McGrory should advance to the CEO slot since he had just completed his term as the president of the New Jersey Savings Bank Association. As a result of Maude's maneuvers, Kress felt saddled with McGrory as his executive vice president. As his retirement neared, Kress seemed totally dedicated to finding a successor other than McGrory. Ideally, he should have started training a successor long ago. Regardless, family banking went just so far. In Kress' mind, in addition to the continuing Maude influence, there was the potential of adverse publicity for the bank arising from a marital conflict involving the president-elect. As a result, the top management of the Howard was locked in a turf battle over succession which would leave its scar on the bank for many years to come.

Somehow, in the course of events, the resume of Bruce Alexander crossed the desk of John Kress. Bruce was the president of a modest sized Massachusetts savings bank and possessed a Harvard Law School degree. Among minimal other data, the resume listed Alexander's phone number. At the next board meeting, Kress presented Alexander's resume and recommended they hire the New England banker with the intention of his eventually becoming president. Undoubtedly impressed by Alexander's Harvard degree, Kress may have sensed that Alexander would be a strong president to advance the Howard in the electronic data processing area. The board and others close to Kress proposed that Alexander be interviewed by the board or at least give more details about his resume. Kress felt that such actions were unnecessary and in fact might embarrass Alexander.

For the time being, John Kress had to eat his own words (i.e., "We grow our own flowers"). He was adamant and his less-than-gentle persuasion prevailed. At the next board meeting, the decision to hire Alexander was made. Throughout its 104-year history, the Howard had always promoted top executives from its qualified list of junior officers. John Kress, however, marched to a different drummer and broke the string. When Kress retired in 1970, Bruce Alexander was named president of the Howard Savings Bank. The Howard soon would be beset with another round of management infighting. The atmosphere was further charged by an article in the *Newark Star Ledger* pointing out the fact that the Howard had selected an outsider to be its new CEO even though it had a reservoir of talent available to fill the gap. By expediting the hire of Alexander, Kress had hoped to limit such media involvement.

Still Mr. Kress could retire knowing he had blunted the lingering Maude influence with his Alexander-for-McGrory substitution. The outwardly easygoing John Kress suppressed a lot of the stress associated with the turbulence at the bank.

Continuing on as a member of the board, he felt uncomfortable as he witnessed the unfolding administration of Bruce Alexander, his own hand-picked successor. Another round of stress overwhelmed Mr. Kress. His own retirement was short-lived. Just three years after stepping down at the bank, John Kress died of a heart attack on September 24, 1973. He was 68 years old.

Chapter 3

The Short Reign of Bruce Alexander 1970–1974

"I didn't enter the banking business to make money. I entered it to make it a better world."

—Bruce Alexander, retired
Greenfield, MA
June 25, 2003

Upon receiving his law degree from Harvard University in 1948*, Bruce Alexander set his sights on a career in the banking industry. Although he eschewed the potential financial rewards of his chosen profession, he nonetheless wanted to be a bank president who had the power to effectuate change. Motivated more like a missionary, Bruce

Alexander was not your standard issue bank executive personality.

Bruce Alexander started his executive job search in Pittsfield, Massachusetts. Located in the western portion of the state, almost 40 miles from Albany New York, the city of Pittsfield was dominated by the General Electric Company for almost three-fourths of the 20th Century. For example, in the 1950s, three out of every four Pittsfield workers had a job with General Electric. The work was primarily defense related and supplied our nation's military efforts in World War I, World War II, and the Cold War.

Bruce remembers his original interview with the Berkshire County Savings Bank very well. The conversation changed when Alexander asked the "purpose" of a mutual savings institution. Gardiner S. Morse, president of the bank, replied that the bank's goals were "eleemosynary" in nature. The concept was quite supportive of Alexander's own business philosophy. Alexander recently said, "I was not in this business to make money. I wanted to make an impact on the banking world."

Pittsfield was obviously vulnerable to any downsizing of the nation's defense budget. Also, over ten years had passed since Bruce started at the Berkshire Bank and Mr. Morse showed no signs of retiring any time soon. Thus, when Alexander had the opportunity to become the president of the New Bedford Five Cent Savings Bank, he quickly opted for the change.

New Bedford was also a city in the transition phase. From the days of *Moby Dick* and Captain Ahab, the city dwelled on its exciting history as a whaling capital. The city in the '60s and '70s was trying to lure industry and to highlight the natural deep sea fishing port on the inner harbor.

When Bruce Alexander took the New Bedford job in 1961, he had many ideas on how the bank could improve the diversity of the local area. When Alexander presented these ideas to the Massachusetts legislature, he was constantly rebuffed. For example, Alexander wanted to impose term limitations on the presidents of mutual savings banks. He felt that 10 years was long enough for any executive to serve as president of a savings bank. The Commonwealth offices responded that Alexander's ideas were sound but just "too ambitious". They turned him down on several branch applications. Soon Alexander decided it was time to rid himself of the Massachusetts yoke. He prepared a resume and selectively circulated it to some banks outside Massachusetts. Following the advice of a friend, Alexander made sure a facsimile of the resume was sent to John Kress, then president and chief executive officer of the Howard Bank in Newark, New Jersey. His thoughts were simply that Mr. Kress could either consider the resume or chuck it into the circular file.

When Alexander's resume crossed the desk of Howard CEO John Kress, he found the contents most interesting. As he reviewed Alexander's credentials, John Kress was impressed by Alexander's two main accomplishments early in life, i.e., a Law Degree from Harvard University and that he was the president of the local bank. In Kress' mind, the Harvard Law connection superficially at least, placed Alexander in the same category as his Barringer High School classmate, William Brennan. With his own retirement fairly imminent, and with his apparent distaste for Norman McGrory, Kress immediately followed up on Alexander's resume. Kress was well aware that intelligent management talent was rarely available from the "labor market." Also, since he received the resume directly, the Howard and John Kress could hire Alexander without the attendant hiring fees attached to such executive placements. For most savings bankers, even the voluntary changing of jobs was a traumatic experience. Without apologies, Kress read Bruce Alexander's resume at the next Howard Board meeting.

Members of the Board suggested to Mr. Kress that they personally interview Mr. Alexander or at the very least obtain more background information. But Kress, fearful that Alexander might be quickly hired by another savings bank, replied, "I don't want to disturb the poor fellow." Kress pressed his case and soon the Board relented. Bruce Alexander, a total unknown in New Jersey banking circles, was elected President & CEO of the Howard Bank.

Alexander was a short man in stature, about 5'6" tall. His Boston accent was quite discernible and immediately labeled him as an "outsider".

When Alexander moved to New Jersey, he settled on buying a house in Montclair. Shortly after making the move, he was mugged on the streets of the somewhat urban community. As a result, he spent the first few weeks of his presidency with an ugly bandage which barely covered the bump on his head.

The bump on the head, the unfamiliar Boston accent, and his short stature all seemed to reconfirm Alexander's status as an outsider. The Howard employees had no preconceived ideas about Bruce Alexander's management style, but they soon discovered he focused on the expense side of the ledger. With ax and pink slips in hand, he immediately set out to reduce the arguably bloated Howard staff. In effect, he went on a purge of the senior officers. As a newcomer, he owed no one any favors, he had no personal favorites. Every department head and every employee was fair game for the Alexander expense cutting plan. Most officers and employees stayed out of his "traffic pattern". Early on, Bruce Alexander started to alienate himself from the Howard family.

One of the casualties of the Alexander onslaught was Bill Grimm, who handled many of the comptroller functions of the bank. Alexander fired him simply because he wasn't a Certified Public Accountant (CPA). Alexander then hired a numbers guy who indeed was a CPA. The CPA knew accounting, but didn't understand the functioning of a savings bank like the Howard. For example, every day Walter Hislop—in the capacity of managing the short term money position of the bank—routinely shifted large amounts of money from bank to bank in order to take advantage of the best rates available in the federal funds market. But the CPA wanted Walter to obtain two signatures before he consummated any trade. Walter stressed the importance of timing "on the wire" executions in the fed funds market, where your word was your bond. Within the market place, the simple words "You're Done" closed an infinite number of multi-million dollar transactions. For a few days, Walter's hands were tied, but eventually he convinced the CPA and Alexander that money market operations should be exempted from the signature requirements.

Alexander seemed to like to meddle in the simplest of bank chores. In 1972, Wally Scanlon, a veteran of many years in the trust department, was missing a key document from one of his files and so he ventured to the rear of the trust area where the extensive files were located. Somehow, Alexander discovered that Scanlon had accomplished this routine task on his own and he scolded Scanlon unmercifully for not "delegating authority" by sending someone else of lesser rank to find the document.

It seemed as if Alexander tried to manage people or events that needed no further management guidance. Scanlon needed no advice on how to allocate his time.

In effect, it seemed that Alexander sought to downsize the Howard so that he could "micro-manage" the bank. Unlike the Berkshire Bank and the New Bedford Five Cent Savings Bank, the Howard retained a relatively large and talented manpower pool and was ideally suited for a "committee rule" style of management. Thus, under the guise of expense slashing, Alexander set out to adapt to the Howard organization. Even if warranted in certain cases, Alexander's cuts were viewed with skepticism. The Howard which John Kress left as CEO was like a huge symphony with all components of the orchestra having a role in its success. Alexander, on the other hand, as conductor of this large personnel assembly, admitted to being involved with a phenomenon that was just too big.

In his first year as President, Alexander scuttled the previous method of producing the Annual Report. While Kress relished the production of a glossy 40 page detailed report of the bank's security holdings and other matters,

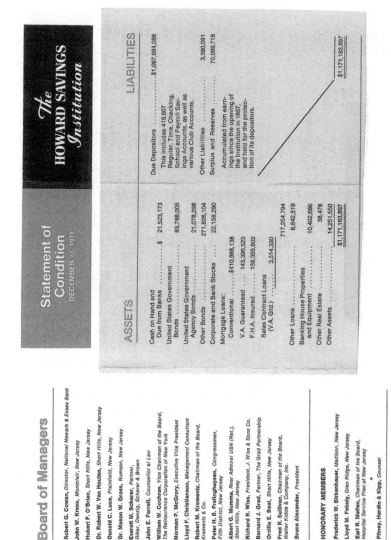

Figure 3-1 Pocket size annual report of 1972—which contrasted with Kress' thirty-page report—typified Alexander's expense cut emphasis.

Figure 3-1 Continued

Alexander opted for a one piece report, folded four ways on relatively inexpensive paper. One virtually needed a magnifying glass to read the numbers. Most of the required financial information was listed and an abbreviated posting of the officers and directors was made. While the Howard family took pride in showcasing itself in the Kress annual reports, the Alexander reports were more in keeping for a modest size bank from Massachusetts. Again, Alexander was grappling with the size of his new banking assignment.

Alexander tried to set the example of a Spartan presidency. He frequently worked until after seven in the evening. While heading the Howard, he never took a vacation. Walt Hislop was able to call him "Bruce", and on many occasions received a call at four o'clock in the afternoon to discuss the economy and the bond market. The two frequently carried on their conversations until well after seven in the evening. Conceivably, Walt Hislop represented an inner circle of one for Alexander.

In one of his after-hours private meetings with Alexander, the CEO asked Walt why the bank was named "The Howard Savings Institution." But without allowing Walt the opportunity to answer his own rhetorical question, Alexander had his answer in hand: "We are a bank, not an institution." The next day, Alexander set in motion the necessary actions to change the name of the bank to "The Howard Savings Bank." For Bruce Alexander, nothing at the Howard was sacred, not even its proud name.

Alexander even "roughed up" the career of his Executive Vice President, Murray Forbes. At the time of Bruce Alexander's selection as President of the Howard, Murray Forbes was working his way through the chairs of the New Jersey Association of Mutual Savings Banks. In a few months, he would assume the presidency of the NJAMSB. In an unprecedented move, overriding the prior endorsement of John Kress and the Howard Board, Alexander forced Forbes to withdraw from the officer sweepstakes of the state association.

"Too much time away from the Bank" captured Alexander's feelings about extra-curricular activities. To save expenses, Alexander also limited the number of executives who could attend the annual conference to a mere four or five, about the equivalent to the tiny Rahway Savings Institution list of attendees. Suddenly, the actions of the strange new CEO reached beyond the walls of the bank itself. Overnight, everyone in the industry was aware of the internal strife taking place at the Howard.

The iconoclast Alexander was like a social outcast at the convention, the grim reaper who had severed the social ties of the middle Howard management with the rest of the NJAMSB management. Many golf foursomes, which had been part of the Conference lineup for years, had to be rearranged.

Before Alexander, almost all members of the Howard staff worked their jobs diligently without fearing any upper management authority interfering or second guessing their achievements. Alexander's job cuts and the Murray Forbes incident changed all that. Alexander was a constant fixture, making observations, as he quietly checked up on the various departments several times a day. The Howard of the early 1970s seemed to function partially out of fear.

Alexander showed a form of paranoia for group gatherings and banking's traditional method of management, i.e., "committee rule." Instead, Alexander favored one-on-one meetings with individual members of his management team. When he found out that Frank Buckworth played college football at Lehigh, he immediately called the burly former lineman into his office. Buckworth was surprised to learn of Alexander's avid interest in football, and the two exchanged generalities about the sport for hours.

In the early 1970s, conformity in business attire was expected of all business leaders, especially of prominent bankers. Individuality and casual days surfaced in the 1980s and advanced in the 1990s with most corporations relaxing their dress code. The advent of companies like Microsoft, whose leader Bill Gates only wore a necktie to Congressional hearings, set the tone for the nation's workers. Bruce Alexander's tendency toward informal attire was probably an outgrowth of his less-than-metropolitan background (i.e., Pittsifield and New Bedford, Massachusetts). Conceivably, he was a man ahead of his time.

In the investment arena, Alexander apparently looked into some of the investment policies of Jack Duerk, whose retirement overlapped his own selection as president. As a result, while Duerk rested in sunny Arizona, Alexander seemed to harbor some harsh criticisms of Duerk's investment policies. Since his rapport with Duerk's successor, Walter Hislop was evolving into a viable relationship. Alexander confided in Hislop and worked as well with him as any of the Howard officers. Alexander had apparently checked out Walter's background and confirmed his knowledge about the market arenas. But Walter was very supportive of Duerk, and when Alexander referred to Duerk in one of their private meetings as being "stupid", Walter immediately challenged his boss' statement. Alexander then rose from his desk, put his hands on Walter's shoulders and said, "We're still friends aren't we?" Alexander told Walter that he had the best IQ in the bank. Rumors of similar activity among other bank employees were rampant.

Leo Rogers was another member of the Howard management team who seemed to work well with Bruce Alexander. Leo and Alexander toiled long hours on the bank marketing program to broaden its depositor base within the metropolitan New York City area. Under Alexander's watch, the slogan "Be Howard Powered" was developed and seemed to launch a new era of growth for the bank. The marketing program enabled Rogers to move up the management ladder, and his office was soon on the 5th Floor of 768 Broad Street.

Bruce Alexander broke the "color barrier" by being the first CEO to name a black member of the Board of Managers. In 1972, he named Dr. James R. Cowan, a prominent physician from Maplewood NJ and the United Hospital Group.

A group of officers led by Norm McGrory attempted to gain support and organize a coup to oust the increasingly unpopular Alexander. Other groups of Howard officers were meeting behind his back, and he was aware of this development. A modest exodus of younger management talent took place, leaving a void that would later impair the bank's succession process. The hiring freeze, the center piece of Alexander's austerity program, added to the problem of who would lead the bank in the future. Kress had been a super-star in bringing the bank to the point it represented as perhaps the strongest bank in the State of NJ. Forbes represented the new era of banking that was just falling into place: extensive statewide branching and interstate banking, varieties of new mortgage products, the construction of the bank's new headquarters in Livingston, and adapting to all the changes wrought by the Reagan administration. In short, quite possibly the unorthodox presidency of Bruce Alexander acted like a buffer enabling the staff to better appreciate the strong regimes of Kress and Forbes.

Alexander's controversial moves all impacted the expense side of the ledger. As far as the use of bank funds, he invested them in the same conservative manner as his predecessors. The ratios that hurt the bank in the 1980s were quite strong in the 1970s. Still, the bank was too much for Alexander to handle. In a few short years, he ruled the bank in total isolation. He couldn't fathom the reasons for his own lack of popularity. Alexander's problems soon impacted his health and he suffered a nervous breakdown.

In January of 1974, the Board of Directors called a special meeting. In a unanimous vote, the Board voted to oust Bruce Alexander and to elect Murray Forbes as the new CEO of the Howard. Rumors abounded that Murray had organized the removal of Alexander. Life at the Howard was getting unbearable and effectively Murray Forbes took charge.

Shortly after the announcement of Alexander's resignation, Walter Hislop received a telephone call from Jack Duerk.

"The news is bad, isn't it Walter?"

Hislop replied, "Yes it is."

Within days, Murray Forbes named George Hughes to be his head of the investment department, thereby replacing Walter as manager of the bank's portfolio. In effect, it seemed like Walter was penalized for his loyalty to the Alexander presidency.

Walter was reassigned to the Corporate Administrative office, where he eventually headed up the Shareholders Relations Department of the demutualized Howard Savings Bank.

For many years following his removal from office, Bruce Alexander spent his time trying to recover from his nervous breakdown and other related ailments. He had no hard feelings about the Howard or his association with Murray Forbes. "They were great people, the Howard was a great bank, and Murray Forbes should have been picked for the job in the first place!" Lastly, he admitted that the job was just overwhelming. "It was a mistake for me to take the job."

He returned to a position at the Greenfield Savings Bank where he worked until age 65. He retired in 1986.[1]

---

[1]Alexander received his undergraduate degree from Colgate University in 1943.

Chapter 4

The Efficient Presidency of Murray Forbes 1974–1982

"The philosophy of service is the principle which guides all of our efforts. From the diverse experience of the Howard's Board of Trustees to the enthusiasm of our newest employees, we believe our human resources are the primary key to our success."

—Murray Forbes, CEO
Annual Report 1978

July 16, 1977
Howard Savings Bank/ Main Office, 768 Broad Street, Newark, New Jersey

The weekly cash management meeting was a veritable institution at the Howard Savings Bank. For over fifty

years, every Friday morning at 9:00 A.M., the entire senior management staff convened in the executive conference room located on the fourth floor of the bank's main office in Newark, New Jersey. The primary purpose of the meeting was to discuss the net inflow (or outflow) of deposits into the bank and the distribution of these funds within the mortgage or securities markets. In other words, the officers of the bank took a look at how much had come into the corporate cookie jar and how the money would be spent.

Generally speaking, the meetings ran for an hour and a half. In fact, during stable interest rate periods, the cash flow aspect of the meeting usually ran for no more than fifteen minutes, possibly to a half an hour. The balance of the time was occupied with evaluating how the Howard's rates compared versus the other mutuals, other commercial banks, and short-term interest-bearing securities. Even though the same group also met once a month for a general staff meeting , the weekly cash meeting was definitely most critical to the operation of the bank.

At 8:57 A.M. on Friday, June 16, 1977, President Murray Forbes was making some notes in the margin of the printed agenda for the meeting about to begin next to his office. Murray also used the NCR computer capability to update himself on the bank's most recent financial figures. Gathering information and making notes to the last minute, Murray finally left his office as the second hand on his watch read thirty seconds before 9:00 A.M. At precisely 9:00 A.M., Murray Forbes arrived at the weekly cash flow meeting. The Forbes Administration ran like clockwork!

With the exception of the CEO's slot at the head of the table, there were no assigned seats at the meeting. As Murray assumed his customary seat, he was flanked by the two recently elected senior vice presidents of the bank—Don McCormick and Leo Rogers. Rogers typically sat motionless and somewhat slumped in his chair, as he appeared absorbed in his notes for the meeting. McCormick, as if in command, signaled for the others to quiet down and get ready for the meeting to begin. Albeit subtle, Mac never missed an opportunity to exercise a modicum of leadership.

"Good morning gentlemen!" said a smiling Murray Forbes as he took his seat. In addition to Forbes, McCormick, and Rogers, there were approximately twelve officers present.

"Good morning Murray," was the informal collective response from the members of the staff.

After dispensing with some housekeeping items, Murray Forbes called on John Quinn for a report on the general investment climate. Seated right next to Donald McCormick, Quinn replied, "My pleasure Mr. Forbes." A characteristic wry smile crossed his face as he began his analysis of the stock and bond markets. While constantly making reference to his weekly lengthy report, Quinn outlined a picture of the economy which implied a very volatile interest rate environment over the next few quarters. Quinn concluded his report with the recommendation that the bank keep its fresh cash in short-term money instruments such as federal funds (one day maturity) and commercial paper (thirty days maturity).

When Quinn concluded his remarks, Forbes opened the floor for discussion. Forever the activist, McCormick was the first to comment on Quinn's assessment of the economy. McCormick felt the near historically high interest rate available on GNMA pass-throughs was an attractive vehicle for the bank to consider and a chance to "lock-up" some yield. Quinn was not afraid to stand up to the McCormick challenge. He quickly alluded to the poor asset-liability match-up of the GNMAs, which were simultaneously callable or could evolve into a much longer maturity. If you wanted a longer bond because you wanted to book the higher yield for some time, the GNMAs were callable on thirty days notice. If you wanted a shorter instrument in the face of rising rates, prepayments slowed and your bond lengthened its maturity. Quinn said he was concerned for the poor asset-liability match-up of the GNMAs.

The remainder of the room was relatively quiet as Mac and John aired their differences. As a genuine student of the fixed-income securities market, Quinn held back the temptation to "upstage" McCormick with some portfolio jargon—he particularly salivated at McCormick's potential reaction to his thoughts about GNMAs as being "negatively convex."

Seeing the stalemate before him, Forbes interrupted the discussion with his analysis of the markets. Ever objective and diplomatic, Forbes smoothly voiced his opinion on the market outlook. On this particular morning, Forbes sided with John Quinn. The conservative Forbes wanted no part of an unhedged bond portfolio. McCormick seemed more inclined to "shoot from the hip" and put some higher yields on the books.

Undaunted by this minor setback, McCormick waited for the next officer to report on his sector.

Upon graduation from high school, Murray Forbes began his business career at the Howard Savings Institution in 1935 when he was 17 years old. His starting salary was $15.00 a week. Murray came very close to beginning and ending his career while serving as a messenger in his entry-level position with the bank. At the time, the Howard kept all its securities in the vault at 768 Broad Street, and the usage of bearer or negotiable securities was widespread. In many respects, these securities were like cash.

The period predated the registration of almost all securities and the central role of the Depository Trust Company. After selling $250,000 of U.S. Treasury notes from its portfolio, the Howard had to remove the bonds from the vault and deliver them to the custody bank acting as agent for the buyer. Thus, Murray Forbes as the messenger involved with the trade had to get on the rail transportation from Newark to New York City while carrying the $250,000 worth of "live securities" in his briefcase. His mission was to deliver the bonds to the Manufacturers Hanover Trust Company which held the securities for C. J. Devine & Company, prominent government bond dealers at the time (C. J. Devine eventually became the government bond subsidiary of Merrill Lynch).[1] Somewhere between the PATH train station and the C. J. Devine offices, Murray discovered he was missing his briefcase. In a panic, he ran back to the terminal but no briefcase had been turned in. His original train was already headed back to Newark.

Fortunately for Murray, the briefcase turned up later the next day. Although the system of numbering the certificates would have protected the bank, it usually takes a mound of paperwork, affadavits, and time before replacement certificates are issued. Although he was embarrassed, there was no harm done. Murray was forgiven and kept his job.

In fact, Murray Forbes kept his job for forty-five more years, and retired at age 65 in 1982. During his career at the bank, he served meaningful terms of duty in the investment, mortgage, and banking departments of the bank. He was fortunate to witness the strong operations of all these areas. His ability to work with people of all professional and personal backgrounds helped move him up the executive ladder. In 1972, during the Alexander administration, he was elected executive vice president. When Alexander left, Murray was elected president and chief executive officer.

While en route to becoming president, Murray built his rapport with many of his coworkers at the Howard. For example, following the Newark riots of 1967, Frank Buckworth decided to move his family from their starter home in the Roseville section of Newark to Cedar Grove, New Jersey, one of the many suburban communities within the Greater Essex County area. The Buckworths were a part of a substantial exodus from Newark as the city's population compressed by almost 200,000.

---

[1]"Chris" who founded C. J. Divine is a famous Jerseyite. He also started as a runner and made a huge fortune in the government bond business. He built the church on the lake at Spring Lake and owned a successful race horse.

When Buckworth inquired about the mortgage financing for his new home, he was directed to the office of Murray Forbes, then the mortgage officer for the Howard. After presenting a short summary of his personal finances, Buckworth watched Forbes quickly dial the telephone of Jim McCracken III, Chairman and CEO of the Orange Savings Bank. At the time, the Orange handled all the personal mortgage inquiry generated by the Howard officers and employees. Forbes outlined the details of Buckworth's background, and McCracken quickly said OK to the mortgage request.

Frank Buckworth then asked Forbes about the prevailing level of long-term fixed rate mortgages.

"They generally are running about 6%," Forbes replied.

"If you could line up a 6% mortgage for me, that would be great," volunteered Buckworth.

"Forget 6%! We are going to set you up with a 5 3/4% mortgage."

Buckworth was ecstatic. As Murray Forbes' responsibilities at the bank grew, Buckworth evolved into one of his strongest supporters. Buckworth liked to call Murray Forbes "coach."

Early on in his administration, Murray Forbes expressed his underlying business philosophy. His mission was to sustain and improve the service provided by the Howard. Expansion of the bank through branches was in support of this service guideline rather than through any "encroachment upon current commercial banking prerogatives."

The Forbes administration was like a honeymoon period for the Howard staff. Following the purges and embarrassments associated with Bruce Alexander, Forbes' soothing personality and effective management style were like a dose of therapy for the Howard.

The NJAMSB also responded to Murray's magnetism. The state association's trade group repositioned Murray in the slot leading to the presidency of the association. As the president of the association, Murray and his wife Marjorie were indeed popular representatives of the Howard and the state of New Jersey mutual savings banks.

The Leo Rogers Factor

A veteran of the Kress and Alexander administrations, Leo Rogers was vice president and head of the marketing department in 1975. Most coworkers respected his intelligence and his vast array of academic achievements. He was always polite, relatively soft-spoken and seemed to avoid conflict at all cost. As an academic, he frequently sympathized with both sides of an issue. Decisions came hard. He was rarely confrontational.

Leo Rogers received a lot of the credit for getting the marketing department up and running by helping to recruit and train staff, develop loan documents, train branch people, and put loan accounting systems in place. Leo also worked well on an advertising campaign, stressing the lending function of the bank. Initially hired by John Kress to write speeches, the academically inclined Rogers was starting to spread his influence around the Howard.

Some differences arose, however, when the consumer loan department achieved some production and they started to submit reports itemizing the reasons for accepting or declining loan applicants. Leo Rogers became quite upset when he noticed that the turn-down ratio of loan applicants was running about 30% of those received. Without discussing the numbers with consumer credit, Leo apparently directly reported to his superiors that the new consumer loan department was discouraging people from becoming bank customers.

Upper management sought to investigate this 30% turn-down ratio, and encouraged a meeting between Rogers and Robert Turrill, head of the consumer loan department. A meeting was scheduled. Rogers sent two representatives and the consumer credit department sent one. In lieu of conversation, Turrill brought all the reject files and asked the marketing representatives to determine which applicants should have been approved.

One of Rogers' subordinates—Edward R. Skoldberg—had just been hired from a commercial bank (The Empire National Bank) and had considerable exposure to the lending markets. Upon investigation, Skoldberg indicated that the consumer credit department was correct, that none of the applicants should have been approved. Although the victory for Bob Turrill's efforts was very gratifying and helped to protect the risk capital of the bank, the likelihood of cooperation when working with Leo Rogers was dramatically diminished.

A degree of alienation evolved between Rogers and Turrill. Still Ed Skoldberg maintained timely contact with Bob Turrill. When Turrill stopped by Skoldberg's cubicle to make sure the credit files were up-to-date, he noticed the expansive office space which lay just beyond the six-foot-high partition designating Ed's office. The office was easily the largest in the department and the windows overlooking Broad Street enhanced the power and prestige associated with the location. When Turrill peeked around the partition, he noticed a large La-Z-Boy reclining chair. The chair was occupied by Walter Hovland, known by his immediate coworkers for his mid-morning naps.

Bob Turrill's sense of the Marine Corps work ethic was immediately aroused. In a normal business voice, Turrill reacted to Skoldberg:

"Hey Ed, the guy is asleep! What the hell is going on here?"

Skoldberg shushed Turrill. He then explained that Rogers had signed off on the chair, the mid-morning naps, and the spacious office in recognition for Walter

Hovland's former stature as long-time head of the marketing department.

Turrill immediately formulated an opinion of Rogers' management style. Rogers' decision was frequently that of no decision. Attempts were made to find the once popular and productive Hovland a useful function within the bank. For example, he was named AVP of public relations. But the naps continued as did the preferential treatment as to office accommodation. Hovland finally retired in 1977.[2]

Ed Skoldberg and many others at the bank felt that the Hovland situation typified the family nature of the Howard organization. During his prime, Walt had been a popular and effective leader. The old Howard held great feelings for its people. Excluding the Alexander experiment, one would have to commit a felony to get fired.

Murray Forbes constantly marked his term of office with personal touches. For example, he annually sent letters to the employees congratulating them on their performance for the year. The culture, the work environment, the pleasant surroundings were all a part of working under Murray Forbes. A strong team of business executives worked in unison to help the Howard fulfill its service oriented profile to the public. Post Alexander, there was little attrition and the bank ran void of any major problems.

Murray explicitly expressed his thoughts about the Howard staff in the 1978 *Annual Report:*

"People are the Howard's most important resource. As a financial institution, the Howard's primary role is to provide services which help our customers attain their individual economic goals and achieve personal financial security. To do this, we have a staff of over 950 dedicated employees all working together to provide these services to our customers."

---

[2]Free of any later working year stress, a well rested Hovland married the considerably younger Betty Macy of the marketing department.

During Forbes' presidency, the bank rose to the position of number seven nationally while retaining its position as the largest mutual in New Jersey. Deposits more than doubled, growing from $1.28 billion to $2.77 while the loan portfolio jumped to $1.8 billion from $984 million. Forbes also moved to reverse a lot of the policy decisions made by Alexander. For example, he gradually worked to enlarge the size of the bank's annual report. Although the report better represented the size and direction of the bank, there was no report of the specific items held in the portfolio. A pie chart depicting the consolidated impact of the various investments was quite effective in summarizing the bank's activities in the securities markets.

In 1977, the bank moved to fortify its capital position by issuing $30 million of capital notes. The Forbes management opted to use the corporate private placement market and sold the entire issue to their neighbor, The Prudential Insurance Company of America. In essence, $30 million crossed Broad Street when the two institutions signed off on the deal. The interest rate of 8.50% for a ten-year bank issue appeared to reflect the perceived high quality of the Howard name. On the closing date of the deal, the Prudential paid +68 versus the ten-year U.S. Treasury note. The rate worked out to be even more attractive for the Howard once the double-digit rates of the 1980s became widespread. Fortunately for Prudential, the notes were subject to a mandatory sinking fund and were all paid off following a balloon payment made in 1987. As the bank's financial problems surfaced in 1988, it might have been helpful if the Howard management had "rolled" into another ten-year capital note arrangement with the Prudential. Apparently, the Howard declined to further access the capital markets because of the high absolute interest rate scenario that prevailed. Once the bank's financial problems were publicized, the capital markets closed this window of opportunity and the bank's ratios suffered accordingly.

The plan to move the bank's administrative headquarters from Newark to Livingston, New Jersey was approved and set in motion during Murray's watch. The bank bought some seventy-two acres opposite the huge Livingston Mall on South Orange Avenue and the Eisenhower Parkway. The actual move of most of the bank's employees took place in 1982.

The balance sheet for the Forbes years reflected the basic savings bank policy of conservative money management and focus on the areas where the bank's staff was knowledgeable and experienced. The balance sheet for year ended 1978 is shown in Table 4-1. The percentage holdings for 1978 are summarized as follows:

Cash, Fed Funds, CDs and other Money Market Instruments	7.3%
Securities (Government, Agencies, Corporate and Stocks)	16.4%
Mortgages (Conventional, GNMA, VA-FHA Insured)	71.5%
Other Investments	4.8%
Total	100%

The Murray Forbes administration indeed ran like clockwork, and it seemed that this well-oiled machine could run forever as a profitable concern. Murray was a business success without being a "greedy bastard." However, while directors, employees, and depositors enjoyed the benevolent leadership of Mr. Forbes, few focused on the succession problem facing the bank as he approached age 65. Murray was a baby-faced, youthful appearing 65 and few at the bank wanted to see him retire. His rosy cheeks added to his youthful appearance. Also his friendship with Arlyn Rus, the youthful and energetic CEO of the Raritan Savings Bank, distracted one's attention from retirement possibilities. Nonetheless, long ago, the Howard had adopted a policy of mandatory retirement for its president at age 65.

Suddenly, the Howard was sent scurrying for a new president. There was no clear-cut candidate among the

TABLE 4-1 BALANCE SHEET FOR YEAR ENDED 1978

DECEMBER 31, 1978

	1978	1977	Increase or (Decrease) Over 1977
Assets			
Cash on Hand and in Banks	$ 65,245,000	$ 54,432,000	$ 10,813,000
Term Federal Funds	82,000,000	30,000,000	52,000,000
Certificates of Deposit	30,233,000	26,248,000	3,985,000
Securities:			
U.S. Government and Agency Bonds	130,024,000	164,787,000	(34,763,000)
Other Bonds	238,206,000	273,814,000	(35,608,000)
Stocks	27,930,000	27,767,000	163,000
Total Securities	396,160,000	466,368,000	(70,208,000)
Mortgage Loans:			
Conventional—Net	1,073,394,000	935,852,000	137,542,000
V.A. Guaranteed	188,618,000	164,871,000	23,747,000
F.H.A. Insured	165,495,000	153,424,000	12,071,000
G.N.M.A. Guaranteed	301,986,000	297,852,000	4,134,000
Total Mortgage Loans	1,729,493,000	1,551,999,000	177,494,000
Other Loans—Net	46,360,000	25,832,000	20,528,000
Bank Premises	26,562,000	19,011,000	7,551,000
Other Assets	41,444,000	37,691,000	3,753,000
Total Assets	**$2,417,497,000**	**$2,211,581,000**	**$205,916,000**
Liabilities and Capital			
Due Depositors:			
Regular Savings Accounts	$ 896,684,000	$ 985,280,000	$ (88,596,000)
Time Savings Accounts	1,238,835,000	976,633,000	262,202,000
School and Club Accounts	5,512,000	5,756,000	(244,000)
Total Savings Accounts	2,141,031,000	1,967,669,000	173,362,000
Checking Accounts	50,372,000	42,578,000	7,794,000
Total Due Depositors	2,191,403,000	2,010,247,000	181,156,000
Borrowings—N.J. Mortgage Finance Agency	12,866,000	13,641,000	(775,000)
Other Liabilities	50,096,000	40,240,000	9,856,000
Capital:			
Subordinated Capital Notes	30,000,000	30,000,000	—
Surplus and Reserves	133,132,000	117,453,000	15,679,000
Total Capital	163,132,000	147,453,000	15,679,000
Total Liabilities and Capital	**$2,417,497,000**	**$2,211,581,000**	**$205,916,000**

YEAR ENDED DECEMBER 31, 1978

	1978	1977	Increase or (Decrease) Over 1977
Revenue:			
Mortgages	$ 135,945,000	$ 109,194,000	$ 26,751,000
Securities	41,202,000	39,858,000	1,344,000
Other Income	5,582,000	3,297,000	2,285,000
Total Revenue	182,729,000	152,349,000	30,380,000
Dividends and Interest:			
Dividends Paid to Depositors	131,438,000	113,618,000	17,820,000
Interest on Borrowed Money	3,561,000	1,087,000	2,474,000
Total Dividends and Interest	134,999,000	114,705,000	20,294,000
Revenue Less Dividends and Interest	47,730,000	37,644,000	10,086,000
Operating Expenses	25,114,000	20,758,000	4,356,000
Operating Income	22,616,000	16,886,000	5,730,000
Gains (Losses):			
Securities Transactions	(322,000)	(120,000)	(202,000)
Other	127,000	310,000	(183,000)
Net Gains	(195,000)	190,000	(385,000)
Net Income before Taxes	22,421,000	17,076,000	5,345,000
Income Taxes	6,302,000	4,497,000	1,805,000
Net Income from Operations	16,119,000	12,579,000	3,540,000
Special Charges to Surplus and Reserves	440,000	163,000	277,000
Net Addition to Surplus and Reserves	$ **15,679,000**	$ **12,416,000**	$ **3,263,000**

Howard senior management. The fact that Don McCormick and Leo Rogers were promoted to executive vice president at the same time may have been designed to imply a race between the two for the top job. Although gaining a modicum of support, the soft-spoken Rogers was not building a power base to rival that of McCormick.

To a certain extent, Rogers exhibited an academic rather than a managerial profile. He was a trustee of Rider College in Lawrenceville, New Jersey, and a member of the development council of Villanova University. He held a master's degree from Temple University. Additionally, he was an active board member of the Blue Cross & Blue Shield of New Jersey, where he was chairman of the finance and investment committee. For the past eight years to the present, Leo Rogers has directed the Rothman Institute of Entrepreneurial Studies from his office at Farleigh Dickinson University. Certainly, he was well qualified to take a strong leadership role at the Howard.

But, as time went on, McCormick—more athletic than academic—had increasingly important assignments come under his wing. Mac had all depository products, electronic data processing, and lending—in other words, the "big stuff"—locked into his corner. Meanwhile, Leo seemed to lack the will to "politic" for the job. He was no match for the Machiavellian tactics of Donald F. McCormick. While Mac was a hands on manager who thrived on confrontation, Leo would more or less "go with the flow" and accept what fate had to offer him. Quite conceivably, Mac relished the advancement of Leo Rogers because in the final analysis, he realized he could easily defeat the one-time college professor in a head-on battle for the top job. Mac also didn't want to do anything to upset Murray Forbes. No sense rocking the boat!

The board of directors virtually waited for someone to step forth and volunteer for the job. The case for McCormick's candidacy seemed to grow stronger by the day, while Rogers' chances seemed to fade into the background.[3]

When Jimmy Carter was elected president of the United States, the nation was on the threshold of a significant inflationary bubble. His appointee to the all-important position of Chairman of the Federal Reserve Bank was

---

[3]Re: Rogers. After the Howard left the scene in 1992, Rogers joined the Rothman Institute for Entrepreneurial Studies at Farleigh Dickinson

G. William Miller. Chairman Miller was assigned the delicate task of slowing down these rampant inflationary forces while not impeding the pace of economic activity. Miller miscalculated the impact of adjustments to money supply growth on the inflation rate, and figures such as the consumer price index and the producer price index began posting double digit gains. Showing an unwillingness to hold anything dollar denominated, the currency markets pummeled the U.S. dollar to historic lows. By adding reserves to the banking system, Chairman Miller was aggravating the processes at work in the economy. In August 1979, President Carter fired G. William Miller and appointed Paul Volcker to head up the Fed. In retrospect, Miller's term (one year and five months) was the shortest for any Fed chairman since that of Eugene Black (one year and three months) back in 1933–34.

Once the Fed gavel was in his hand, Paul Volcker was anything but "delicate" as he quickly slammed a tight monetary grip on the nation's economy. During his early rule, Volcker was described by many publications (*Time, Newsweek*, et al.) as the most powerful man in the United States. Slowing demand was his main thrust as he attacked demand pull inflation.

Following his victory in the presidential election in 1980, Ronald Reagan impacted the inflationary scene early in his administration when he confronted the air traffic controllers union and ordered the striking technicians back to work. By his actions, Reagan sent a strong message to the labor movement as the president stood by his word and hired a whole new collection of controllers. In short, Reagan had attacked the issue of cost push inflation and emerged a winner.

University, where he became director of a fast-moving program. Rogers found his niche in life!

Part Two:

"The environment was more hostile for thrifts than for banks . . . Indeed, one could say the industry was bifurcated; either the thrift was strong or very weak. Few could be characterized as average."

—Ryan Beck & Co.
New Jersey Bank & Thrift Stock Manual 1991,
Volume #28

The Fall of the Howard Savings Bank 1982–1992

Chapter 5

The Changing Economic Environment of the 1980s

"American regulation at the state and federal level caused fossilization in the banking system and there simply was no capacity for change. When Reg Q came down, it was like sending two-year-olds out to play in heavy traffic."

—*Ronald Geesey, retired VP Citibank*

Given the very difficult economic environment that prevailed between 1979 and 1990, examining the motivations of most corporate managers during this period should provide an interesting perspective to the fate of the Howard Savings Bank. Initially, these managers were hit by an unprecedented tight monetary policy implemented by the Federal Reserve Bank. Double-digit inflation was public enemy number one. To Fed Chairman Paul Volcker, all other economic phenomena were of secondary importance. The severity of Volcker's actions implied that there might be some casualties among the nation's financial institutions, but this was all part of the cost and process of eliminating virulent inflationary forces. At the same time, a huge volume of legislative proposals was grinding its way through Congress. Some bills sought to rid the nation of unnecessarily restrictive laws, while others granted corporations and banking institutions many new arenas of operation. As the corporate and bank CEOs of the nation collectively adjusted to these events, a break from the patterns of the 1970s and earlier became readily apparent.

Some say the CEOs changed from "benevolent despots" to "greedy bastards." Indeed, the corporate executive of the 1980s played the game by a different set of rules when compared to those of his predecessors. For most of the twentieth century, say from 1900 to 1980, the fundamental purpose of a business corporation was to maximize profits, plain and simple. The concept implied a maximizing period equivalent to a normal business cycle, say about four years in duration. Employee and client loyalty were deemed as important contributors to the process. Large companies functioned more like family than efficient machines. The concept of a "better mousetrap" was expected to raise the overall standard of living, and research and development budgets were structured accordingly. Management knew its business, anticipated the challenges within its industry, and made changes to enable the corporation to adapt to long-term changes spawned by the business cycle.

Early in the 1980s, the corporate emphasis swung away from the idea of maximizing profits to the concept of enhancing shareholder value. The time frame of this process was abbreviated to as soon as possible. Corporations compromised long term goals to bump up their stock. One method to quickly impact earnings was to implement wage cuts and hiring freezes. Upper management used euphemisms such as "human engineering" and "corporate restructuring" to disguise the zeal of corporate executives in their quest for instant success. As increasing numbers of corporations announced similar lay-off policies, the guilt trips associated with such programs were lessened at the management level. Dealing with the replacement of key personnel sacked in the purges was put off to some undefined time in the future. Journalists gradually subordinated such almost commonplace announcements to the inner pages of the finance section of their respective publications.

The specter of being laid off led to the American worker being more resilient when the inevitable pink slip presented itself. Most workers kept an updated resume in their briefcase at all times. Networking, whereby workers maintained contacts at rival companies, became very common. Career paths were diverted in order to stay on the employment rolls. Health insurance and retirement benefits were judged to be more important than achieving basic job satisfaction. "No more Mister Nice Guy" became a common management expression, and crass materialism was a way of life.

Even on the rebound, many of the rehired workers were classified as "temps" or "consultants." Many recycled workers found that they were entitled to none of the benefits covered at their previous jobs. Or possibly, they were faced with a year-long time delay before the benefits kicked in.

Although culminating in their market importance in the 1990s, corporate buyback programs symbolized the thinking of the period. Opting to forgo potentially lucrative research on new product development, many corporate CEOs used the ready funds to buy the corporation's own common stock. In a corporate stock purchase plan, the corporation simply bought their stock in the open market, perhaps on the New York Stock Exchange, then reclassified the same amount of shares outstanding to treasury stock—stock which was issued, authorized, but no longer in the hands of public investors. The acquired stock was immediately stashed in the vault. The math was fairly simple.

Once a buyback program was approved by the board of directors, the program could be quickly implemented. Depending on price restrictions set by the board, the program could be completed in minutes. Generally, it entailed no more than one call by the treasurer to a major investment banker involved with trading large blocks of common stocks (such as Goldman Sachs or Morgan Stanley). The investment banker, perhaps aware of pending approval of a buyback plan by the corporation, may have stock lined up in advance of the actual order. A slick operation, corporate buybacks functioned like reverse dilution. In some cases, the reduction in "float" of the common

Basic Example of Corporate Buyback Program
Corporation XYZ

Phase I:

Number of shares outstanding	1,000,000
Earnings of the corporation	$1,000,000
Earnings per share of the corp.	$1.00
Market value of common stock	$10.00 per share
Price/earnings ratio of common stock	10 times earnings

Phase II:

Corporate treasurer buys back
  250,000 shares (25% buyback)
Corporate treasurer reduces the number
  of shares outstanding and credits the
  "treasury stock" account with the
  same number.

Number of shares outstanding	750,000
Earnings of the corporation (no change)	$1,000.000
Earnings per share of the corp.	$1.333
Assume constant price/earnings ratio	10x
Market value of common should go to	$13.33
Net Impact: Instant market value increase of 33.3%	

led to an even stronger multiple than the constant ratio assumed in the above example. Some stock investors became buyers based on the announcement of such programs—before they were ever implemented, and soon tailgated the quick rise in the stock. Expediency was king as due process took a back seat. Earnings were pumped up to maximize their current impact.

The use of the stock buyback depends on there being surplus cash in the treasury of the corporation. In the 1990s, as the economic cycle remained strong beyond any perception of a normal time period, corporate profits rolled in and buybacks were deemed an expedient use of cash. In 2002, however, the downturn in profitability and the specter of underfunded pension fund liabilities threatened to dominate the use of corporate cash.

Pegging executive compensation to the value of the corporation's stock added fuel to the fire. Actual shares or common stock options were awarded to the CEO who could substantially increase the price of his company's shares. Using options, they could thus reward their employees now but not realize an expense until the option was exercised. Quite often, the source of the shares delivered in these programs was the corporate buyback program. Thus, many companies were constantly buying and selling their own shares, recycling them to meet their current needs. It was not until the summer of 2002 that Coca-Cola Corporation announced it would expense the use of options in the years awarded rather than exercised. While masses of unemployed workers scurried for new jobs, many top executives received total compensation packages beyond their wildest dreams. Most corporations jettisoned the policy of paying its top executives a constant salary plus an annual pay increase consistent with some inflation number.

The executives who hit the home-run ball were those who linked their compensation to the price of their company's common. It was almost as if all corporate chief executive officers were on commission with the base figure being the trading value of their common.

Another aspect of the fast buck era within the corporate arena was the trend evolving in mergers and acquisitions. Especially true in the field of banking, many CEOs apparently went public with an eye toward flipping the bank at a sizable premium to the issue price. Going public enabled senior management executives to cash in their chips. For the mutual savings bank industry, prior to the evolution of demutualization, no currency existed which possessed the firepower of common stock. Among the New Jersey mutuals going public in the 1980s but lasting 10 years or less before being sold to larger banks were the Montclair Savings, Morris County Savings, Savings Bank of Central Jersey (or Starpointe), and Harmonia, to name just a few. The Howard Bank may have been a takeover candidate as late as 1988, but once the bank exposed its dirty laundry and the extent of its non-performing assets, the potential acquirer backed away.

In almost all cases, the banks that were acquired saw their chief executive officer elevated to the slot of vice chairman of the board of the surviving bank. The job entailed a fat paycheck with little other responsibilities.

In roughly 90% of the cases, the remaining personnel at the acquired bank didn't fare so well, as most were fired either immediately or on a phase out program so as not to shake up the regulatory authorities. Many of those receiving pink slips held impressive titles (i.e., executive vice president) and shouldered a lot of responsibilities at the acquired institution. When duplication with the acquiring bank became visible, the acquired bank's staff became the "jayvees." For example, merging banks only require one human resource department or one legal department. The second team department was ultimately unceremoniously dismissed as a unit. Loyalty and length of service to the company meant nothing. Even if the acquired bank's personnel were ranked as smarter or better than the acquiring bank, they were generally fired regardless. Reflecting these developments, the nation's unemployment rate hovered around 9%.

For financial and banking related entities, feeling the pressure to maintain constantly improving earnings quarter after quarter created intense competition for the highest yielding mortgage product, commercial loans, and other potential investments. A "buy now, check the credit later" attitude evolved within the banking industry. A veritable feeding frenzy took place as the most attractive paper traded quickly. Research support just couldn't generate the information soon enough. Perhaps most importantly, in their haste to accumulate what appeared to be attractive lending opportunities, many banks put the fundamental principle of *diversification* on the back burner.

Diversification is perhaps the simplest but possibly the most important of all the principles which guide investment and lending policy. Diversifying means spreading risk over a broad spectrum of lending and investment alternatives in order to limit exposure to a tolerable level. Buying 100 line items with the ultimate experience of three failures versus buying six loans with three defaults illustrates how diversification works in the extreme. The residential mortgage portfolio for the Howard Savings gave the bank substantial diversification, and in 1970 they carried 41,604 separate mortgages valued at $622.3 million. However, in many cases, the need to diversify was disregarded. In the intense competition of the marketplace, portfolio managers became obsessed with capturing yield, and in many cases led to an institution buying more of a single project than was necessary. Prudent investor tests remained buried in the textbook as traders accumulating larger blocks of high risk investments. Diversification was for sissies!

Nonetheless, instant gratification was available as long as these questionable investments accrued and immediately impacted the bank's earnings. Construction loans were particularly attractive because of their two- to three-year duration and high rate of return. These loans paid off once long-term financing was arranged and the project was up and running. Earnings short-falls in a particular quarter could be quickly remedied by putting a few large construction loans on the books. Handsome bonus "commitment" fees were also enticing. The Howard apparently viewed these loans as "self-liquidating."

Common stock investors, who saw only these early accretions, were unaware of the risks entailed in the bank's quest for higher earnings. As the Wall Street broker community endorsed these successes, a meaningful sector of the investment public bought into the common stocks of these entities, and prices moved up accordingly.

The high interest rate levels of the 1980s spawned several new fixed income products, many of which directly competed with the passbook accounts of the mutual savings banks. One such security was the zero coupon bond. As a synthetic U.S. Treasury, the stripped zero market soon became an ideal method of capturing the compounding impact of the double-digit rates offered in the 1980s.

Many immunized portfolios were structured to capitalize on these securities. In fact, my daughters built their educational funds dynamically through the use of zeros which matched the maturity dates of their scheduled college years.

Zeros also proved to be suitable trading vehicles for those interested in playing the interest rate cycle. Unhampered by the premium deterrent of a standard bond (i.e., many bond buyers object to paying more than 104 for a bond regardless of the yield), zeros can trade anywhere but over par! For the depositors of mutual savings banks, zeros were an attractive passbook alternative and aggravated the disintermediation process at work in the economy. Alternatively, some savings banks offset this process as they experienced positive deposit trends in anticipation of their going public.

The Howard was one of the forerunners of selling insurance products to its depositors, and the concept of a tax-deferred annuity was marketed through its 30% investment in "Compu Plan" as a possible zero bond look-alike.

Meanwhile, the bondologists at Salomon Brothers were broadening the market for another new product—the collateralized mortgage backed security. Thus, if you were new in the bond business, chances are you would get assigned to zeros or CMOs. Originally conceived by a mortgage team at Lehman Brothers, CMOs were an outgrowth of the need of the banking system to fund its operations while at the same time meeting the borrowing demands of their own customers. As such, a commercial bank could take a portion of its loan or mortgage portfolio, and sell it as a package to Lehman or Salomon Brothers. The hometown bank would continue to service the Mortgage (collect P&I) but they would "flow-through" those payments to the ultimate investor. Lehman or Salomon, in turn, would take the packaged items and create a security (usually having several "traunches" or buckets of maturities) which it peddled to the non-banking clients of the investing public (i.e., insurance companies, pension funds, foundations, etc.). Banks responded to this market arena by offering huge volumes or packages of their securities for sale to Lehman and Salomon and a growing list of dealers. The process also added to the fee based revenue of the banks. Following the peaks in interest rates in the mid-1980s and with an aggressive easing of rates in the early 1990s, while the market for zeros functioned relatively smoothly, the market for CMOs exhibited some inefficiencies and irregularities. CMOs, with their multitude of bells and whistles, call features, indices, etc., became a different animal at lower rates versus higher rates. Longer dated paper started to trade on a yield to call basis, and most of the bonds stalled out at 100. Dealers and investors who hedged their positions with bullet Treasuries faced huge losses. Bankers Trust Company's dealer woes and the municipal government of Orange County, (California's) market losses were front page financial news.

The broad-based market generally referred to as the mortgage market was severely affected by this CMO phenomenon. Although the subsector market for real estate development loans involved a different set of participants, it nonetheless was hurt by the willingness of Wall Street to commit capital to support this area. At most dealerships, the two markets were linked and most likely both head traders reported to the same executive on the manning chart. The executives overseeing the trading operations of Wall Street's market makers lost their appetite for additional risk. Almost overnight, the market shut down. Wall Street had no bid.

For those operating in the new product areas of Wall Street, this was their first experience with the vague mysteries of the business cycle.

The Role of Demutualization for the Mutual Savings Banks

Those electing to convert from a depositor-owned to a shareholder-owned institution (previously described as the process of *demutualization*) threw themselves into the feeding frenzy associated with a constantly improving stock price. One more piranha in the pool! The challenge of producing ever improving earnings—quarter after quarter after quarter—undoubtedly warped many executive decisions. Forced to produce or else, many banks reached out on the risk curve in order to maintain or at least modestly improve income streams. As the historically high interest rates of the 1980s gave way to more realistic levels, this process of sacrificing quality for higher income became more prevalent. For those financial institutions electing to find that "extra yield" by making commitments in the real estate development loan markets, the consequences were severe. Unfortunately, for many of the participants, there was little focus made on the concept of risk based pricing. The price differentials paid by these aggressive buyers of real estate loans were too narrow versus quality loans in the sector. Spreads were tight! When the market turned and the professional mortgage crowd was making the bids, to the extent they were able to make bids, the higher yielding paper sank more than proportionately as it found its proper level.

Prior to the enactment of the Tax Law of 1986, the nation's real estate market provided vast tax shelters to individuals opting to invest in second and third homes. Allowances for depreciation and deductions for interest costs were all part of the stimulation. Construction projects, based on this bulge in demand for luxury homes, abounded and required financing. Changes impacting their own investment laws lured many savings banks into making loans in this sector.

The favorable tax treatment spawned excessive abuses and led to widespread uses of tax shelters. When Congress met to evaluate the tax law and its impact on the real estate markets, it was more concerned with the proliferation of these shelters than curtailing overall real estate activity. But when the dust had settled and all the fine print and footnotes were explained, it was clear Congress had acted unilaterally. To the surprise of many market participants, the Tax Law of 1986, without allowing for any exceptions, effectively eliminated the deductibility of mortgage interest on second homes or luxury houses. By 1988, this provision had drastically reduced the demand for development projects. While demand stopped on a dime, supply kept on going, blinded to a large extent by the need to meet production schedules. Very quickly, the mortgage market was awash with unwanted or nonperforming paper. The unforeseen risk of the mortgage market became a reality and only a policy of diversification could have limited its negative impact. Almost overnight, banks participating in this market arena had serious problems on their hands.

Dating back to the mid 1960s, bank management began to deemphasize the role of its securities portfolio. While previously active buyers of municipal bonds for their own account, commercial banks—particularly larger commercial banks—found they could temper their tax liability through mechanisms other than tying up huge capital dollars for low yielding tax-frees. The identification of the portfolio as a residual of the bank's other operations evolved and investment officers became more passive. The concept of the commercial bank as an investment trust became an anachronism. The main purpose of the commercial bank was to service its clients and to make loans. Once this mission was accomplished, the bank portfolio came into play.

Likewise, mutual savings banks and S&Ls were created as mortgage lenders to "Mom and Pop" America. Tax incentives were rendered unto these institutions to maximize their participation to at least 65% of their asset base.

The passive commercial bank or thrift institution portfolio was called into action during the 1980s. In many cases, the decade of the 1980s was marked by a preference for trading the interest rate cycles stemming from the volatility implicit in Volcker monetary policy. Interest rates didn't just go straight up and come straight down. Unlike in today's marketplace, where the target for Fed funds and other critical FRB objectives are outlined immediately after regularly scheduled Federal Open Market Committee meetings, monetary policy was filtered into the market by a series of maneuvers in the securities markets. Traders had no preannounced numbers to work with. What was critical was what the Open Market desk did at the middle of the trading day. Usually at 11:45 A.M. EST, the street wanted to know if the Fed was a buyer or seller of securities, was it for system or customer account, was it intended to correct a previous days excess either short or long, and so forth. Try as they might, the Fed had difficulty in fine tuning their objectives and frequently overshot or under-supplied the amount of reserves they wanted to provide the banking system.

Money center banks employed the services of some savvy "Fed Watchers" to help then trade the market on a short-term basis. Ed Heinmann of C. J. Lawrence & Co., David Jones of Aubrey Lanston, and Ed Yardeni of Prudential Bache Securities were constantly in print with an assessment of the Federal Reserve Bank monetary policy. Soon the volume of this activity gained to the point that many commercial banks made considerably more by trading their bond portfolios than they did in their basic operations. Some savings banks were also active in this regard. Many of the savings banks also traded the common stock market (and the IPO market for new issues of bank-shares). In either case, the banks which successfully traded the securities markets in the 1980s had the luxuries of market liquidity and the opportunity to spread their risks over a vast spectrum of issues and maturities. New issue corporate bonds, term issues of municipals, governments, and agencies all were arenas which witnessed substantial portfolio turnover.

It is important to note that the banks which played the trading game used securities which were consistent with their basic policy guidelines. Most all of the action was in the sector known as investment grade securities, i.e., rated Baa-BBB or better. When the trading game ended, few if any of the banks faced any severe problems resulting in nonperforming assets. While booking profits throughout the period, the banks that so traded the market continuously sold their higher coupon investments, and perhaps deprived their institutions of higher future earnings. Such was the mentality of the fast buck era.

The regulatory authorities eventually changed the accounting laws and the banks had to classify each investment as to whether it was intended for investment or held for sale. Those held for sale were marked to market quarterly and potentially could have a negative impact on earnings. Prior to the Federal Accounting Standards Board (FASB) change, the banks carried such positions at cost. Be that as it may, the syndrome of the trading bank was quite prevalent in the 1980s, but then quieted down to a virtual standstill once the FASB rules became effective.

When the Fed changed to a system of announcing its target for federal funds and other matters, the traders changed their focus to betting on a "consensus view" of what the announcement would be rather than trying to interpret a series of money market operations by the Open Market desk.

Junk bonds and the activities of Mike Milken at Drexel Burnham were a dramatic part of the big picture of the 1980s and early 1990s. In New Jersey, however, legal investor tests kept the savings banks from investing in this marketplace to any extent. West Coast savings & loan associations were active in the junk market and in many cases functioned as "parking spots" for Drexel issues. For a full yet entertaining description of this activity, read Connie Bruck's stimulating book entitled *"The Predators Ball—The Junk Bond Raiders and the Man Who Staked Them."*

Chapter 6

The McCormick Years 1982–1990

"We look forward to 1989 and beyond with a great deal of optimism. As the market continues to change, and we know it will, we will continue to evaluate our operations and adjust our strategic thinking to the benefit of our shareholders and customers."

—Donald McCormick, CEO
Howard Savings Bank 1988
Annual Report

McCormick's Route to the Position of CEO

In 1949, the University of North Carolina football team posted a 7–4 record and won the Southern Conference

championship. The Tar Heels were led by the legendary Charlie "Choo Choo" Justice, perhaps the best player in UNC history. With Justice leading the way, Carolina posted a 24-7-1 record for the three years he played at Chapel Hill. He finished second in the Heisman Trophy voting in 1948 and 1949, and lost his final collegiate game in the Sugar Bowl against number 2 Oklahoma University, which was coached by perpetual winner Bud Wilkinson.

Don McCormick was a freshman and therefore ineligible under then prevailing NCAA rules to play at UNC when Justice was a senior captain of the 1949 football team. When Justice graduated, Carolina disappeared from the national rankings and subsisted through seven lean seasons of losing records. McCormick was a defensive tackle on the 1950–1951–1952 teams which posted an aggregate 7-19-2 mark during his playing career. The media guide published by UNC listed his playing weight at 225 and his height at 6'2". In a very brief thumbnail sketch, the guide described Mac as being a "tough guy."

Throughout his life, McCormick loved football. Before entering UNC, he had starred for Bloomfield High School and went on to earn All State Prep Honors at Newark Academy. Although football was his best sport, he also loved basketball, and played golf. He relished portraying himself as a "real jock type."

Don McCormick graduated from UNC in 1953 with a bachelor of arts degree in economics. As his career evolved, he did some graduate work at Montclair State College and attended Rutgers University. Subsequently, Mac entered the United States Navy as an enlisted man. His sea duty was aboard the USS *Currituck,* a sea plane tender.

McCormick then took a position with the New Jersey Bell Telephone Company, which was a subsidiary of the AT&T company. After working for New Jersey Bell about twenty years, McCormick held a modest position equivalent to the rank of assistant vice president or commercial management in the credit department. The department's main responsibility was to focus on seeing that unpaid telephone bills were eventually paid off. Job pressures were minimal and afforded McCormick a lot of free time to pursue the athletic and social pastimes of his life. As part of its natural monopoly, the telephone company paid its employees well and most workers were on board essentially for life. Pension allowances and vacation time were reported to be among the most generous of any offered by American industry. After twenty years, there was no compelling reason for Don McCormick to leave New Jersey Bell. It seemed his business career was set on cruise control.

But one day early in 1974, the division manager of the marketing department at New Jersey Bell—Don Stevenson—suddenly announced that Don McCormick was leaving New Jersey Bell for personal reasons. To his co-workers, it seemed odd that there was no going away party, no final handshakes with old friends. Just an abrupt departure. After twenty years with a company, more was expected than a brief one-liner.

Meanwhile, just a few blocks away at 768 Broad Street, the Howard was just adjusting to the legacy of changes brought about by Bruce Alexander. Newly appointed President Murray Forbes was just a few months into his first year in office. The bank certainly wasn't in a hiring mode, and generally speaking the executive staff seemed in balance. All executive slots on the bank's manning chart were occupied. Murray's management style implied a gradual approach as a sedative to the turbulent Alexander era. According to one reporter, Murray met McCormick at an outside study of the Newark system and conceivably invited him to join the Howard as part of its reorganization from the Alexander period.

On May 21, 1974, or roughly midway through the first year of Murray Forbes's presidency, an announcement in the ***Newark Star Ledger*** said that the Howard had hired Donald F. McCormick as a vice president for planning with no other specific details being mentioned. Mac was apparently given the assignment of finding someone to start up and head a consumer credit department, at the VP level. Otherwise, no one knew what McCormick's plan would be. He had no subordinates to manage, just a fancy office, and a plaque advertising his new title.

Executive Vice President J. Edward Boylan was McCormick's pivot man in the transaction. Boylan strongly urged the bank to hire Don McCormick. With virtually no other supporting recommendations, Boylan was quite convincing in making his case to the board of directors.

However, Boylan was less than candid in pointing out to the board that he was related to McCormick by marriage. Ed Boylan's daughter was married to William McCormick, Don McCormick's younger brother. The implicit nepotism of the Boylan-McCormick relation resulted in an air of skepticism about McCormick's credentials. The "whisper circuit" among the bank employees was very active once the McCormick announcement was made public.

The media was less aroused by McCormick's hire. Alexander Milch, veteran financial columnist for the **Newark Star Ledger,** wrote that McCormick "joined the Howard in 1974 as a vice president for planning after many years of service with the New Jersey Bell Telephone Company of Newark, New Jersey." Another article represented him as an "expert in management."

McCormick's own resume apparently did not delve into the details of his departure from New Jersey Bell. The term "sabbatical" served the purpose of underplaying his disconnection from the telephone company. Few if any objections to McCormick's background were formally raised.

Around this time, Tom Keegan—a Howard vice president—was transferred out of the electronic data processing department and installed as head of the future planning department. When McCormick was hired, there appeared to be a redundancy of the two officers' responsibilities. In one of his early assignments, Keegan headed a so-called "long range planning task force" consisting of 12 or so senior-level people, which included McCormick. Their assignment was to create a five-year plan for the bank. Most of the members thought it was important while some others thought it was a big waste of time.

At any rate, the task force for future planning drew up a document that echoed many of the proposals espoused by Donald McCormick. For example, the group recommended that the bank convert to stock. A small minority opposed the conversion proposal.

Generally speaking, nepotism was frowned upon or was expressly forbidden at many banking institutions. The Howard might be alive today if Murray could have selected his son Charlie as president! Charlie was an easy going, well-mannered correspondent banking executive at the Chemical Bank. His travels nationally gave him a strong background in the overall world of banking. Previous administrations at the Howard had prided themselves on the absence of nepotism in executive appointments. In looking back at McCormick's hire, Investment Officer John Quinn remarked: "The impact of the nepotism factor had a demoralizing effect on the entire senior management corps." The traditional method of hiring and grooming Howard execs had been violated. It seemed the entire bank waited to see what the consequences would be.

Once Don McCormick had his foot in the door, he used his seemingly innocuous title of VP-planning to strategic advantage. McCormick was a smart cookie. As an action oriented person, McCormick spent most of his days visiting the other fifteen officers who represented the inner management circle. For sure, every manager needed a business plan for the department's operation, and Don McCormick was there to offer advice. At first, some managers resisted Mac's intervention, but his persistence overcame these barriers. He seemed genuinely interested in everyone else's operation, and his knowledge of the big picture at the Howard expanded rapidly. Before long, everyone in the bank knew he existed. In Charlie Forbes' words, Don McCormick was the "consummate corporate politician." Don McCormick was ubiquitous.

Oddly enough, if he had assumed a title heading up a specific operation, McCormick probably would have been swept away by the minutiae of his separate department. He was in no way a specialist or a bean counter. His role as a generalist was a natural fit to his personality.

McCormick soon discovered that the fifteen managers worked very well as a team. Most had spent a large portion of their careers at the bank and regarded the Howard almost as a family business. They were proud of the Howard's history and its position as the largest banking institution in the state. Early on in the Forbes administration, there was no apparent power struggle for the number two slot at the bank. The two executive vice presidents of the bank were Ed Boylan and George Hughes, head of the investment and trust departments. Ironically, both had started at the bank in the same year and both were scheduled for mandatory retirement (i.e., age 65) at the same time. Although the board of directors extended their retirement by one year, both finished their careers in the very late 1970s. Regardless, Don McCormick knew that neither would be around to succeed Forbes.

As McCormick instinctively viewed the overall profile of the bank, and as a relative newcomer unaccustomed to the relaxed work ethic of the Howard managers, he intuitively sensed an opportunity to assert his "Type A" personality and move up the management ladder.

At first, after New Jersey Bell, he needed a job. Now, he was becoming obsessed with the power that might be his if he played his cards right. In the eyes of Ed Boylan, Mac was the "fair-haired boy."

McCormick's gains within the Howard hierarchy were a tribute to his persistent nature. Additionally, Mac benefited from his day-to-day commute with Ed Boylan, who also lived in Glen Ridge. Boylan became McCormick's mentor as they drove to and from the bank in Mac's car. At the time, Boylan was recovering from cataract surgery which precluded him from driving. It was a great opportunity for Don to broaden his knowledge of banking in general and the Howard Savings Bank in particular.

Also, he gained some technical knowledge of the savings bank industry through his attending the highly regarded Graduate School of Savings Banking at Brown University in Providence, Rhode Island. For three years, he was listed as a student at the school's two-week sessions. Just how serious a student was Don McCormick? Kevin Ward, presently the CFO of the Provident Savings Bank, was a classmate of his and Kevin said he rarely saw him at any classes. Somewhat enviously, Kevin surmised that Mac was out on the local golf course.

When the time was appropriate, Mac apparently bore down and completed his term paper(s) and received his certificate from this very tough school.

McCormick was often the center of attention at Howard-related social functions. His outgoing nature and tall physical frame set him apart from the crowd. He consciously limited his alcohol intake to a few white-wine spritzers. His memory for conversations that took place over cocktails was like a locked trap. Many an officer taken with "loud mouth soup" found his conversations repeated to him by a relatively sober McCormick at a later date. He seemed to have a mental dossier on everyone at the bank.

At these social events, he was the master of working a room. He was perpetual motion as he touched base with everyone that mattered. He never missed the opportunity to "schmooze" with a member of the board of directors who might be in attendance. Prior to being selected CEO of the bank, Mac behaved himself very nicely as far as his rapport with women was concerned. But once selected CEO, usually he was accompanied to the party by one of two possible females, both of them being employees of the bank. Since his wife Sheila was bedridden for much of his career, Mac usually circulated quite openly with either of these two women. The occasion could be a small gathering at the Brothers Restaurant in Newark or a UNC vs Army football game at Michie Stadium (seating capacity 45,000) in West Point, New York. Once he had the CEO job in hand, McCormick never hid his friendships with these women.

McCormick maintained a consistent devotion for his wife, and constantly expressed his feelings that he would never divorce Sheila. Despite her propensity to shop extensively on the Home Shopping Network, Sheila was the love of his life.

Elissa T. Uber, popularly known as "Toni," was a senior trust officer at the bank during the McCormick years. An attractive blond, "Toni" was listed in McCormick's obituary as his fiancee.[1] Ironically, Sheila's name was not mentioned in the obituary. Throughout the 1980s, Sheila was very sick, and continuously bedridden. As far as the consensus is concerned, Mac never got a divorce from his wife Sheila.

After working three years at the bank, McCormick had constructed a meaningful power base for himself. A number of the staff officers reported Mac as their link to the president. In 1977, his fraternizing with various board members paid off, as he was named a director himself. Mac's fellow EVP—Leo Rogers—was selected for the board as well.

McCormick always was very sensitive about his own personal appearance. At 6'2" tall, he was an imposing figure in most any crowd. He fought to keep his weight within certain tolerance limits, and he never let himself get fat or overweight. Smoking two packs per day of *Vantage* cigarettes might have curbed his otherwise training table appetite. His use of profanity probably was a defense mechanism designed to portray his "macho jocko" image.

The McCormicks had two children, Linda and Donny. Away from the bank, Don McCormick's true passion became his son's very promising basketball career. At 6'5" and weighing 200 pounds, Donny McCormick started all four years for Glen Ridge High School, and led his team to a 23-3 record in his senior year. He was an All-State selection of the **Herald News** in his senior year while averaging 22 points and 14.8 rebounds per game. Donny often cited Kelly Tripucka (Notre Dame, Detroit Pistons) as the most influential player on his career. Upon gradu-

---

[1]See obituary on p. 169.

"We help our Trust cus-
tomers manage and invest
their money for growth and
profit. Our ability to design
investment strategies to
meet individual needs is
based on six decades of asset
management experience."
Elissa T. Uber,
Senior Trust Officer
(from 1980 Annual Report)

ation from high school in 1982, Donny selected Fordham
University as the venue for his basketball talents.

Fordham Coach Tom Penders assessed young
McCormick's talents as he was about to launch his college
career: "Don is quite advanced technically. He's a tough
rebounder, a solid defensive player, and has a good
medium range jump shot."[2] The main campus of Fordham
University, located in the shadow of the Bronx Zoo and the
New York Botanical Gardens, was less than an hour's
drive from the McCormick's home. Additionally, Fordham

---

[2]Quote from 1982 Fordham Basketball Media Guide.

played several colleges within short driving distance (Iona, Manhattan, St. Peters, Seton Hall, etc). Thus, Don McCormick saw every one of his son's home games and more than half of his away games while he played for the Rams. In addition to his basketball achievements, Donny was an honor roll student and a Citizenship Award winner at Glen Ridge High School.

Once at Fordham, it took Donny just six games to break into the starting lineup as a freshman. Playing in all thirty of the Rams games, his scoring highlight occurred when he registered 17 points against St. John's University. However, in between his freshman and sophomore years, he strained the tendons in his right thumb and the injury limited his scoring average to 7.7 points per game. His highlight game in his sophomore year was a 19 point effort against Notre Dame.

As a senior, his strongest game was against Seton Hall University when, playing before many local fans at the Meadowlands Arena, he returned home to have the game of his college career. He scored 27 points as the Rams lost to the Pirates from the rugged Big East Conference by 73–66.[3]

Don McCormick was, as noted, extremely supportive of his son's basketball career at Fordham. As the fortunes of history would dictate, his son's career overlapped the initial four years of his presidency at the Howard. Perhaps the slippage of his son's scoring and rebounding statistics from when he played in high school plus the Rams record of 13–17 in the 1985–1986 season might have been a source of inner frustration for the leader of the Howard Savings Bank. Conceivably, McCormick became more aggressive in the lending area as an outlet for these frustrations. Don McCormick loved his son, his son played his heart out, but the Howard Bank may have suffered by this transfer of emotions once the elder Mac was back in

---

[3]Two years later Seton Hall lost to Michigan in the final game for the NCAA championship.

his executive offices. The dream of young Don advancing to the NBA faded as the four years at Fordham University rolled by.

Since his days in Bloomfield, New Jersey Don McCormick maintained a close friendship with the Tripucka family. The patriarch of the family was Frank Tripucka, who was the star quarterback for Notre Dame (class of 1949) and the New York Giants in the early 1950s. He sired six athletic children, including the aforementioned Kelly Tripucka. Two of his sons—Tracy and Todd— were standout basketball players at Lafayette College and subsequently were elected to the school's athletic hall of fame. While Tracy opted for a coaching position at Utah State University, Todd entered the business world, and his outgoing personality and almost natural sales ability attracted Don McCormick. The perpetually positive McCormick outlined some opportunities at the Howard, offered him a job, and Todd accepted. In 1976, Todd entered the Howard Savings Bank training program.

Glen Ridge, New Jersey was and continues to be an attractive Essex County community known for its antique gas lamps which line the major streets. Don was a member of the Glen Ridge Country Club. His physique rendered him a lot of power but frequently kept him in the rough at the fairly tight course which unfolds on both sides of Ridgewood Avenue. Don carried a high teen handicap, implying an average score of around 88–95.

Backtracking to 1970, Ed Boylan was one of two EVPs at the bank. The second EVP was Walter D. Tombs. But Tombs seemed unsure of his future role as co-EVP, and soon left the Howard to take a high executive position at the Harmonia Savings Bank in Elizabeth, New Jersey. The hyper-tense Tombs eventually became the CEO of the Harmonia where he ran a more-or-less "squeaky clean" operation until the bank merged with the Sovereign Bancorporation in the mid-1990s. Hindsight is 20-20, but the "upwardly mobile" Tombs might have provided strong competition for the CEO post when Murray Forbes eventually stepped down. George Hughes then succeeded

Tombs in the EVP slot. Hughes was head of the investment department and highly regarded among his peers at
the bank. But Hughes was not a "political animal" and
seemed disinterested in becoming the CEO.

In 1980 McCormick was selected executive vice president. In essence, he was one title away from being chief
executive officer of the bank. To most of the other officers
and employees of the Howard, Don McCormick's intentions were obvious. He often dressed for work in his black
business suit with a red power tie, as if rehearsing for
his pending promotion. Don wanted the job, and it
seemed that no one else cared on the Howard staff. Under
Forbes, life was good and there seemed no reason to
rock the boat. In a period of eight years, Don McCormick
rose from the newly created position of vice president-
planning to CEO in mid-1982. Like a case study of a
Machiavellian power play, Don McCormick took advantage of the content management team and the tolerant
Howard board and finessed his way to the top of the list.
Don McCormick indeed *was* the consummate corporate
politician.

Perhaps this somewhat ruthless expression of ambi-
tion turned off the regulatory authorities. In the early
1980s, two Fed-assisted merger situations arose which
awarded basic franchises to the Hudson City Savings
Bank. The "Mighty Hudson" was led by mild mannered,
tactful Ken Birchby who had been in banking his entire
life. He had served as president of the national association and the New Jersey group. Meanwhile, McCormick
seemed more interested in his pending IPO, which would
convert the Howard to a shareholder institution. The IPO
had the potential of making McCormick a very rich man.

At the time of his election, McCormick was 51 years old.

Throughout the process, Murry Forbes quietly favored
the younger Leo Rogers (then 45) over McCormick as his
successor. He supposedly agonized over the prospects of a
McCormick presidency. Walter Hislop also disapproved of
Mac's selection. His personal choice was Arlyn Rus, the
young personable president of the Raritan Savings Bank.

Walter actually had more than a casual understanding of how Arlyn Rus worked with people. When Bernie Allecks, the executive director of the NJAMSB, died suddenly in a car accident, the official affairs of the association fell into a state of disarray. Arlyn Rus was the chairman of the state association at the time, and feared that the time lost with a search for a new director would lead to even further inefficiencies. Arlyn telephoned his friend Murray Forbes and obtained the services of Walter Hislop, who took a leave from the Howard to assume the temporary duties of the executive director. Walter held the position for a few months and finally the search produced Samuel Damiano, who continues to this day as the association's full-time director. In the meantime, Walter and Arlyn worked closely together in pulling the NJAMSB back to rights. But once back at the Howard, given the contrast of working with Arlyn Rus versus Donald McCormick, Walter—a veteran survivor of many of the turf battles at the bank—certainly anticipated that the Howard would have its difficulties in adapting to McCormick's style. Despite some fairly significant objections, the Don McCormick freight train moved ahead.

As Ronald Reagan assumed the presidency of the United States, a general spirit of deregulation was sweeping the nation. Tax laws, banking and utility regulation, rules governing markets, an overlay of legal restrictions and footnotes seemed ready to strangle the country's economic entrepreneurial spirit. Reagan and his supporters pledged to get rid of many of the loopholes in the tax code, to eliminate the basic monopolistic franchises of utilities, to free banks to invest in heretofore restricted areas, and to generally speaking create a free flow of capital throughout the nation's marketplace. In his pursuit of a level economic playing field, Reagan—in effect—reshuffled the deck known as the United States economy.

☆ ☆ ☆

In the final analysis, Fed Chairman Paul Volcker's plan to defeat inflation was effective and ultimately succeeded in wringing the inflationary bias out of the economy. By slowing the growth in the money supply and subsequently raising interest rates to the highest levels ever recorded, Volcker delivered the knock-out punch which initially drove back the measures of inflation (such as the consumer price index or the wholesale price index) from their double-digit gains for the late 1970s and early 1980s to a point ultimately in the mid 1990s where they showed zero or negative inflationary performances within the economy.

Undoubtedly the inflation rate called for strong action on the part of the Fed. To have continued otherwise would have aggravated the situation. But some would question the extent of the Fed moves and, although somewhat expected, was it necessary to take so many of our financial institutions down in order to accomplish these gains?

One of the basic—truly basic—fundamentals of all fixed income markets relates to the calculation of yields and prices. One of the first tautologies learned by a Wall Street trainee entering the fixed income market is that:

"When interest rates go up, bond prices go down"

By definition, when Volcker raised interest rates so dramatically, he also lowered bond prices by a significant amount. From 1980–1983, the entire commercial and savings bank industry saw every one of its portfolios simultaneously nose-dive purely as an arithmetic consequence of the Fed's action.[4] In New Jersey, the accounting firm of Peat Marwick held an emergency seminar for all the mutual savings banks in the state. If you "marked to mar-

---

[4]Theoretically, a portfolio fully invested in "inverse floaters"—a novel security born in the period—would have appreciated in the bear market for bonds.

ket" the various portfolios of these banks, they all would have been in deficit positions as far as their surplus accounts were concerned.

Almost every bank from Citicorp to the Raritan Savings Bank was technically bankrupt. Although solvent, the best quality banks were posting losses. The strongest banking system in the world was teetering on the edge.

A tower of strength, a Democrat, and an imposing physical person, Volcker would not waver from his tight monetary policies. Reagan and his principal advisers soon became concerned that the Fed chairman had gone too far. They feared that a policy-induced recession might take place as the 1984 elections approached. Secretary of the Treasury James Baker tried to be subtle and convince Volcker to ease rates, but the chairman deflected any forays which threatened Fed independence. To Volcker, the independence issue was as important as the inflation issue itself.

Although Volcker resigned in 1987, the longer term impact of his policies was locked into place and would influence the course of banking for at least another decade.

McCormick as CEO of the Howard

At first, the activities of the NJAMSB were not overly exciting for Don McCormick. The initial convention he attended as president was held in Hershey, Pennsylvania, and he spent most of his time on the golf course including one round with me. Actually, my friend Bill Bellott from the Orange Savings Bank and I had signed up as a twosome with the intent of playing in the conference's annual golf tournament. McCormick was assigned to our twosome, having signed up as a single golfer. Bellott and I were pleased to have the opportunity to play with such a man of rank, but found it unusual for him to be playing alone. Most CEOs travel in entourages and are anxiously sought as golfing partners, particularly in the annual tournament. The night before the tourney, we discovered

Foursome consisting of Don McCormick, Bill Bellott of the Orange Savings, Paul Luscombe of Prudential Bache, and Charlie Forbes of the Chemical Bank prepare to tee off in the NJAMSB annual golf tournament at Hershey, Pennsylvania, in 1983.

that Murray Forbes' son (a correspondent banker with the Chemical Bank) was looking for a game and he gladly rounded out our foursome the next day. As our golf round evolved, we found McCormick to be intent on his game and a minimum of conversation took place. Perhaps our expectations were too high as we envisioned a more out-going leader. In fact, at first glance, Charley Forbes, Bill Bellott, and I were not impressed with the social skills of the new CEO of the Howard Savings. He apparently saved his "best stuff" for internal events at the Howard. We were not a part of his political aspirations at the bank. Somehow, we were external to his world.

Still, McCormick's rank almost immediately qualified him to be part of the industry group's trade organization. Because of the consolidation in the thrift industry and the banking business overall, the NJAMSB changed its title to be The New Jersey Council of Savings Institutions. As the CEO of the largest savings bank in New Jersey, McCormick was soon in the annual ascension of leaders within the group, and the slate of officers was chosen for the 1986 year, and those selected were:

Chairman	Donald McCormick	Howard Savings Bank
First Vice Chairman	C. William Kulthau	New Brunswick Savings Bank
Second Vice Chairman	Charles W. Frost	Morris County Savings Bank
*President	Samuel Damiano	New Jersey Council

*essentially executive director of the council and its predecessor NJAMSB

As a nontraditional banker, McCormick was intrigued by all the new legislative proposals being faced by the Howard and the rest of New Jersey's savings banks. Besides, there wasn't much he could do to significantly improve the retail operations of the bank. Most of the bank's operation could run on auto-pilot. He was, however, captivated by the possibility of the bank raising equity capital by way of issuing an initial public offering of common stock. From the standpoint of greed alone, McCormick could alter his compensation arrangement from that of an incremental increase per year to one based on awards of stock options and the like. Don McCormick was motivated beyond the level of the stereotypical "3-6-3" mutual savings bank president. With equity shares outstanding, the sky was the limit as far as his compensation was concerned.

Donald McCormick was a buyer of assets and subsidiaries. In his decision to acquire the relatively small ($30 million) Citizens Federal S&L of Berlin, New Jersey, Mac relished the thought of his bank being the first

"Our subsidiaries have been a key element in The Howard's development into a full service financial company. They have expanded our product line to include non-traditional services and made it possible to satisfy virtually all of our customers' personal and business requirements."
—Frank Buckworth, Vice President (from 1980 Annual Report)

mutual savings bank to ever acquire a S&L. Because Citizens already had shares outstanding, actually a shareholder institution since 1967, and the HWRD's issue was being processed, the newly acquired bank became one more of a growing list of Howard subsidiaries. Actually, the Citizens subsidiary operated fairly independently of its new parent. President Ernest L. Previto remained in charge and no immediate effort to change the name of the bank was made. In many respects, the attraction to buying the beleaguered Citizens was its federal charter, whereas the Howard and the other mutual savings banks in New Jersey all possessed state charters. Although the media tabbed the move as a "rescue operation," in McCormick's grand design, this small Berlin, New Jersey operation may have been the conduit for expanding into profitable out-of-state areas such as Florida.

Shortly thereafter, the Citizens name was changed to Howard Federal Savings, F.A. and the new subsidiary made an application for a branch in Haddonfield, bringing its total number of branches to two. By 1987, the tiny bank subsidiary was operating at a profit and contributed modestly to the overall very successful year of the Howard.

Back in 1970, the Hoboken Institution for Savings resembled a geriatric home. Most of the bank's senior management was over 60 years old and their CEO Peter Verdicia was over 70. When the bank examination team headed by Jim Pinto wrote his critique of the bank, he cited their inadequate program of providing a management succession for the future. Pinto was shocked by the reply of the Hoboken Bank's CEO. In short, he offered the job to Pinto. And, after some deliberation, Pinto accepted! For about ten years (1972–1982) Pinto was the charismatic leader of the Hoboken Bank, subsequently renamed the Washington Savings Bank.

Although his record was comparable to his peer group, in 1982, Pinto had had enough of Volckernomics and stepped down as president. He was succeeded by Paul Rotondi as CEO and another bank examiner, Anthony Callebrese, as president. Like most thrift institutions in the 1980s, the Washington Savings Bank struggled, tried to satisfy its customer loan demand, and survived. In 1987, when at least twelve New Jersey thrifts went public, the Washington joined in the party.

In May of 1989, the Howard made an attempt to buy the Washington Savings Bank. Essentially, the Howard agreed to pay $20.59, or 1.35 times the book value of Washington common shares. Prior to the announcement, the last trade on NASDAQ was $14.25. The total cash outlay by the Howard would be $47 million for the $362 million franchise. The Howard was most interested in the Washington's presence in Hudson County and Bergen County.

Paul Rotondi, CEO of the Washington, liked the proposal and soon the merger was about to be completed, and required only the approval of the FDIC, the state banking department, and the stockholders. The merger, if finalized, would mark the shortest life of a demutualized New Jersey savings bank. The Washington Savings went public in 1987 at $10.50 per share and was scheduled to lose its corporate identity just two years later. Anthony Calabrese, president of the Washington, said that all 100 employees of the Washingon (including officers) would retain their jobs if they chose.

As 1989 progressed, the negative news on the Howard began to roll in on a fairly constant basis and the HWRD stock began to sharply trade downward. Soon the implicit takeover price had slipped below the minimum price of $18.58 per share and the Washington terminated the transaction. Also in 1989, a similar market phenomenon was experienced by the Montclair Savings Bank, which had agreed to a merger with First Fidelity Bancorporation. When FFB's stock traded dramatically lower in 1989, the merger with Montclair was canceled.

Ultimately, the Washington Savings Bank was acquired by the Hudson United Bancorporation headquartered in Mahwah, New Jersey. Times had changed, and most of the WSB employees lost their jobs.

So, Donald McCormick would bat one for two in the bank merger game. There also were other discussions but none came as close as the Washigton Savings deal.

Almost simultaneous with the Citizens acquisition, the Howard bought Mortgage Services of America, with offices in Cherry Hill and Elmwood Park, New Jersey. MSA was a residential mortgage banking company which originated over $70 million in loans in 1982 and was servicing over 1400 mortgages valued at $75 million.

Another subsidiary was added when the Howard bought controlling interest in Potere Inc., an executive relocation firm based in Elizabeth, New Jersey. The company was family owned and was led by its president Daniel I. Hanrahan. The company held the distinction of being the first national third-party home-buying company involved with the relocation of executives. McCormick liked the investment and felt that job-related transfers would remain stable over the business cycle. To his credit, McCormick was adding a subsidiary which produced new avenues of fee income and service diversification.

But McCormick had bigger fish to fry, and he was quickly on the move to set his plans for converting the Howard to a shareholder institution. McCormick wasted no time. On July 19, 1983, just one year after being elected president of the Howard, the bank became the first mutual savings bank in New Jersey to go public.

The Initial Public Offering (IPO) of HWRD common stock

The capital-raising effort of a mutual savings bank's initial public offering of common stock differs sharply from the IPOs issued by other corporate entities such as industrial companies. In the case of the mutual savings banks, the shares are first offered to its depositors. In essence, this stage is comparable to the preemptive right of existing shareholders in non-bank financings, and represents the rights of the previous owners of the bank to be the first to fund the newly organized capital structure of the shareholder institution. Savvy investors in states where mutual savings banks are apt to issue IPOs circulate aggressively around the state and make deposits at as many banks as they can.

In 1983, the deposit game was not as fine-tuned as later on in the cycle. Nonetheless, the Howard Savings tapped its depositor base for 1.3 million shares at $20.00. The price of the initial phase was similar to a "maximum filing price" and later on would be adjusted (via refund) to match the official and final offering price. The next phase of the marketing of the new issue was the amount of

Offering Circular

4,000,000 Shares

═══ the Howard ═══

Common Stock

The 4,000,000 shares being offered hereby constitute the balance of the 5,500,000 shares of common stock (the "Stock") of The Howard Savings Bank ("The Howard" or the "Bank") to be issued upon its conversion from a state mutual to a state stock savings bank (the "Conversion"). The remaining 1,500,000 shares have been either subscribed for in a Subscription Offering by depositors of The Howard at April 30, 1983 or ordered in a Direct Community Offering by individuals who are residents of New Jersey. The purchase price in the Subscription and Direct Community Offerings, which ended on June 30, 1983, will be the same price as the Public Offering Price set forth below.

Various limitations have been placed on the number of shares that may be purchased by any person together with associates and persons acting in concert. See "Conversion—Purchase Limitations."

The Stock has been approved for quotation on the National Association of Securities Dealers Automated Quotation ("NASDAQ") System. Its NASDAQ symbol is "HWRD." Prior to this offering there has been no public market for the Stock and there can be no assurance that an active and liquid market for the Stock will develop.

THESE SHARES HAVE NOT BEEN APPROVED OR DISAPPROVED BY THE DEPARTMENT OF BANKING OF THE STATE OF NEW JERSEY OR THE FEDERAL DEPOSIT INSURANCE CORPORATION NOR HAS SUCH DEPARTMENT OR CORPORATION PASSED UPON THE ACCURACY OR ADEQUACY OF THIS OFFERING CIRCULAR. ANY REPRESENTATION TO THE CONTRARY IS UNLAWFUL.

	Public Offering Price	Underwriting Discount(1)	Proceeds to Bank(2)
Per Share	$15.00	$.96	$14.04
Total	$60,000,000	$3,840,000	$56,160,000
Total, as Adjusted (3)	$68,250,000	$4,368,000	$63,882,000

(1) The Bank has agreed to indemnify the Underwriters against certain liabilities.
(2) Before deducting Conversion related expenses payable by the Bank, which if allocated on a pro rata basis to the shares in this Public Offering are estimated at $872,727. Net proceeds to the Bank from the sale of the 5,500,000 shares are estimated at $77,278,000. See "Net Conversion Proceeds."
(3) Assuming full exercise of a 30-day over-allotment option granted to the Underwriters to purchase up to 550,000 additional shares in the Conversion. See "Underwriting."

The above shares are offered by the Underwriters named herein subject to prior sale when, as and if delivered to and accepted by the Underwriters and subject to their right to reject orders in whole or in part. It is expected that certificates for the shares will be ready for delivery at the offices of E. F. Hutton & Company Inc., New York, New York, on or about July 26, 1983.

E. F. Hutton & Company Inc.   **Dean Witter Reynolds Inc.**

July 19, 1983

Figure 6.1 New issue circular

shares acquired by state of New Jersey residents who were not depositors of the bank and also general investors (including institutions) who resided outside the state's borders. About 4 million shares were sold in phase II and quickly $15 per share was established as the price of the IPO. The sum of phase I and phase II brought the total size of the HWRD offering to 5.3 million shares. Those who subscribed in Phase I received a $5 refund per share plus a token amount of interest. Since the IPO was oversubscribed, the underwriters exercised the right to issue 550,000 additional shares (historically referred to as the "Green Shoe" provision) bringing the total equity base of

1,150,000 Shares

the Howard

Common Stock

The shares of Common Stock offered hereby are newly issued shares of The Howard Savings Bank ("The Howard" or "the Bank"). On February 6, 1986, the closing sale price for the Common Stock, which is traded on the NASDAQ National Market System under the symbol "HWRD," was $35¼ per share.

THE MERITS OF THESE SECURITIES HAVE NOT BEEN PASSED UPON BY THE DEPARTMENT OF BANKING OF THE STATE OF NEW JERSEY OR THE FEDERAL DEPOSIT INSURANCE CORPORATION NOR HAS SUCH DEPARTMENT OR CORPORATION PASSED UPON THE ACCURACY OR ADEQUACY OF THIS OFFERING CIRCULAR. ANY REPRESENTATION TO THE CONTRARY IS UNLAWFUL.

	Price to the Public	Underwriting Discounts and Commissions(1)	Proceeds to the Bank(2)
Per Share	$35.25	$1.90	$33.35
Total(3)	$40,537,500	$2,185,000	$38,352,500

(1) See "Underwriting" for information relating to indemnification of the Underwriters and other matters.
(2) Before deducting other expenses payable by the Bank, estimated at $250,000.
(3) The Bank has granted the Underwriters an over-allotment option to purchase, within 30 days after the date hereof, up to an additional 150,000 shares of Common Stock at the same Price to the Public less the Underwriting Discounts and Commissions shown above. If such option is exercised in full by the Underwriters, the total Price to the Public, Underwriting Discounts and Commissions and Proceeds to the Bank will be increased to $45,825,000, $2,470,000 and $43,355,000, respectively. See "Underwriting."

The shares offered by this Offering Circular are offered by the Underwriters subject to prior sale, to withdrawal, cancellation or modification of the offer without notice, to delivery to and acceptance by the Underwriters and to certain other conditions. It is anticipated that delivery of the certificates for the shares will be made at the offices of Shearson Lehman Brothers Inc., New York, New York, on or about February 13, 1986.

Shearson Lehman Brothers Inc.   Alex. Brown & Sons
Incorporated

February 7, 1986

Figure 6.1 Continued

the bank to 5.850 million shares. Donald McCormick succinctly summarized the effect of the financing and said it "completes the bank's conversion from a mutual to a capital stock form of organization."

E.F. Hutton & Co. and Dean Witter Reynolds managed the financing for the underwriters. Among the various Wall Street investment banking firms, there existed an extensive amount of competition to earn the right to represent a preeminent bank such as the Howard in its capital financings. Members of the board heard presentations from a multitude of Wall Street firms on how they could most efficiently serve the bank. The bank management ruled out some of the larger firms which made presentations. "Too slick" was the only negative comment on record. The final selection of E.F. Hutton was based on its strength as a retail firm. It ranked second only to Merrill Lynch in the number of registered representatives, although the gap was a fairly wide difference (i.e., Merrill had 8,600 reps while E.F. Hutton had 4,000).

As a prelude to the marketing period of the Howard offering, the news on E.F. Hutton revolved around its president George Ball. In a surprise to Wall Street insiders, George Ball resigned suddenly in July 1982 to become CEO of Bache Halsey Stuart Shields. His raiding of his alma mater EFH whereby he attracted the head of stock research, the firm's national economist, and its head of institutional research must have affected the focus of the Hutton sales reps. The quotable Ball (i.e., he used to remark as to the profile he sought for Bache, "We want to be sizable and sinewy rather than large and languid") remarked that he wouldn't raid any other Hutton employees, although he admitted that "hundreds" of EFH employees had contacted him regarding potential employment at Bache. E.F. Hutton disappeared from the Wall Street list of firms in the late 1980s.

E.F. Hutton's marginal underwriting effort may have been a partial reason for the Howard selling 4 million out of a proposed 8 million shares. In 1986, E.F. Hutton was replaced by Shearson Lehman and Alex Brown & Sons when the Howard came to market with a secondary issue of common.

As a co-manager, Dean Witter Reynolds performed the function as a distributor stemming from its strong branch office system in Northern New Jersey and on the West Coast. Like Hutton, Dean Witter boasted a solid sales force of close to 4,000 retail representatives. Additionally, Dean Witter apparently filled a void for the Howard Savings Bank trust department which resulted from the bank's move to Livingston, New Jersey in 1982. With the advent of the Depository Trust Company and all institutions clearing their stock positions through the DTC, the suburban location of Livingston, New Jersey found itself out of the loop on proceed checks from sales of stocks in its trust department. Tom Gilligan, one of the top salesmen at Dean Witter, covered the Howard Trust and volunteered to act as agent out of his Millburn, New Jersey office in all sales of equities from the Howard accounts. Gilligen smothered the bank with "service" and may have been part of Dean Witter's selection. At the very least, Gilligen's actions made the Dean Witter efforts more visible than others seeking the underwriting fees available on a Howard new issue.

Actually, the Howard management perceived the Hutton-Witter team to represent an effective effort on a retail basis, with Hutton being a strong distributor on the East Coast and Dean Witter being a power on the West Coast. And so the team was selected.

The 5,850,000 share offering enabled the bank, after underwriting expenses, to raise approximately $80 million in equity capital and was accorded a satisfactory welcome by the capital markets at $15 per share. Using the ticker symbol HWRD, the Howard's new common was approved for quotation on the National Association of Securities Dealers Automated Quotation (NASDAQ) System. In secondary market trading, once price restrictions had been removed, the stock was initially quoted by the dealer community as 15 bid or—in the language of the street traders—"issue price bid." Stock was offered at 15.25 per share or as the traders would say, "stock offered at a quarter."

In the IPO market, it is almost taken for granted that a quality stock will open at a premium and advance in price when the free market opens for trading. The speculators (such as hedge funds) which subscribed for the stock were greeted with a market that essentially enabled them to break even on their commitment. Although many downplay the role of such speculators, they perform a role in creating a sense of urgency for long-term buyers to commit at the offering price. Whereas the very recent Provident Savings Bank jumped 55% (i.e., from 10 to

15.50) when it opened for trading, the HWRD offering, obviously critical to the management and staff of the bank, drew a so-so amount of national attention as the calendar for equity issues bulged with new financings. Competition from double-digit yielding fixed income instruments may have siphoned off potential investment funds from the Howard offering. Investment bankers might have advised the Howard to delay its offering and possibly perform better in a stronger market. In many respects, raising equity capital via an IPO is more an art than a science.

The officers and directors of the Howard pledged to buy (for their own account) approximately 750,000 or 12.8% of the newly offered shares. Directors Luis H. Meyer and Dr. James R. Cowan each purchased 100,000 shares on the offfering. Former U.S. Congressman Peter H.B. Frelinghuysen (5th District—NJ) subscribed for 40,000 shares. Don McCormick was the largest investor among the officers/employees of the bank with an initial commitment of 30,000 shares or $45,000 of his own money. All purchasers listed as directors and/or officers of the stock were locked into a one-year holding period before they could sell their stock, a common provision of initial public offerings of stock.

The circular for the common stock also listed the compensation for the highest paid officers of the bank for 1982. The remuneration paid was:

Name	Capacity	Total Compensation
Donald F. McCormick	Chairman of Board (CEO)	$139,116
Leo J. Rogers, Jr.	President, Board Member	116,734
*Andrew V. Aldi	Pres. Howco Investment Corp.	75,379
Tom Garratana	Exec. Vice President	69,035
Louis Selitto	Exec. Vice President	68,643

*Hired as a result of recommendation by Donald McCormick.

The 1983 *Annual Report* for the bank credited the initial public offering with increasing the bank's supply of available capital enabling it to provide a more diversified package of services to its customers. The report also alluded to the increased lending and investment capacity of the bank. Ultimately, a grand total of 17,000 investors were owners of the new issue of HWRD common.

But the $80 million raised through the capital markets was far less than the $150–$200 million that the McCormick team had originally contemplated when they filed registration statements with the SEC. The Howard, like many other banks, was issuing stock not only to create a new payroll currency but also to respond to the regulatory authorities' demands for stronger capital. Also, the lesser amount of equity capital implied taking additional risks in order to have a meaningful impact on earnings.

Among the banking law changes, McCormick also seized upon the provision allowing mutual savings banks the right to invest in real estate development loans. Just prior to his election to the Howard CEO post, McCormick organized a subsidiary in 1981 carrying the name Howco Investment Corporation. He subsequently brought in Andrew V. Aldi from the outside to run the group. Aldi, as shown in the list, immediately became the third highest officer of the bank. Aldi listed on his resume that he had held executive positions with the Bellemead Corporation, the Prudential Insurance Company of America and Planned Resident Communities Inc. The function of Howco and its sister subsidiary named The 768 Broad Corporation was to research the quality of the loans available in this area.

Originally, Howco met with stiff competition from the investment alternatives available to the bank in the public market. As the negative yield curve worked its way into place, the Howard could make a substantially better spread in the securities arena than in the mortgage market. In December 1981, rates on federal funds, commercial paper, and other short-term securities averaged 14.11% compared with a 9.88% return on loan instruments. As the yield curve flattened, the two sectors essentially traded at the same level in September 1983 (i.e., 9.70%).

Notwithstanding McCormick's preference for mortgage product, the Howard fared very well during his early reign as CEO because of the high rates of return available on top quality short-term investments. At this point in the cycle, following John Quinn's recommendation, the bank made a historic move and shifted a large portion of its assets from the mortgage area to the arena of money market instruments. At one point, 63% of the Howard's assets were invested in cash, money market instruments, and securities which matched the duration of their liabilities. In fact, research firms which followed the HWRD stock were quoted in the *Wall Street Journal* as saying that the bank looked more like a money market fund than a savings bank. The shift in liquidity is illustrated by the bank's holdings of money market instruments in 1983 ($959.7 million) versus its holdings in 1985 ($413.5 million). Meanwhile, the bank's deposit base grew by $272 million.

The time lag dictated by the market made McCormick just the more anxious to get his pet Howco project into full operational status. He spent a large portion of 1984 studying the viability of several large real estate development projects. These projects could be extensive and entail a multitude of payment sources. Many projects approximated the construction of an entire city or a large section thereof. Subcontractors for sewer construction, roads, street lighting, road access, and various utility connections dealt separately with the project manager, the lending bank's main contact in working with the loan. Project managers were a harried bunch. They were all experts in crisis management.

The Garden City (Long Island) project entailed close to 100 acres being developed for private use. McCormick devoted much of his attention to studying the viability of the loan. The project had two towers of luxury apartments, and initially, speculation was rampant that the condominiums on an individual basis might have appreciation potential.

McCormick's reputation as a braggard was reconfirmed when he, along with Aldi, exchanged "high fives" after the bank landed a huge participation (between $50–$110 million) in the Garden City project. The thrill of making the loan gave the two officers a "rush" and sustained their ego trip. An oddity of this transaction was that only one other investor participated (the Mitsubishi Bank). Two institutions, the Howard and the Mitsubishi Bank, owned the entire piece.

The high attained while buying this loan propelled the Howard into comparable commitments on several similar projects. Buying $25 million loan participations, accompanied by handsome commitment fees, surely was more efficient than putting the bank's money to work in the consumer credit area where money flowed out at a "Neanderthal pace." Included in the Howard's larger acquisitions was a hotel in Washington, D.C. Then, a hotel in the Meadowlands-Secaucus area was added to the portfolio. As McCormick and his mortgage team focused on these large takedowns, they lost sight of the time-tested principle of risk investing: *diversification*. Within a very short period of time, the Howard had a concentrated residential development project portfolio which exceeded the surplus of the entire bank. No problem, thought Mr. McCormick. To McCormick, these loans were "no brainers!"

While focusing on size and quality of their investments, the Howard team seemed to overlook the nature of the mortgage market mechanism itself. The Howard team projected an efficient level of liquidity for the blocks of paper that they held. For years, the Wall Street community had been trading mortgage backed securities using GNMA issues as the bellwether security. As the market matured in the 1977–1983 period, trading and secondary market activity began to intensify in other mortgage related areas. At times, this market was very efficient. But the mortgage market had yet to experience a real crisis. Few at the Howard anticipated that this market arena could experience a total shutdown. As long as this market functioned, and the newly acquired mortgage portfolio was current, the Howard had no problems. The problems came later in the decade when the impact of the national recession and the depressed real estate market virtually closed down the marketplace. When the music stopped in 1989, there was no chair for the Howard Savings Bank.

Meanwhile, the capital markets continued to trade HWRD common within a few points—over or under—of the original issue price. In 1984, for example, the low was 11 1/8 and the high was 18. As the positive earnings impact of the HWRDs trading activities became known, the common stock registered this performance in 1986:

	High	*Low*
First Quarter	21⅝	18⅛
Second Quarter	26½	19⅝
Third Quarter	27½	23⅛
Fourth Quarter	35⅝	26⅝

☆ ☆ ☆

Playing golf, in many respects, resembles playing the game of life. If you suspect your golf opponent of cheating at golf, he probably cheats in the business world as well. If he loses his temper or throws a club after a missed shot, he is more than likely apt to break out in a verbal tirade when confronted with frustrations at the office. Some golfers take big risks—they go for the green with a three-wood from 230 yards out—while others play more conservatively and use a five-iron to lay up in front of the pond guarding the green. An 18-hole golf course presents a myriad of challenges, and you get to know the personality of your opponent or partner pretty well by the end of a round.

In the 1970s, the thinly capitalized trucking industry continuously lived on the edge as surging oil prices threatened its very existence. The Cooper Jarrett Trucking Company was one of the casualties as it started the decade with a bankruptcy filing. Joseph G. Wojak was the president and CEO of Cooper Jarrett. He also was a golfing friend of Donald McCormick and a fellow member of the Glen Ridge Country Club.

When McCormick became aware of Wojak's corporate destiny, he jumped at the opportunity to hire his pal at the Howard. He had sufficient character background information on Wojak just from the many rounds they had played together. Wojak had also earned his CPA.

At this time, McCormick was grappling with the decision of who to select as his chief financial officer, a highly visible position of upper management which carried the title of executive vice president and implied a seat on the all-important Loan Review Committee. In McCormick's mind, Wojak's credentials and the vacancy at the Howard were a match. Mac moved quickly before his friend found another position in the marketplace. In less than 24 hours, prompted by a call from Donald McCormick, the Howard's human relations department was in touch with Joe Wojak. He was quickly interviewed and hired.

The collective response to Wojak's hire by the officer corps at the Howard was one of skepticism and disappointment. Although Mac was confident of his decision, the reservoir of potential talent from within the bank felt underappreciated. Surely one of them deserved a crack at the six-figure plus income and the prestige that the CFO title implied. Instead, a feeling of jealousy and resentment faced Wojak when he joined the bank.

When Ed Boylan first convinced the Howard board to hire Donald McCormick, his convictions seemed motivated by his daughter's husband being Mac's brother. And now, he was hiring a golfing buddy from the Glen Ridge Country Club. In many respects, McCormick's leadership was built on nepotism and personal friendships.

McCormick underestimated the complexities of the real estate market and probably exaggerated the quality characteristics of his loans, misleading Wojak into thinking these loans were self-liquidating. In Don McCormick's eyes, the bank could have its cake (in the form of a high rate of return) and eat it too (since it was sure to get its principal back!). The bank instead got a case of acute indigestion.

Based on his successful three-year college basketball career at Maryland University, Buck Williams was selected as the third player taken in the National Basketball Association (NBA) draft. He was the number one choice of the New Jersey Nets based on his fantastic rebounding ability. While playing at Maryland, he averaged 10.9 rebounds per game and averaged 13.6 points per game while sinking 61.5% of his shots from the field. A successful professional player as well, Williams was selected three times for All-Pro honors during his 18-year career, most of which was played with the Nets.

During his early years with the Nets, Williams was introduced to Donald McCormick. Mac, who relished the opportunity to "hang out" with professional sports figures, cultivated a friendship with Williams. Two or three months later, Williams was hired by McCormick as a part of the staff in the bank's real estate department. Once on board, Mac invited Williams to attend senior loan committee meetings. Because of Williams' lack of lending responsibilities, Mac's actions were regarded as "showcasing" his basketball star to the distraction of this vital committee.

Utter euphoria abounded at the annual meeting of the stockholders in April 1987. The Howard reported that the first quarter earnings of the bank surged a record 42.3% while posting a record $0.56 per share versus $0.44 for the same period in 1986. McCormick also announced at the meeting that the board of managers had voted to pay a $0.10 dividend to holders of record on May 4, 1987. The dividend would be the first paid by the bank since its issuance of shares in 1983. McCormick alluded to the contribution of the commercial mortgage loans in the bank's improved earnings. He also mentioned that these types of investments had reached the $1 billion mark.

In his comments at the 1987 Annual Meeting, McCormick informed the shareholders that the bank had "restructured its assets and liabilities to protect against interest rate swings as a result of the bank's increasing profitability. We run a conservative bank."

In his remarks about the quarter, Chief Financial Officer Joseph Wojak said that "the growth had been achieved without loss of asset quality. Write-offs were only $1.9 million, or 0.7% of the total."

In the footnotes of the 1987 Annual Report, the Howard management made a comment on its loan performance: "A continuing expansion of the New Jersey economy with sustained demand for commercial and residential real estate development, a higher per capita income than the national average, and an ongoing high level of consumer and capital spending have supported this loan growth and given The Howard an excellent environment in which to expand its lending services. Since 1983, gross loans outstanding have increased at an annual compound growth rate of 25.5%."

The statistical growth in the Howard's lending activity is illustrated in Table 6-1. The substantial increase recorded in the categories of Commercial Mortgages (+64.8%), Construction Loans (+155%), Home Equity Loans (+258%), and Commercial Loan Participations is illustrated by this table. Table 6-2 provides the different levels of interest rates that prevailed in the marketplace for fixed income securities and loan product areas. By emphasizing the better yielding (but generally more risky) loan areas, the bank was able to widen its interest rate margin by almost 100 basis points over a three-year period.

As a vice president in the Potere division of the Howard, Todd Tripucka participated in several staff meetings headed by Don McCormick and other senior officers. Those attending the meetings were posted on the various loans that the Howard was adding to its portfolio. As he monitored the details of these items, Todd was quite adamant in insisting that the bank was making investment loans in areas where they had no knowledge. "I

TABLE 6-1 DISTRIBUTION OF LOAN DEMAND BY HOWARD SAVINGS BANK FOR THE PERIOD BETWEEN 1985–1989

Gross Loans	1989	1988	1987	1986	1985
Residential Mortgages	766.7	702.9	632.4	631.9	668.4
Commercial Mortgages	751.7	795.2	849.3	684.7	559.7
Construction Loans	525.8	502.6	454.0	274.3	205.5
Total Mortgage Loans	2,039.4	2000.7	1,986.6	1,648.1	1,481.9
Indirect Auto Loans	114.3	149.1	126.3	126.5	83.9
Floor Plan Loans	38.6	45.0	42.0	32.4	10.0
Home Equity Loans	620.8	615.6	552.2	396.4	173.1
Total Consumer Loans	790.01	833.9	745.4	580.0	506.3
Student Loans	260.7	225.5	193.8	185.2	179.7
Commercial Loans	309.0	231.5	271.9	239.5	189.0
Commercial Loan Participations	165.3	118.9	140.3	97.0	33.5
TOTAL ALL LOANS	$3,610 million	$3,422 million	$3,338 million	$2,750 million	$2,190 million

Sources: Various annual reports between 1985 and 1989.

remember it like it was yesterday." He blamed a large portion of the high-risk lending activity on the persuasive influence of Andrew Aldi, who, according to Todd, painted very rosy pictures of the prospects for all of his loan proposals. An article in the *Newark Star Ledger* echoed Todd's remarks and criticized the Howard "for jumping into a market it knew little about. Too often, in its love affair with real estate lending, the Howard bet on the wrong developers and the wrong projects."

During the 1980s and particularly during Donald McCormick's reign, the basic culture of the Howard Savings Bank was changing.

During Mac's regime, there seemed to evolve an A team and a B team. The A team consisted of McCormick's recent hires. Their resumes were well polished, probably professionally prepared, but most had to stretch to find any real accomplishments in the field of banking. They confidently spoke about critical matters such as lending as if they had memorized the book on the fundamentals of extending credit. It appeared that the A team learned

**TABLE 6-2 AVERAGE INTEREST RATES
EARNED & PAID BY THE HOWARD
SAVINGS BANK PERIOD BETWEEN
1985–1987**

	1987	*1986*	*1985*
Average Rates on Loans			
Real Estate	9.39%	9.70%	10.03%
Student Loans	9.60	9.88	11.08
Consumer Loans	10.04	11.03	12.41
Commercial	9.26	9.37	10.88
Avg. Rates Investments			
Money Mkt. Instrumt.	7.29	7.20	8.80
Investment Securities	6.98	7.12	8.21
Mortgage Backed Secs.	8.13	8.49	8.51
Total Earning Assets	8.98%	9.16%	9.64
Rates on Liabilities			
Savings Deposits	5.55%	5.75%	6.25%
Time Deposits (CDs)	7.03	7.99	9.33
Reverse Repos	5.68	6.06	8.67
Other Borrowings	7.02	7.24	7.88
TOTAL INT LIABS	6.46%	7.16%	8.27%
INTEREST RATE SPREAD	2.52%	2.00%	1.57%

Source: 1987 annual report for the Howard Savings Bank.

on the job often at the expense of the bank's new corps of shareholders. The A team was made up of "talkers." The B team, essentially veterans remaining from the Forbes and prior administrations, got the job done with little or no fanfare. The B team consisted of "doers."

McCormick's cronies—the members of the A team—mirrored his confidence and exhibited substantial bravado in the execution of their duties. As the decade of the 1980s rolled on, the A team gained more sway, began to believe in itself, and soon alienated itself from the B team. The people at EVP and above (including Mac to some extent) were not perceptive enough to give credit to the doers. Mac's A team lieutenants failed to recognize those that could do more than talk a good game.

Soon, top management lost confidence in several department heads, and the bank hired many "consultants," a sure sign of weakness. With the incumbent managers and the consultants working in the same area, they were almost stumbling over one another. The double standard employed in many areas weakened the heretofore sound structure of the bank. Once the pride of New Jersey, the Howard management lost its touch and found it lacked the ability to judge its own people.

McCormick's hand-picked EVPs were hired from outside the world of banking. They possessed virtually no experience in running a strong department from within the organization. They seemed to achieve their position because of their friendships and/or their ability to glibly talk abut the banking business. The Howard was the classic example of cronyism operating at its very worst.

In fact, one of the consultants did a lot of harm. The student-loan market, by its very nature, is capital and labor intensive. The veteran management of the Howard was well aware of the time and effort required to build a prominent position in this market arena. Other banks applauded the Howard's effort and the state of New Jersey was relieved to have the loans handled by the private sector. But in one ill-advised sweep of the broom, the consultant severed the servicing agent for all student loans from the Howard's books. The consultant was surprised to find that while saving a nominal fee, he immediately reclassified $10.5 million as nonperforming assets—just when the Howard's balance sheet was starting to unravel on other fronts.

Over the years, the student loan program had been one of the bank's huge success stories. But that success was suddenly reversed based upon an operational technicality. The B team members understood the implications of dispensing with the servicing agent (known as PHEAA, or the Pennsylvania Higher Education Assistance Authority) while the A team relied on their under-informed consultant whose case was built around saving the bank a nominal amount of servicing fees. Without giving the decision much thought, McCormick & Co. sided with the consultant preferring to focus their attention on the more exciting mortgage market. Given its inexperience in the sector, the A team could not fathom how a change in the servicing agent could possibly have disastrous implications for the bank, and so the consultant's plan was adopted. When added to the nonperforming assets of the bank, the $10.5 million loss was a huge blow. In effect, the student loan program was the story of the Howard in a microcosm. (Note: see section on student loans for further details.)

As the Howard's problems accelerated into a downward spiral toward possible bankruptcy, they needed all the support in Trenton they could muster. The acknowledged leadership of the bank in the student loan market might have served them well in their darkest hour. The B team leaders might have played on the many years of support for this socially desirable but relatively low profit sector. They might have immediately dispatched a bank representative to Trenton. Instead, the McCormick-led management delegated this area to a misinformed consultant who overnight let this area evaporate into yet another financial embarrassment.

Also, the Howard may have been less diplomatic than some of its competition when moving its headquarters from politically sensitive Newark, New Jersey, to the friendly multi-acre campus located in Livingston, New Jersey. Although conceptually the move was orchestrated by Murray Forbes, McCormick was the first chief executive officer to serve his full term at the new corporate headquarters. For political purposes, the bank assigned the sobriquet of "administrative offices" to the huge suburban facility, while leaving its historic but antiquated Newark office with the "legal offices" designation. The lack of subtlety insulted the intellect of the Trenton politician, and would come back to haunt the HWRD management later on.

From the outside looking in, the first full six years (1983–88) of the McCormick reign appear relatively successful. After going public in 1983, the bank began to report earnings on a quarterly basis. The below-listed earnings figures were reported thus:

Annual Earnings / Share (adjusted for 2-for-1 stock split)

1983	1984	1985	1986	1987	1988
N.A.	$0.91	$1.40	$1.71	$2.41	$2.43

The bank's ability to produce constant increases in quarterly earnings was just as they wrote it in the textbook.

In part sparked by a 19.9% increase in loan activities, which brought the total amount of loans on the books to $2.2 billion, the quantum leap in earnings occurred in the 1985 calendar year when the bank reported earning $2.86 per share versus $1.86 a year for 1984. For the entire year this represented a 55% increase. Most of the gain was logged in the fourth quarter of 1985 which contributed $1.16 against $0.36—virtually a three times increase. At the end of 1985, the bank had a capital ratio of 6.43%. The bank noted that $232 million of its capital was tangible.

The bank's common stock responded accordingly, and the HWRD shares logged a 98% gain for the period between December 31, 1984, and 1985. On February 7, 1986, the Howard sold 1,150,000 additional shares at a price to the public of $35.25, providing the bank with $43 million in additional capital.

Although only selling 1.3 million shares in the secondary, the bank raised approximately 51% of the capital forthcoming when it sold 5.85 million shares in the primary market as an IPO. The combined total equity infusion during the McCormick years was over $125 million. Wall Street underwriters of the second offering were Shearson Lehman and Alex. Brown & Sons., replacing the Hutton-Witter team which underwrote the original IPO shares. Using extensive financial information already on file, secondaries are executed much more quickly than

IPOs and can be quite effective for the issuer from the standpoint of timing market highs. Given the latter events that impacted the HWRD capital and surplus accounts, the bank should have sold even more stock at this time. Even so, the Howard employed the investment banking tool of an "equity secondary" to sound advantage in 1986.

McCormick applauded the second leg of the Howard's financing, and said that the proceeds would be used to "facilitate growth and expansion of our operations." Unfortunately, the investment of these proceeds did not pan out as well as had been anticipated. The newly found capital funds were lumped with funds which the bank poured into real estate commercial loans and investments.

The number of HWRD stockholders apparently peaked in 1987 when approximately 18,000 investors owned the stock. The high dollar price for the stock was posted in September 1987 when the HWRD shares traded at 38⅛. Previously in January of 1987, the Howard Board had voted a 100% stock dividend (in other words a 2 for 1 stock split) which effectively meant the stock touched a pre-split price of 76.25 in September 1987. Don McCormick had the Howard franchise on a roll, and the approval of stockholders was indeed quite supportive.

The Loan Review Committee

As the 1980s unfolded, the inexperience of thrift institutions with the new forms of credit instruments became quickly apparent. Given the distinct tax incentives and regulatory encouragement, the thrift industry's 65–70% average asset holdings caused them to focus almost exclusively on the traditional mortgage analysis. According to Ronald Geesey, VP at Citicorp for over 30 years, "These managements simply had no training or background in lending that was not secured by real estate . . . Cash flows were what repaid loans, not liens and foreclosures."

In the mid-1980s, the loan review committee consisted primarily of officers from the bank who had never made a loan in their career. Wojak had been the CEO of a defunct trucking company, Lyons was "in house" counsel, Aldi was an expert on real estate development, Leo Rogers was an academic, John Quinn was a securities man, and McCormick was from the telephone company. The one executive whose experience came closest to lending was Louis Selitto, but he had been promoted into the position of senior lending officer from head of residential mortgage servicing department. Even Selitto had no experience in making loans. Further handicapping the committee, Selitto died from a brain tumor and was replaced by Peter Sammon whose background was marketing. Accordingly, the loan review committee for the bank lacked schooling in the fundamentals of lending, especially in the area of evaluating the character of a loan prospect. The committee was prone to lending funds to shell corporations, which were historically less disciplined than individuals with respect to loan repayments.

The loan review committee also approved the expansion of the Howard into the area of home equity loans and these instruments exploded from a zero base in 1983 to where $1.2 billion had been approved by year-end 1987. The product (dubbed with the acronym HERO, which stood for Home Equity Reserve Option) grew dramatically (+258.7 per cent!) between 1985 and 1988. The Howard and other banks in New Jersey were very aggressive in making these loans and apparently compromised their otherwise strict credit standards in order to put some numbers on the books. May Stern was a loan officer at Approved Finance Corp. (AFC), mortgage bankers who specialized in the home equity loan area. She recalls that once the traditional banking industry got involved with this area, they started to take business away from the mortgage bankers such as AFC. As a rule, the mortgage bankers are considered less critical of loan applicants than their banking counterparts.

Ms. Stern was shocked at how lax the Howard Savings and others had become in granting these Home Equity Loans, in effect second mortgage loans. "It was almost as if they set up a booth on the Garden State Parkway and handed out the money."

In 1986, the Howard borrowed $100 million from the federal agency known as the Student Loan Marketing Association (a.k.a. Sallie Mae). The terms of the loan included a 5-year fixed maturity at a spread of +63 basis points to the comparable U.S. Treasury issue. John Quinn negotiated the terms and he was intent on using the proceeds to shorten his asset-liability match in what he anticipated to be a reflattening of the yield curve. He left on a short vacation, relaxed and confident that the move would fall into place shortly after his return two weeks hence.

In his absence, however, Don McCormick just couldn't bear to see the proceeds sit in short-term investments, and so he placed the proceeds out long in various out-of-state real estate projects including a rehabilitated office building, and a warehouse in relatively remote locations. Generally speaking, Mac earned a spread of +200 for his investments but he exposed the bank to substantial risk. And who was to say if +200 was sufficient compensation in the world of risk-based asset pricing.

John Quinn was most unhappy when he returned from his vacation to find his plans for the SLMA proceeds had been overruled by the "Big Guy."

The Fall of Donald McCormick and the Howard Savings (1988–1990)

The Howard Savings Bank Annual Report of 1987, which was delivered to investors about March or April of 1988, was another glowing report of the bank's successes in the commercial real estate loan market and how the earnings had grown dramatically over the last six years. The report showed how the bank had increased these loans by $344 million, thus bringing said mortgage loans to $1.3 billion. The 1987 report also dwelled on the power structure of the bank by listing short thumbnail sketches of all its presidents since its foundation in 1857. The report added creditability to the Howard's reputation as a quality provider of bank services and leader in the data processing area.

But on October 19, 1987, the Dow Jones Industrial Average plunged over 22% in value, losing 504 points in the largest single decline in the market's history. Prior to "Black Monday," the HWRD stock had struck a historic high in 1987 when it traded at 38 1/4. To a large extent, the "crash of '87" was attributable to technical factors such as program trading by the Goldmans and the Morgans of the world. An insecurity complex settled over the securities business and Black Monday of 1987 definitely had a ripple effect in causing an economic slowdown. As earnings started to slide for 1989, consumers and corporations started to find it a little snug covering their interest charges on debt. Soon, as 1989 progressed, those charges gathered momentum and led to many bank loans being classified as nonperforming assets. The Howard's NPAs rose rapidly and the price of HWRD common stock spiked down sharply.

Following his graduation from North Arlington (New Jersey) High School, Walter Hislop began his career as a junior clerk at the Howard Savings Institution. He was 17 years old. At the time, the Howard listed $100 million in assets, three offices in Newark only, and roughly 105 employees. During Walter's 50 years at the bank, its footings had grown to $4.5 billion, 74 branches statewide, and 1,500 employees. On October 16, 1987, Walt was cited as one of five employees who had worked for the HWRD for 50 years or more since the bank's founding in 1857.

A little more than two years after receiving his award, on December 12, 1989, Walt Hislop was working on some projects in connection with his position of VP stockholder relations. His office was in Newark, New Jersey which the bank claimed to be its legal offices. At about 1:15 P.M., Walt received a telephone call from the administrative offices in Livingston, requesting his presence at a meeting to be started as soon as possible. A sense of urgency prevailed. Simultaneously, seven or eight senior officers at the administrative headquarters in Livingston received similar calls and they dropped everything and set off for the meeting.

As the officers entered the meeting, one of the secretaries handed out a sheet of paper resembling a press release. As Walt Hislop and the others read the report, you could see a changed expression come over their faces. The main point of the statement was that the Howard Savings Bank would soon report a shocking $65 million loss for the fourth quarter of 1989, and that the bank would report a $45 million loss for the entire year. The annual loss meant a negative earnings per share figure of $3.00. Just a few months prior, at an analysts' meeting in late October in New York, the management of the bank said it "felt comfortable" projecting a $1.75–$2.00 earnings figure for the year.

Henry S. Peltz, thrift analyst for Keefe, Bruyette & Woods of New York, attributed the problems revealed at the Howard to the weakening real estate market in New Jersey and along the eastern seaboard. "The Howard was willing to take a large hit in the fourth quarter, and hopefully this may be enough."

The timing of the announcement virtually coincided with the seizure of the $9.3 billion City Federal Savings & Loan Association of Somerset, New Jersey. City Federal was the largest thrift in the State of New Jersey and had registered losses of $234 million for the first nine months of the year. Real estate woes in New Jersey and Florida were primarily responsible for $747 million in nonperforming assets. William Seidman, chairman of the FDIC, voiced his concern about the real estate market in northern central New Jersey, stating that the area had perhaps the highest commercial real estate vacancy rates in the country.

For the Howard Savings Bank, this was the first real setback for the bank since going public in 1983.

Previously, its record as a mutual had been rock solid. To many, selling because of one year's number, a single figure of a $65 million loss, was a panic move. As such, HWRD shares fell from a closing quote of 10.50 prior to the announcement to 7.75 and then rebounded slightly to the 8.125 level. Although management made few if any confidence-inspiring remarks in the media, most investors long on HWRD stock felt the bank was "too big to fail" and would soon return to profitability. The motto of the bank listed in the 1985 Annual Report read, "Your Bank for Life" and many investors continued to hold their shares.

With the bank stock trading so low, a potential buyer of the stock could buy the basic franchise of the bank "real cheap." Ned Jesser, then chairman of the United Jersey Bank indicated that the largest single shareholder of HWRD approached him to see if he had any interest in acquiring the HWRD. Jesser found it interesting but declined because his bank was just then absorbing another banking institution. First Fidelity Bank had apparently accumulated in excess of 850,000 shares perhaps anticipating a hostile bid for their state rival.

Further investigation of HWRD's numbers, however, revealed the depth of the problems. The bank had forty commercial real estate loans of $25 million or larger on the books. Collateral for the loans included hotels, luxury condominiums, office parks and shopping malls. McCormick announced a 60% increase in nonperforming loans and the total for the year of $400 million. The likelihood of a "white knight" who could save the bank faded quickly. This was more than one self-correcting bad quarter. At the same time, nationwide, banks were dropping like flies and the mortgage market was totally drained of liquidity.

In an attempt to calm investors, McCormick made the following statements in the *Newark Star Ledger* as reported by writer Alexander Milch:

> "The real estate markets are in bad shape, and we're taking a market-driven but prudent response in dealing

with potential losses . . . Our bank is exceptionally strong and fully able to deal with this situation. Our ratio of tangible capital assets is far above regulatory requirements . . . We have the financial strength to deal with these losses."

Meanwhile, the media continued to work on McCormick's psyche. The concern about HWRD's mortgage portfolio was expressed by New Jersey's Commissioner of Banking Jeff Connor:

"It was quite a departure from the traditional Howard, which bought bonds and invested in mortgages . . . In the aggregate, that was a much less risky business than the commercial real estate business."

Classifying its $50-plus million loan to the Garden City project as a nonperforming asset was especially rough on the Howard. But the Garden City twin tower complex of luxury condominiums encountered problems of its own. The word spread that the builder was using less than best quality new appliances. Sheet rock at the foundation of the project was rumored to be of substandard composition. Initially thought to be a strong bet in the real estate spec market, the Garden City condos became suddenly available. Many potential condo owners clamored for the return of their deposits. When they took their fight into the courts, the judge ruled in favor of the condo owners over the Howard. The Howard would have to return all condo deposits on the Garden City project, if requested. The Howard was tapped very quickly as even depositors not involved with the Garden City project withdrew their accounts from the Howard. The "whisper" circuit spread rumors of a run on the Howard.

Howard alumnus Walter Tombs, president of the Harmonia Bank in Elizabeth, reported a sudden $10 million increase in deposits, which he attributed solely to problems at the Howard. The corps of Howard shareholders responded with a flurry of lawsuits, which basically charged the bank with misleading them as to the prospect for future earnings and the condition of its loan portfolio.

As the adverse numbers rolled in, Wojak increasingly took on the role of "enforcer" as he sought to stem the tide of losses and unnecessary expenses. For example, in the Potere subsidiary, he had a confrontation with Todd Tripucka, whose sales success had generated a sizable commission check. The check was properly earned in accordance with the contractual agreement between Todd and the bank. But Wojak felt the commission check was exorbitant, and in a private meeting with Tripucka, he threw the check at the former college basketball player and stated Todd would receive no more commissions, retroactive or otherwise. Todd politely mentioned the matter of his contract with the bank. Still Wojak stood his ground. Todd then mentioned that he would have to sue the bank if his contract terms weren't met. Wojak quickly replied, "No one sues the Howard Savings Bank!"

Undaunted, Todd Tripucka *did* sue the bank and was awarded a six-figure settlement. The Howard, in addition to being out the court settlement, also had to pay legal fees roughly estimated at between $25,000–$50,000.

As the once powerful Howard structure started to unravel, the role of the board of directors came into question. As the creators of this structure, could they also set in motion the forces of a turnaround?

Barring a crisis, most boards tend to be reactive rather than proactive. Indeed, most are passive in nature and act as review or monitoring agents for the management team they have put into place. The responsibility of being a corporate director is often thought of as an honorary rather than a real functional position. Directors rarely if ever get their hands dirty and instead tend to rubber stamp the proposals of their personally chosen CEOs and other top management personnel. Being a director gets one invited to all the industry conventions, which incidentally can include sizable travel and entertainment expenses, and adds prestige to one's resume.

Members of the board receive a fee (at the Howard, these were $550 for a full meeting, $400 for a committee meeting) for attending quarterly and monthly meetings. From the standpoint of the corporation, some of the prestige of the board members rubs off and gives an impression of a stronger financial institution. The practice of window dressing comes to mind.

Actually, if a corporation is performing effectively in the economy, if it is generating profits and dividends at an expected or better than expected level, if its stock price is moving up in line with or better than stock market indices or its peer group, then most directors lean back and enjoy their responsibilities and essentially become "yes men" for the CEOs policies. The cliché "If it aint broke, don't fix it" aptly applies.

But if the corporation falls short of attaining any or all of these accomplishments, how quickly should the board dig in and get directly involved? In the Howard's situation, only Murray Forbes had any direct experience in the lending area, but his term of service ended in 1984—a critical year for loan formation for the bank. Murray's reappointment to the board came after the loans were already on the books and were mostly nonperforming or about to nonperform.

Despite the tradition of passivity, the members of the board had enough clues without banking expert knowledge to have hemmed in McCormick. They could have set a standard of requiring full board approval for McCormick's deals which exceeded a certain size individually or in the aggregate. It seems this procedure would have been preferable to that of delegating responsibility to a committee he controlled.

Allowing Donald McCormick to fly as an "unguided missile" in the area of real estate development lending probably could have been prevented. At the time of the Howard IPO, McCormick and Forbes were the only inside directors. The outside board members and their respective business associations, as published in the circular filed in support of the bank's IPO, were:

As of 4-30-1981

Member/Affiliation	Age	Date of Board Appt.
Saul K. Fenster	50	1986
President New Jersey Institute of Technology		
Bernhard Grad	74	1968
The Grad Institute (architects)		
Carl W. Menk	61	1980
CEO Boyden Associates (executive search & management consultant firm)		
Donald A. Peterson	48	1976
CEO Continental Electric (manufacturer of electric motors and generators)		
Peter H. B. Frelinghuysen	67	1966
Former member of Congress (5th District)		
Robert M. Krementz	70	1965
Retired Chmn., Krementz & Co. (jewelry manufacturer)		
Gordom W. McKinley	68	1977
William F. Marfuggi	59	1980
CEO, Victory Optical Mfg. Corp (eyeglass frame manufacturer; served as Treasurer of State of, New Jersey, 1973 and 1974)		
James C. Pitney	56	1980
Partner, Pitney, Hardin, Kipp & Szuch (law firm)		

Orville C. Beal   74   1969
CEO, Prudential Insurance Co. of America

Robert J. Boutillier   59   1982
Vice Chmn., Peat Marwick Mitchell & Co.

Lloyd F. Christenson   69   1964
CEO (retired) and founder of Electronic
Associates, Inc.

James M.Cowan, M.D.   66   1972
CEO, United Hospitals Medical Center; former
New Jersey commissioner of health

Louis H. Meyer   60   1975
CEO, Loumey Management Company
(consultants)

John J. Unkles, Jr.   52   1979
Managing director, Tucker Anthony & Day
(securities)

When some of the directors retired from the board or became honorary members thereof, McCormick added the following outside directors to the team: Leonard Coleman of Kidder Peabody & Co.; Richard Ellwood, who ran his own investment management company; Natalie I. Koether, partner of the law firm of Keck, Mahin, & Koether (she also was involved with various investment groups); Frank T. Reilly, CEO of Brooks Brothers; and Sidney F. Wentz, CEO of Crum & Forster Insurance Companies.

It is easy to play Monday morning quarterback, but perhaps the big picture problem that should have been addressed by the Howard board in 1983 was: How far should the bank go in implementing the new powers authorized by congress in the Reagan presidency? From all appearances, the board granted Don McCormick too much latitude and virtually gave him carte blanche to plunge rather than wade into these areas. A ceiling on the amount permitted per loan—as applied in the investment area—might have been the only policy required. An outside director with some experience in the real estate lending field might have raised some red flags.

In retrospect, certain ironies surround McCormick's appointment of Frank Reilly, the chief executive officer of Brooks Brothers to the Howard board. The Brooks Brothers stores have always been the symbol of the standard men's business suit, rarely if ever changing style, always emphasizing conservative colors, and above all long-lasting high quality material. Although somewhat more expensive than some other retailers, BB was where executives young and old bought their suits. A Brooks Brothers suit seemed to last a lifetime!

This conservative, durable profile is what characterized the Howard's approach to business for so many years. On the surface, Frank Reilly was short on banking knowledge but long on "style points." Perhaps some desire of McCormick to return to fundamental savings bank practices prompted him to name Reilly to the board.

It is also interesting to note that McCormick gave credit to the board of directors, the officers and staff of the bank for their *guidance, leadership, and customer service performance* during the mid-1980s.

Jeff Connor, the commissioner of banking in New Jersey, was most upset with the Howard's board of directors when fourteen of its members opted to collect lump-sum payments of deferred compensation totaling $1.58 million. He publicly denounced the move and criticized the members for taking their cash rather than staying with the bank. Connor saw the directors as "unsecured creditors" and felt such monies belonged in the corpus of the bank to be ultimately divided up among the shareholders. Connor referred the matter to the FDIC for investigation. Connor's reaction to the directors' move may have precipitated an earlier action on his part to close the bank. The Howard definitely needed time to work out its problems.

☆   ☆   ☆

By going public, the Howard Savings Bank in essence started from the same point when it was organized in 1857. The bank's history resembled a successful basketball team which played extremely well in the regulation portion of the game, but was tied at the buzzer to send the game into overtime. The overtime was decisive and considerably shorter than regulation. The pressure to produce was severe. Going for the three-point play wasn't necessarily the wisest strategy.

In the overtime, between 1983 and 1988, the Howard coaching staff substituted freely and fired from behind the arc. The conservative game plan used in regulation was scuttled for a more aggressive style. When the final score was tallied, Coach McCormick's strategy had failed. Investors, employees, directors and the people of New Jersey lost in the end.

Actually, in mid-1989, McCormick had triple bypass surgery and subsequently returned to his post as CEO. He implored his upper management to keep his operation a secret. He didn't want it to become the excuse for the bank's poor performance. A few months later, in January 1990, the board of managers of the Howard Savings Bank accepted the resignation of Donald McCormick for "personal reasons." No further explanation was necessary. The one-time gritty lineman, the fast moving corporate executive, and the CEO of the once most prestigious bank in New Jersey had been humbled by the forces of a marketplace he thought he understood. Leo J. Rogers, Jr., president and chief operating officer, was elected to the added post of acting chief executive.

The Howard's long history of success may actually have led to its undoing. The investment public and the board were probably mesmerized by these successes, felt they were automatic, and assumed that the bank was invincible or bulletproof.

The bank honored the golden parachute severance terms of McCormick's contract. Mac received $1.3 million when he resigned. McCormick's contract called for payment of three times his annual salary. His cash compensation for

1989 had been $401,766 and his severance even included the $10,000 fee to McCormick's attorney who negotiated his severance arrangement. He apparently even retained use of the car service available to him as CEO. The general public and shareholders were outraged at the award by the board.

Ironically, the CEO of Brooks Brothers—Frank Reilly—was named head of the search committee to find the bank its next permanent CEO.

McCormick moved from his house in Glen Ridge to Manasquan, New Jersey, in January 1996. Shortly thereafter, at age 65, he died in the Jersey Shore Medical Center in Neptune of a stress-related heart attack. (See Figure 6-2.)

☆ ☆ ☆

By way of comparison, it is interesting to follow the career of mutual savings bank executive Charley Smith, who took over the reins of the Keene Savings Bank (NH) in 1983—the same year that the Howard converted from a mutual charter. Charley had built a solid reputation as executive vice president of the Raritan Savings Bank (NJ), but moved up to New Hampshire to accept the challenge of bringing the tiny ($62 million) institution to the point of profitability. Almost twenty years later, the original Keene Savings Bank—subsequently renamed "The Granite Bank"—boasted some $1 billion in assets and was the largest bank (commercial, savings or otherwise) domiciled in the state of New Hampshire.

Certainly Charley Smith had to work his way through some tough real estate markets. In fact, on October 10, 1991, the five largest banks in New Hampshire failed on the same day, presumably all because of real estate debacles. For sure, Charley had to write off some bad loans, but these were held in check and never jeopardized the survival of the bank. The bank focused on expanding its customer branches and erecting ATM machines at convenient locations. The bank bought back its own stock at low

Figure 6-2   Obituary of Donald McCormick from the Glen Ridge *Voice* of July 11, 1996.

Donald McCormick

A prayer service for Donald F. McCormick Sr. of Manasquan was held July 6 in the Van Tassel Chickene Funeral Home, Bloomfield. Mr. McCormick, who died July 3 in the Jersey Shore Medical Center, Neptune, served as chairman of the board and chief executive officer of Howard Savings Bank in Livingston for 8 years, retiring in 1990. He also served as chairman of the New Jersey Council of Savings Banks.

Earlier, he had been employed with New Jersey Bell for 20 years.

Mr. McCormick was a 1953 graduate of the University of North Carolina, with a bachelor of arts degree in economics.

He was a member of the Thrift Institutions Advisory Council in Washington, D.C., the New Jersey Chamber of Commerce, and the Board of Trustees of the United Hospitals of Newark.

He was a past president of the Society to Prevent Blindness and the 200 Club of Essex. Mr. McCormick also served as a board member of the University of Medicine and Dentistry of New Jersey and director of the Metro Newark Chamber of Commerce, and was a past recipient of the Boy Scouts of America Distinguished Citizen's Award.

Born in East Orange, he lived in Bloomfield and Glen Ridge before moving to Manasquan six months ago.

Surviving are a son, Donald Jr.; a daughter, Linda; his fiancée, Elissa Uber; a brother, William; a sister, Ann McCormick, and two grandchildren.

points in the marketplace. Once a year, the bank treated its client base to an economic seminar followed by a golf tournament. The Keene Economic Seminar was quite a show and represented the bank's centerpiece as far as public relations were concerned.

But above all, Charley conservatively managed the assets of the bank. A five-year maturity was about as long as he would go. He used his own knowledge and instincts to trade the volatility of the stock and bond markets of the 1980s. Most of the bank officers were already in place when Charley arrived at the bank in 1983. Bill Henson, who had never traded a bond before, became the chief investment officer while Charlie Paquette was in charge of overseeing the mortgage operation. Both young officers were given broad latitudes in the execution of their duties. As the bank grew, the management team grew along with it. Charley built his team from the sources available to him. He encouraged a management training program for young college graduates, and Steve Witt (vice president in Portsmouth, New Hampshire) has emerged as one of the outstanding products of this program.

Many of Charley's friends from New Jersey have enjoyed the fruits of stock ownership in the bank. The stock has split several times and has appreciated from an adjusted cost basis of $9 to $33 over the 17 years it has been outstanding. Many of the same friends have also participated in the economic seminar, but none of these "friends" have been superimposed on the management framework of the bank. In merger situations, humanitarian efforts to find positions for displaced employees such as Whalen Dunn also worked out to be sound business decisions.

In November 2002, the Granite Bank announced it would be acquired by the Chittendon Trust Company for approximately $46 per share. For an original investor in the Granite Bank stock at an adjusted price of $9 per share, the Chittendon take-out represented over a 500% return over the life of his holding.

When Donald McCormick retired from the Howard Savings Bank, it seemed obvious—especially to outsiders—that the next chief executive officer would be Leo Rogers. In all the photographs of McCormick in the Annual Reports of the 1980s, there was Rogers by his side dressed in the symbolic uniform of a bank CEO—i.e., a black suit and a red power tie. Rogers also cosigned the letters that Mac addressed to the stockholders within reports. Leo, however, was not a political creature and he literally had no power base. Also, he publicly disavowed any interest in the CEO position. Soon, the board appointed recent member of the Howard family Frank Reilly of Brooks Brothers to head the search committee for a new chairman and CEO.

Succession was again the order of business for the Howard board. This time, the matter included "survival and succession." The board temporarily decided to tap one of its own members, Donald Peterson, president of the Continental Electric company and a director since 1976. Peterson thus assumed many of the responsibilities of Interim CEO, advancing from his position of vice chairman of the board to which he was elected in December 1989.

The bizarre story surrounding Mr. Peterson's life will be told in a later chapter. By way of background, he was an MIT graduate, had served on the Howard board of directors for fourteen years, and admitted to having a relatively modest background in banking. As the crisis facing the Howard intensified, Peterson became frustrated and overwhelmed. He opted to bring in an experienced banker as his own replacement. Bill Tuggle, vice chairman of the First Fidelity Bank, the largest commercial bank in the state and one of the Howard's main competitors, was selected.

Chapter 7

A Special Analysis of Guaranteed Student Loans and a Comparison with Hudson City Savings

"When the Howard Savings Bank failed, it took a part of New Jersey with it."

—Sam Damiano, President
New Jersey Council of Savings Banks

The enduring profile of the Howard Savings Bank was that of a "service oriented" institution. From its very origin, it sought to help immigrants by accepting the smallest of savings accounts. The bank adopted the name of John Howard, a man who literally gave his life to achieve advances in the proper treatment of prisoners in eighteenth century England and Europe.

At the heart of the Howard image was its program to promote savings among young school-age children as well as its student loan program. The Howard business plan was based on a long-term objective which included encouraging the virtue of savings as a means of stockpiling a financial nest egg. The student loan program was an extension of this concept. While other banks spurned the student loan business, the Howard took up the slack and became one of the largest lenders in the United States.

The Howard also supported its program with a large staff which maintained contact with the principals and guidance counselors from every high school in New Jersey.

Many of these same representatives set up booths at "Back to School Nights" attended by students and parents. The program and the promotion were highly successful, and soon the Howard portfolio grew to just under $300 million. The Howard had the largest portfolio of student loans in the state of New Jersey and ranked eighth largest in the nation. In addition to the Howard, some New York City banks and West Coast banks aggressively built their guaranteed student loan portfolios (GSLs) as well.

Compared to the rest of the banks in New Jersey and across the nation, the Howard was a bit unusual with its affinity for the federal government's guaranteed student loan program. The program entailed considerable paperwork and was fairly costly to maintain. Additionally, the base or fixed rate of 7% was in itself an anachronism sustained by the need to simplify matters for the neophyte borrower. As banks sought to match their assets and liabilities, a rate indexed to a market rate (such as the prevailing level on the five-year U.S. Treasury note) rather than a 7% "forever" might have made the student loan a more attractive outlet for the banking industry in general.

At first, the U.S. Department of Education created a quarter-annual supplement known as the "special allowance" to the base rate. Initially, there was no formula used to derive the *special allowance* and many potential lenders regarded this as a negative attribute of the program. Most banks maintained just a token effort in the program, and in many cases restricted their use to children of depositors. Several banks limited the amount they would lend to under the $1000 limit allowable by the program.

Finally, the U.S. Department of Education changed its policy and they announced that it would use a formula to determine the *special allowance (SA)*. The Department of Education would use the 91-day U.S. Treasury bill rate (using the basis of the "bond equivalent yield") minus 3.5 %. Applied in today's absurdly low short-term interest rates, the SA results in a negative figure. Regardless, most banks regarded this as inadequate compensation for their efforts.

With so many defectors from the program, the Howard saw the opportunity to become the best in the field and thereby benefit from its established leadership in the area. The bank's conspicuous advertising campaign (including Banner Airways) added to this profile. Banks which backed away from the student loan business often referred their inquiries to the Howard staff because they knew their clients would be professionally treated.

The Howard's upgraded position in the GSL market also was well received in Trenton, New Jersey, the state's capitol and location of the local GSL program. Prior to the Howard stepping up its activities, the local agency acted as a "lender of last resort" for students who were unable to find a bank lender. This role was deemed to be outside the role of its originally intended scope. The Howard Savings Bank, by announcing its willingness to make GSLs to all qualified students, effectively replaced the state agency as the lender of last resort.

In compiling the state's largest portfolio of almost $300 million and by its recognition of its status as the lender of last resort, the Howard Savings Bank's reference to its advertising slogan "HOWARD POWERED" certainly seemed justified.

☆   ☆   ☆

Since the Kress administration, the Howard was also recognized as a leader in the area of bank computerized systems and services. This was a key to the Howard GSL program, and the bank's consumer credit department installed effective systems to service the loans properly, once they were on the books. These systems also guided the bank in following the very specific rules of the state's local regulatory unit in servicing GSLs as codified in its Manual of Policies & Procedures.

Servicing a student loan takes place in two distinct phases; i.e., (1) while the student is in school, and (2) after he or she graduates. During Phase 1, the role of the servicer is fairly simple. The only requirement of the bank is that it contact the student borrower at least once annually. Given the secular trend toward the higher cost of education, most students continuously are in need of more money and the bank readily fills this requirement when the student applies for another loan. No interest payments are paid by the student during his/her years in college. In many cases, Phase 1 continues on through graduate school. The bank receives 7% interest plus the special allowance from the federal government via the Department of Education (DE).

But once the student graduates and enters the job market, servicing his/her loan becomes a lot more labor intensive. There is suddenly no built-in contact mechanism for the student. The difficulty is particularly magnified in the early stages of phase two. The bank typically sends a letter to the student outlining the requirements that take place upon graduation. Coupon books are also sent along to the student, who signs a note and starts to pay off the loan. Often the letters are ignored by the students.

Nationwide, regulatory agencies similar to the New Jersey Department of Education were confronted with this phase two problem of servicing GSLs. The best operation across the nation functioned in the Commonwealth of Pennsylvania. The Pennsylvania GSL agency was called PHEAA, which stood for the Pennsylvania Higher Education Assistance Authority. PHEAA built a GSL servicing operation to work not only with loans made within its home state but also to service loans by other lenders throughout the United States. PHEAA was a very efficient operation supported by a *data processing system* that had been custom designed for GSLs.

PHEAA's service fees were very reasonable, so much so that most lenders (including the Howard) felt that self service was more costly than paying PHEAA's rates. Even more important, PHEAA provided a performance guaranty. Thus, if the New Jersey agency decrees that PHEAA's service was not in compliance with New Jersey's minimum standards on any single GSL or group of GSLs, the resulting guarantee would be lost. PHEAA would then have to buy the loan from the lender. In effect, PHEAA's quality of service was backed by the Commonwealth of Pennsylvania. At the inception of PHEAA's GSL servicing operation, they had proven themselves to be effective. At the time of the Howard's search for a servicer, the New Jersey guarantee agency was contacted. The agency was very familiar with the PHEAA and recommended it highly.

Additionally, PHEAA serviced GSLs possessed strong *liquidity*. PHEAA loans were more competitive in the resale market or fit within securitization programs—should either of those options become beneficial to the Howard.

The Howard staff established a routine whereby GSLs would be shipped to PHEAA for service, from 4 to 6 months before the student was scheduled to complete his/her studies. This gave PHEAA adequate time to contact the student for the purpose of having an installment promissory note signed, and complete the process of converting the loan from in-school status to repayment status. By the way, using PHEAA as a servicer did not cause the lender to lose identity with the student.

PHEAA's customer service people would speak to the student as if they were Howard people. And the borrowers would make monthly payments to the Howard Savings Bank and mail them to a post office box serviced by PHEAA.

The Howard's GSL program was a source of pride among the bank's employees. On the surface, it seemed the program was a great means of reeling in clients at a very young, impressionable age. The GSL program contributed to the long-term objectives of the bank by building its client base and by providing a distinct service to these clients. Finally, the program was very good to the bank in terms of income.

After 1983, short-term objectives became considerably more important to the Howard. Once the bank was a shareholder owned institution, the important role of quarterly earnings reports started to dominate management decisions. In the mid-1980s, Robert Turrill, the head of the consumer credit department, was informed by Leo Rogers, the president of the bank (Don McCormick was CEO), that a consultant had been retained to review the Howard's student loan operations. The consultant worked alone and represented that he was an expert in office systems and operations. He was paid $700 per day, which, annualized, was more than Rogers made.

It turned out, curiously, that the Howard had hired a consultant for the student loan review who had absolutely no prior experience with the government's GSL program. He educated himself on the subject through discussions with Bob Turrill, other members of the bank staff, and contacts at the New Jersey guarantee agency and the PHEAA.

After a few weeks, the consultant issued a report that was critical of the bank's student loan operation. He recommended that the bank build a student loan servicing operation, and to stop sending loans to PHEAA for service. He supported his recommendation with numbers that showed that approximately $6.00 per loan per year could be saved by self service. In addition to recommending a total in house servicing department for GSLs, the consultant offered to personally assist in the endeavor.

The Howard executive management (Rogers and McCormick) bought the whole package. The two executives apparently focused on the relatively paltry amount of PHEAA service fees which would be saved rather than looking at the significant dollars that would be invested to create the new student loan servicing operation. The process to build a student loan service center started with the consultant's continuing involvement. The process took about two years.

Curiously, Rogers and McCormick also bought the consultant's position that the PHEAA performance guarantee was of little value. The Howard did not need the liquidity that the PHEAA provided.

Although the student loan operations remained on the bank's organization chart as part of the consumer credit department, the consultant was calling all the shots. Turrill's authority with respect to student loans had been completely removed. Turrill respected the chain of command and asked Rogers to establish student loans as a department separate from consumer credit. But Rogers, in keeping with his deliberate management style, let several weeks' time elapse. During this time, the consultant ordered that no more loans be shipped to PHEAA. He gave that order even though the Howard was not yet prepared to self service the loans. He claimed that the data processing system and the staff would be in place by the time (two to three months hence) service on the loans would have to be started.

At this point, Rogers still had not acted on Turrill's request, so Turrill sent a memo to McCormick asking to be released from accountability for student loans. He reasoned that without the authority to prevent potential problems, he should not be held accountable for their performance. Up to this point, Turrill had no communications with McCormick about the student loan consultant or the changes that were taking place. He felt sure that McCormick would call him upon receipt of the memo and ask for Turrill's version of the situation.

McCormick had coordinated Turrill's hire in 1975, and McCormick had always respected Turrill's opinion of bank activities. On one occasion, the Howard had announced in the New Jersey newspapers that it was negotiating the purchase of another bank. Fairly late in the process, Turrill was asked by McCormick to take a look at the merger prospect's consumer loans. Peat Marwick and others seemed satisfied that the merger would be positive for the Howard. In just one day at looking at the bank's books, Turrill found enough to be concerned about. Irregularities were reported to McCormick and the bank's auditor, with the opinion that Peat Marwick's loan review was faulty. Turrill suggested that he be assigned to the reviews of other loan portfolios at the bank to be purchased. He was not taken up on the offer, but McCormick asked Turrill to attend the meeting of executive management at

Peat Marwick, to discuss whether or not Howard would recommend the purchase to the board, and if so, at what price. Peat Marwick's recommendation was positive, with only token discounting of the loans. Turrill opined that Peat Marwick's loan review was faulty, with a few examples. With one notable exception, the members of the executive management team were unanimous that the purchase should be recommended. Donald McCormick abstained and remained silent.

Later on, McCormick and Turrill met one-on-one and Turrill went into greater detail on the subject bank's lending irregularities and the poor quality of the Peat Marwick loan review. Turrill closed the session with the following remark: "Don, if you buy that bank based on the work that's been done for you, some people probably will get fired, and you could be one of them." McCormick thanked him without additional comment. Two weeks later, *The Newark Star Ledger* reported that purchase negotiations between the Howard and the subject bank had been terminated.

At any rate, McCormick never did ask Turrill for his assessment of the student loan situation. Approximately one week after Turrill's memo to McCormick asking for release from accountability for student loans, Rogers called Turrill and informed him that he no longer had responsibility for that product.

Triggered by the mere technicality of swapping PHEAA servicing for supposed "in house" capability, the timing of the announcement could not have been worse for the Howard. Diversified by their very nature, student loans were not supposed to "throw off" big losses. As a national leader in this sector, GSLs were perceived to be a strong suit of the Howard's operation. Most bank analysts expected the positive income stream from these loans to at least in part offset some of the red ink flowing in from real estate lending.

Instead, the $10.5 million loss compounded the negative results in the commercial mortgage area. The Howard Savings Bank was definitely snakebit.

In 1989, New Jersey's GSL agency informed the Howard that because of substandard servicing, it had lost the guaranty on hundreds of loans that were in default. To accommodate these charge-offs, the Howard was forced to add $10.5 million to the allowance for bad debt account. The timing of these losses could not have been worse for the Howard Savings Bank.

The Hudson City Savings Bank Successful Savings Bank Survivor 1868–Present

"We are not flashy. We do not trade securities, our fee income is nominal and we do not have a venture capital arm. With us, day in and day out, it is interest received minus interest expenses."

—*Len Gudelski, Chief Executive Officer*
Hudson City Savings Bank 2000

John J. Roe (affectionately known as "Johnny Roe") was a man who wore many hats. In the mid 1950s–1960s, Johnny was the president of two banks—a mutual savings bank and a commercial bank (the Hudson City Savings Bank and the First National Bank of North Bergen). He also was the mayor of North Bergen. He owned a team of race horses, who were often on the card at the Monmouth race track. Additionally, Johnny Roe played golf. He was a member of the Deal Country Club and always looked very distinguished on the course. He usually wore a straw hat, white business shirt, and a bow tie when he played. Throughout a round, he gnawed on a well-broken-in cigar.

When not preoccupied with some of these activities, Johnny Roe's main function was to run the FNB of North Bergen and the Hudson City Savings Bank.[1] His

---

[1] The relatively small FNB of North Bergen was in essence an investment trust, almost entirely invested in public securities, mostly bonds.

management philosophy for the bank was fairly simple. First, he supplied the local residential (1–4 family homes) mortgage market with the funding it required. Second, he invested in government and federal agency securities plus a modest amount of short maturity corporate bonds, including railroad equipment trust certificates.

Miss Emma Rackey was Johnny Roe's executive secretary. A veteran of many years, it often seemed like she was the CEO of the bank.

The Hudson City Savings Bank was chartered in 1868 when it opened its doors in Jersey City, New Jersey. Since then, the financial histories of the two institutions paralleled one another until the early 1980s. More specifically, the years 1982 and 1983 mark when this similarity disappeared. The separation point occurred when (a) Don McCormick was elected chief executive officer of the Howard and (b) the Howard converted to a shareholder based institution.

While the Howard adopted the plan of creating subsidiaries and adding staff, as the Howard increasingly took on the appearances of a commercial bank, the Hudson City stayed its course as an old line savings bank. The Hudson City held $1.784 billion (or 64.6%) of its total footings of $2.7 billion in residential mortgage paper in June of 1987. For the entire decade of the 1990s, the Hudson City kept this ratio about the same.

As Johnny Roe approached retirement in the mid-1960s, the Hudson City board hired Kenneth L. Birchby as the heir-apparent to the CEO slot. In February 1936, Birchby began his banking career with the Brevoort Savings Bank (subsequently renamed tbe Crossland Savings Bank) of Brooklyn. During World War II, he served for three-and-a-half years as a special agent for the Federal Bureau of Investigation. He returned to the Brevoort in 1945. In 1948, he left Brevoort and joined the Jamaica Savings Bank as auditor and later on became a vice president. He received his undergraduate liberal arts degree from St. John's University and his LL.B from the St. John's School of Law.

When Ken Birchby arrived at the Hudson City, he had twenty-six-and-a-half years of experience working for various mutual savings banks. In comparison, Don Mc-Cormick spent twenty years for New Jersey Bell. Birchby logged sixteen years at the HCSB while McCormick registered eight years before 1982.

One of Birchby's coups was in the area of FDIC assisted mergers. Two franchise banks from the original twenty mutual savings banks in New Jersey were in deep financial trouble as probable casualties of Volckernomics. The thrift industry in New Jersey and nationally was hemorrhaging losses in 1981. The combined losses of the 135 savings and loan associations and twenty mutual savings banks was estimated to be $220.7 million in 1981. The mighty Hudson City even lost $9.04 million, which trimmed its net worth to $61.0 million. The largest loss in the state ($14.9 million) was sustained by the United States Savings Bank, whose CEO—Rudy Novotny—ironically held the position as head of the NJAMSB. The capital ratio of the United States Savings fell to 1.21% of assets. Without a merger, it was estimated that United States Savings would exhaust its capital by the end of 1981. Like many of the thrifts nationwide, the United States Savings Bank was on a death watch in 1981.

As the eleventh hour of United States Savings' existence approached, an arrangement was worked out with the FDIC, New Jersey Commissioner of Banking Mike Horn, and the two banks (i.e., Hudson City and United States Savings). The highlights of the deal were that the Hudson City would receive $65 million in capital funds as well as the deposits and the eleven offices of the United States Savings. While most of the thrifts in New Jersey were gasping for capital, the Hudson City Savings doubled its amount by virtue of its taking on the United States Savings. Ken Birchby now headed an institution with a surplus-to-deposit ratio of 6.3%.

Next on the block when its ratios dropped well below industry standards was the Orange Savings Bank. By 1984, the net worth of the Orange had dwindled to $5.8 million, representing 1.13% of its total assets of $513 million. When the Hudson City captured the Orange franchise, it received $26 million from the FDIC and its surplus account jumped to $156 million.

The two mergers netted the HCSB close to $95 million in capital or surplus funds. Meanwhile, Don McCormick focused on going public. In 1983, the initial public offering of HWRD stock netted the bank about $80 million and implied a whole new business philosophy. The IPO for the Howard entailed substantial lending and/or market risks in order to achieve the quarter-to-quarter gains customarily demanded by the stock market. Whereas Hudson City had no ax to grind, the Howard was constantly striving to enhance shareholder value.

The award of the two beleaguered Jersey thrifts to the HCSB was apparently based on them having the "best bids" for the near failing institutions. One wonders, where was the Howard's bid for either the United States Savings or the Orange?

Ken Birchby indeed was "the strong silent type." He had served as past president of the New Jersey and national associations. His calm, reassuring personality definitely played a role in the Hudson being awarded the United States and Orange operations. On the other hand, McCormick's aggressive type A personality might have turned off Commissioner of Banking Mike Horn. Birchby focused on the more meaningful opportunity at the time. The stock market would live on forever whereas the United States Savings and the Orange would not.

Chapter 8

Tuggle Struggles to Save the Bank 1990–1992

For the first year or two after the Howard Savings Bank failed, I thought about the experience a lot. An exhaustive push on the part of the entire staff fell short of saving the bank. But once reality of the bank's demise set in, it was time to move on in life. The memory of the Howard, once vivid, grows fainter every day.

—Bill Tuggle, retired at age 70
May 14, 2003

For Bill Tuggle, the *de facto* closing of the once powerful Howard would be disappointing but hardly a scar on his

otherwise flawless record in New Jersey banking. The fact that the Howard was on the brink of bankruptcy could be traced to the real estate lending policies of Donald Mc-Cormick, who had been forced to resign as chairman and CEO in early 1990. With Leo Rogers declining a leadership role in the post-McCormick Howard Savings Bank, vice chairman of the board Donald Peterson, a fourteen-year veteran member of the Howard board and a president of a local manufacturing corporation, assumed the leadership role of trying to rescue the bank. He possessed positive executive skills but was a newcomer to the New Jersey banking scene. Expedient action rather than "on the job training" was required. Peterson activated retired President Murray Forbes to the board in an effort to get to the root of the Howard's problems. Overwhelmed by an accelerated increase of nonperforming loans, the bank's capital ratios headed toward zero. Peterson soon summoned the board to seek help from the outside.

Bob Ferguson was president and chief executive officer of the First Fidelity Bancorporation (FFB), which in 1990 was the largest commercial banking institution in New Jersey. Utilizing the conduit of the bank holding company, First Fidelity accumulated a substantial investment in the Howard Savings Bank common stock. Sources close to the situation estimate that at one point FFB owned between 800,000 and 900,000 shares, representing an initial investment of about $20 million. Given the 14.3 million shares outstanding, the bank owned about 6.3% of the Howard.

Throughout the 1970s and 1980s, the First Fidelitiy Bancorp (and its predecessor names First National State Bank of New Jersey and National State Bank) was a veritable merger machine. Up to 1984, FFB's main conquest had been New Jersey's third largest commercial bank—Fidelity Union Trust Company. As a follow-up, apparently, Bob Ferguson was enamored with the possibility of taking over the Howard Savings Bank, then the state's largest mutual savings bank. Given its size, the perceived quality of its loan and investment portfolio and its extensive branch system, the Howard was definitely a prime target within the New Jersey thrift sector. Ferguson also saw synergies between the Howard trust department and that of the combined First National State—Fidelity Union Trust Company. Based on all these factors, Ferguson justified an extensive investment by the First Fidelity Bancorporation in the Howard Savings Bank.

In 1986, as a warm-up drill to the Howard involvement, First Fidelity Bank took over the Morris County Savings Bank—the second mutual savings bank to go public in New Jersey. Shortly thereafter, they made a proposal to acquire the Montclair Savings Bank, which represented an exchange of common stock at a particularly attractive level for the Montclair. But as the banks proceeded through the "quiet period" (i.e., when the accountants check the books of the merging institutions and their respective executives are precluded from making public statements about their banks) the stock market dropped substantially and the Montclair merger slipped "out of the money." Negotiations broke off and ultimately the Collective Savings & Loan Association of Little Egg Harbor (NJ) acquired the Montclair franchise several years later. Ferguson firmly believed that the stronger mutual savings banks in the state of New Jersey were an efficient mechanism for obtaining deeper penetration of the retail market. When the common stocks of these institutions became available at attractive prices, Ferguson was always a buyer.

Another theory of the First Fidelity involvement with the Howard common was the perception that the HWRD shares were simply undervalued. Exclusive of any takeover possibilities, it is possible that Ferguson bought into the Howard shares for what he calculated to be a fundamentally sound investment which over time would achieve a higher rate of return than other investment alternatives. Eddie Knapp, executive VP at FFB, counseled Ferguson against purchasing the HWRD shares after looking at the numbers for the thrift.

More than likely, Ferguson's appetite for HWRD shares was part of his overall empire building plan. He was convinced that "bigger was better" as far as banking was concerned.

Generally speaking, bank buy-outs were a regular diet of the equity markets throughout the 1980s and early 1990s. The First Fidelity and other acquiring banks held positions in the stocks on their merger target list. The era (say, from 1979–1992) culminated with the merger of the Chemical Bank and the Manufacturers Hanover Trust Company in 1990. It was the largest bank merger ever in the United States! More recent mergers have surpassed the Chemical-MHC totals. In fact, the Chemical joined forces with the Chase and then the Morgan Guaranty Trust. Citicorp aside, the four largest banks in New York City became one bank (Chase-Morgan) in the decade of the 1990s. Ironically, the surviving name of the Chase Bank probably represented the least efficient operation as the nation entered the decade. Within this context, the First Fidelity Bank calculated a take-out premium for the Howard and probably concluded that if their own acquisition efforts failed, a more aggressive suitor would in turn bail them out. As the merger syndrome evolved into a game of larger players, the pure asset size of the Howard (peaking slightly over $5.2 billion[1]) added to its investment allure.

Bill Tuggle's Role at First Fidelity Bank

Bill Tuggle, like Donald McCormick, was a Tar Heel. They both graduated from the University of North Carolina in Chapel Hill with Tuggle receiving his B.S. degree in 1955 and McCormick his in 1953. Tuggle went on to obtain his M.B.A. at UNC and also completed his studies at the University of Virginia School of Bank Management in 1961.

---

[1] The $5.2 billion figure did not include the value of the trust assets under management, which also was a bonus for a commercial bank looking at the Howard shares.

Tuggle began his New Jersey banking career in 1964 when he took the position of senior lending officer at the Somerset Hills National Bank in Bernardsville. Within a year, at the tender age of 35, he was elected president and chief executive officer of the bank. After successfully guiding the bank for ten years, Tuggle sold his bank to the First National State Bancorporation. He retained several titles within the First National State system for close to fourteen years.

When Donald Peterson of the Howard called looking for FFB's help, Bob Ferguson had a stable of executives carrying the transparent title of "vice chairman of the board." They were mostly figureheads who were effectively capitalizing on sweetheart deals consummated when their once independent banks were integrated into the FFB system.

Unlike many of the executives absorbed in the merger process, Bill Tuggle was named president and chief executive officer of the First National State Bank of West Jersey. Later, when the First National State Bank merger with the Fidelity Union Trust became effective in 1984, Tuggle was named executive vice president of the First Fidelity Bancorp.

Motivated more by professional pride than a need for financial gain, Bill Tuggle easily out-performed the other "vice chairmen." At first, he was dispatched to rectify the problem loans and other matters attendant to the mergers of the Burlington Trust Company of New Jersey (Moorestown) and the First National Bank of South Jersey (Atlantic City) into the FFB system. For months on end, Tuggle commuted to these locations from his home in Bernardsville and brought the local banks' problems under control. As Bob Ferguson contemplated retirement, he was impressed by Tuggle's work ethic and overall performance and genuinely considered Tuggle as a possible successor to his own title. Tuggle's principal competition seemed to be Eddie Knapp who rose through the New Jersey division of the bank after graduating from Lafayette College in 1955, where he was a standout basketball player for the 23–3 Leopards.

The other favorite was a 38-year-old banking "whiz kid" by the name of Harold Pote. Pote built his reputation as the CEO of the highly profitable Fidelcor Bancorporation (nee Fidelity Bank of Philadelphia). When the First Fidelity Bank (NJ) merged with the Fidelity Bank (PA), Pote quickly emerged as the likely heir apparent to Ferguson's title. The center of gravity for the combined bank seemed to lean toward Philadelphia and several operating units began moving personnel from Newark to Philly.

While Titanic-like problems beset the Howard, the FFB was not without its own headaches. In a shocker to the marketplace, Pote's division (i.e., the former Fidelity of Philadelphia)—once a powerful earnings engine—began hemorrhaging losses in its extensive international currency trading operation in London. Another source of substantial losses was attributable to delinquent collateralized loans to African nation fishing companies. Foreclosure possibilities painted an embarrassing picture of a bank with a fleet of fishing boats in its lobby.

Anguished by the vertical decline in FFB's common stock, Ferguson felt compelled to take some drastic action to turn the stock around. Pote—the Philadelphia "Whiz Kid"—was fired.

The earnings period of the late 1980s and early 1990s spawned a number of infamous turnaround specialists within the corporate sector of the economy. These specialists were noted for unceremoniously laying off huge chunks of a company's work force, spinning off profitable subsidiaries as a cash vehicle, and reducing employee benefits to the minimum required by law. Some were noted for firing personnel whose pension benefits were about to kick in. Whenever possible, outsourcing of responsibilities previously handled internally was part of the overall strategy.

As Bob Ferguson contemplated a change in top management that would reverse the slide of First Fidelity Bank common stock, he bypassed the normal channels (which might have included Knapp or Tuggle) and went outside the bank hierarchy to pick his own corporate turnaround specialist. Drastic action was the order of the day! Soon, Fergy hired Anthony P. "Tough Tony" Terracciano of the Mellon Bank and two supporting executives from the Chase Bank. Ferguson not only paid up for the Terracciano team but he also relinquished substantial power, essentially making him CEO.

Tough Tony's reputation was that of a job slasher. Upon assuming the controls at FFB, he immediately cut the staff to the bone. Within a month, he had eliminated close to 15% of the bank's total payroll. By year end, the number was around 22%. Before long, Tough Tony's expense slashing was reflected in improved earnings (and subsequent favorable price action) for FFB's common stock.

Tony Terracciano presented an "austere" image as CEO of First Fidelity. He constantly drank black regular coffee while he chain-smoked two or three packs of *Camel* cigarettes a day. His eyes looked like they were underscored by a pair of tea bags. He started his day by arriving at 7:30 A.M. and worked at his desk right through the day, never leaving for lunch or a snack. Given his pale complexion and frail 155-pound physique, he literally looked like he was about to keel over.

Tony and his wife lived in a basic apartment in Bayonne, New Jersey. When Tony left the Chase Bank to join Mellon, she refused to make the move to Pittsburgh, and so Tony commuted to New Jersey on weekends. She must have known he would be back in the New York City metropolitan area.

Tony, however, possessed a very effective baritone quality speaking voice. When he spoke before a group, his ideas sounded very believable.

Compromise was not a quality of Tough Tony's repertoire. He was swift and decisive. His power was unilateral. Most of the other executives stayed out of Tony's traffic pattern.

The challenge of rescuing the Howard Savings Bank appealed more to Bill Tuggle than serving Tony Terracciano in a supporting role. Perhaps Tuggle might even have felt like he was "expendable" given the wide spectrum of

Tough Tony's plan. When the Howard Board of Directors indicated its interest in Tuggle's services, he listened very carefully. The Howard offered him the following package:

- A salary of $600,000 per year
- A signing bonus of $400,000
- A three-year employment contract
- Options to buy 220,000 shares of HWRD common stock

The risk of the Howard's ability to pay these enticements was neutralized by their being backed by an irrevocable letter of credit issued by a major commercial bank. Tuggle readily accepted. For the partial year of 1990, Tuggle's total compensation from the Howard brought him a combined compensation of $553,840. Tough Tony was glad to see one more high salary off the books.

Howard Director Jack Unkles was ecstatic when he heard that Tuggle had accepted the offer. Hopefully, the Howard had found the "white knight" to turn around its ship of state. In some respects, Tuggle resembled Ken Birchby in his tactful yet firm management style.

Unlike Bill Tuggle, Tom Albright was not a member of the "good old boy" club of New Jersey bankers. While pursuing his degree at St. Bonaventure University in Olean, New York, he had been a collegiate swimmer. Subsequently, he actively played basketball in the Chatham Borough Men's Basketball League. Early in his financial career, he worked in the executive training area of American Express before taking a position with the United Counties Trust Company, a mid-sized bank controlled by the Bauer family in Elizabeth, New Jersey. Working with the market makers of Wall Street, Albright built a reputation for aggressive and original market actions, and soon he was hired away by the First Fidelity Bank before Tony Terracciano arrived on the scene. Tuggle liked the macho of the 36-year-old Albright, and invited him to be his right-hand man at the Howard. Albright accepted and immediately moved into the chief financial officer's position.

After eight years featuring the tightest monetary policy and the highest interest rates in the nation's history, Paul Volcker was succeeded by Alan Greenspan, graduate of the Juliard Music Conservatory, as chairman of the Federal Reserve Bank on August 11, 1987.

When Bill Tuggle and Tom Albright made their moves to the Howard Savings Bank, the Federal Reserve Bank monetary policy under Chairman Alan Greenspan was a friendly force at work within the economy. A classic example of "easy monetary policy," the Fed had persistently lowered the federal funds rate and the discount rate to a cyclical low of 3%, primarily in response to a very fragile banking climate. As the number and extent of bank failures began to surface, the expectation of even further lower rates spread throughout the money and capital markets.

The Fed actions sparked an extensive rally in the short-to-intermediate maturity range of the bond market. As the rally in the bond market spread to the longer end, the Howard's higher coupon bonds had appreciated substantially to the point that the bank could essentially bail out of corporate bonds and pass along nominal gains to its surplus account and shrinking cash reserves. In addition to the corporate bond sales, the Howard sold approximately $155 million from its residential mortgage portfolio and $235 million from its student loans.

The excitement of seeing the gauge on the bank's surplus account bounce off empty gave some of Tuggle's staff members a "warm and fuzzy" feeling that the bank might be saved after all. Everything revolved around the surplus account as a percentage of the total size of the bank. From a historical viewpoint, the surplus of the bank included the original amount invested in the bank plus any proceeds from new financing in the debt and equity areas. Sometimes referred to as capital and surplus, the critical account also represented a bank's accumulated retained earnings, referred to by many bank accountants as paid in surplus. Investment of the retained earnings of a bank also flowed back to the account itself. The size and frequency of changes within the surplus account was also a matter of importance to the regulatory authorities.

Tuggle kept his focus and put into effect a cost cutting program which cut the bank's work force by 23%. Though tactful Tuggle's cuts were more severe than Tough Tony's, they were viewed in the context of survival rather than enhancing shareholder value. Essentially, 440 workers were released. As expected, the board of directors voted to suspend dividends.

In the early 1990s, the state of New Jersey had several banks and financial institutions whose ability to survive the vicissitudes of the business cycle were somewhat suspect. A pending financial collapse at Mutual Benefit Life—the thirteenth largest life company in the nation— was about to broadly impact the New Jersey economy. The resignation of Donald Daniels, the president of the Blue Cross & Blue Shield of New Jersey, aggravated the financial woes of the state. The New Jersey commissioner of banking, in the face of these swirling forces, established a 3% minimum "core" capital ratio as a precondition for staying in business by the end of 1992. As this date approached, the Howard's capital ratio stood at 2.44%. The commissioner started a rough draft for the "Cease & Desist" order for the Howard. He hoped that he would never have to edit the document.

Undaunted, Bill Tuggle and his lieutenants plodded away. Tuggle moved to shrink the bank, thus reducing the denominator in the capital ratio. The Tuggle plan trimmed the asset size of the Howard from $5.2 billion to $4.3 billion. The execution of this plan implied aggressive sales of branches—the brick and mortar—to rival banking institutions. In one day, the Howard sold two solid franchises in the Bergen County market to its commercial bank rival, the United Jersey Banks. Ned Jesser, the CEO of UJB, salivated at the opportunity to fortify his competitive position within the county lines of his home office. The one-day sale reduced deposits by $110 million alone. Branch sales, though accomplishing a quick and significant impact on the bank's capital ratio, sustained a fundamental blow to the operation of the bank in the event it did survive this crisis.

The normal method of fine tuning the rate of deposit formation is by changing the rates set on certificates of deposits. By posting rates higher than the competition, the bank can attract CD buyers and by being less than competitive they experience a reduction in the number of CD holders. The Howard, in its darkest hour, deliberately let a sizable amount of the CD money recycle to other institutions. Here again, the focus of the Tuggle program was survival. If the plan worked, they could go after this "hot money" simply by raising its rates to a more competitive level.

Despite the presence of Tuggle and Albright, skeptics and bears dominated the market for HWRD common stock as it continued to languish at an extremely low dollar price. In the equity market, it was demeaning (as well as financially painful) for a one-time quality stock to trade below $1 per share, or in trader's parlance, "without a handle." A bank's deposit base is built on confidence. A bank whose common stock trades at 50 cents a share does not inspire confidence. As a more-or-less efficient discounting mechanism of forward events, the marketplace was sending out the message that the Howard would not and could not be rescued.

Once the First Fidelity Bancorporation managed to rectify its own problems, it exacerbated the HWRD equity price action as it started to unload a seemingly endless volume of the HWRD shares. For days on end, FFB sold 10,000–20,000 blocks of the HWRD stock around 1¼ per share.

The New Jersey Bankers Association annual convention reflected the difficulty of the times. Originally scheduled for Bermuda, the convention site was shifted to Atlantic City, New Jersey, because of the adverse banking environment. Attendance at the 1991 event was down and the social events which invited all delegates were reduced to just one. Many CEOs were back at their banks reconciling their capital positions or trying to seek possible merger candidates. Social activity was mostly limited to "one on one" networking at remote restaurants. Tony Terracciano, who was voted to the association's executive committee to fill the vacancy of Bill Tuggle, bagged the convention while he monitored the First National Bank of Toms River negotiations. It was no time for fun and games.

At the annual meeting of the Howard Savings Bank on April 24, 1992, Bill Tuggle emphasized the effort and extent of the programs he had put into place. He reiterated the goal of all these programs was to pull the bank's capital ratios into compliance with the regulators. In *The Newark Star Ledger* account of the meeting, they quoted Tuggle as saying:

"There is still much work to be done and the real estate markets are still a long way from recovery. Each of us has to realize that we are dealing with a market that's in very bad shape. No one can predict where it's going short-term."

Following the formal presentation by Tuggle, he was deluged with questions from shareholders and the media. Tuggle did emphasize that there was no evidence of any improper activity on the part of the bank's loan officers.

The Howard was advised by its investment bankers that it could not access the capital markets.

Nonetheless, Tuggle had accomplished a positive turn in the "ship of state" of the Howard Savings Bank. To his credit, he had reprogrammed the factors within his control and seemed to have the bank at least partially on track to survival. But no single management action or assortment of actions could offset the impact of the malfunctioning mortgage market.

☆ ☆ ☆

Time, patience, and calm were wearing thin. Jeff Connor, the commissioner of banking, recognized the efforts of Tuggle and Albright, but felt their programs would still leave the Howard in a deficit capital position. The selfish action of fourteen Howard board members to withdraw their deferred compensation in the midst of the crisis seemed to expedite the commissioner's decision. The FDIC was notified, the die was cast, the "Cease & Desist" order was drawn up, and soon the caravan headed by Deputy Commissioner Szabatin was on its way to Livingston.

Depositors of the Howard were moderately inconvenienced, but otherwise unaffected by the transition to the First Fidelity Bank. Over time, Tuggle and Albright found new positions in bank related areas.

Some employees of the Howard found it particularly difficult in finding new positions in banking because of the industry's saturating consolidation phase. The redundancy of many bank functions created a float of bankers around the state. For example, individual banks have their own investment officer(s) and/or investment staff, depending on their size. Two merged banks require only one investment department, thus making the second department redundant. As such, most of the Howard investment personnel found slots outside the field of banking. One exception was Rich Donnelly, who was retained by the FFB trust department possibly in an effort to retain the Howard trust accounts. Shortly thereafter, Rich was hired by the Peapack-Gladstone Bank NJ in the bank's surprisingly large trust department. Craig Spengemann, senior vice president and subsequently named to the bank's board, and formerly of the Howard trust department, was the key to Donnelly's hire at the P-G Bank.

P. T. Steffens, the member of the state of New Jersey bank examination staff who took away the bank's charter, later on would become the president of the Chatham Savings & Loan Association. The Peapack-Gladstone Bank subsequently acquired the Chatham S&L.

Hardest hit of all were the Howard stockholders. After the regulators and the liquidaters moved in, those holding the stock from the time it was issued to the date of the "cease & desist order" lost all but $0.70 of their entire investment (or $14.30 per share). Those who paid up in the secondary market to a peak of $38¼ in 1987 lost even more. Speculators banking on a "white knight" to rescue the Howard lost the least of all, and entered the market knowing the bank was facing extreme difficulties.

The federal and state regulators had set a 7% minimum capital ratio for the Howard and they fell short of this number by reporting a 6.56% ratio. By the end of 1992, the Feds were expecting a 7.50% ratio. Did the regulators want to set an example with the Howard? Although they were short of capital, they were within 100 basis points. The new management led by Bill Tuggle was conservative and was gradually correcting the mistakes of Mr. McCormick & Co.

The once powerful Howard Savings Bank was power-*less*. It's asset base had shrunk from $5.2 billion to $3.6 billion. The $700 million of nonperforming assets were nonsalable and remained a constant drain on the bank's capital base. On September 20, 1992, the HWRD common stock posted its last trade at 37.50 cents.

From its very foundation in 1857, the Howard Savings Institution was created by a group of twenty-seven men seeking a banking organization that could service its financial needs. Throughout its mostly successful history, the bank supplied mortgages to its clients, fought the restrictive branching laws of New Jersey, sought to pay higher rates on deposits, set up small savers accounts for students, and on and on. For all the years that it functioned, the Howard embraced the role of serving the public. While the profit motivation was evident and indeed important to the managers throughout its history, it was not an overriding concern.

John Kress was the epitome of the successful CEO. He sought to pay the bank's clients the highest rates possible. He worked to make the bank more profitable by computerizing the expense side of the ledger. The Howard is generally recognized as being the first to put its full operations on line. As the EVP of the bank, he took a risk and proposed to the Board, in 1944, that they sell longer dated U.S. Treasuries and buy high quality common stocks. The Board approved the Kress plan, and history proved this to be the proper course of action. In essence, the bank was subsequently better able to sustain its deposit expansion because of appreciation in the stock portfolio. Whereas historically the bank had been run with longer-term objectives in mind, Don McCormick ran the bank with his eyes zeroed in on short-term results. Once the bank shed its depositor ownership and became beholden unto a large group of profit-seeking shareholders, the pressure on the bank management to take inordinate risks in order to raise interest income intensified. The pressure to boost earnings, quarter after quarter after quarter, caused the bank to deviate from its normal uses of funds. Outsiders from the consulting world came into the bank to supposedly help it achieve its goals. McCormick hired some old pals into high places, pals who knew nothing in particular about savings bank operations. His entire management focus was dedicated to construction lending in the real estate market. Loans from Long Island, Washington, D.C., and North Carolina decorated the books of the Howard. Commitment fees on construction loans acted as a quick fix to artificially inflate quarterly earnings.

Prior to the McCormick administration, residential mortgages and student loans were viewed as a means of servicing the bank's lucrative New Jersey client base. Practically all of these loans were domiciled within the boundaries of New Jersey. The new lending activity of the 1980s emphasized yield and short payback periods. There was no service factor implicit in the Howard's purchase of construction loans. Enhancing stockholder value was all that mattered. Life was a series of short-term goals encompassed in quarterly earnings reports. Perpetuating this cycle of constantly improving quarterly earnings reports was more important than establishing short-term objectives as a means to achieving long-term goals.

Many would argue that the FDIC gave away the store in selling the bare bones structure of the Howard to the First Fidelity Bank. Though in severe pain, the mortgage market had to eventually turn around. Even if the process took another year or so, the Howard was worth saving. Bill Tuggle was a solid citizen who evoked a banking style not unlike that of Ken Birchby.

Bill Tuggle was not a greedy bastard.

Any special place of the Howard Savings Bank in the hearts and minds of the regulators seemed to get lost in the whirlwind of bank failures at the time. Basically, the FDIC lumped the Howard with some other options, absorbed the bad assets, and sold the bank for $73 million, essentially just $10 million more than what the bank went public for in 1983. Regardless, the FDIC's action was a *fait accompli* and the identity of one of New Jersey's proudest financial institutions had been swallowed up by the carnivorous First Fidelity Bank. The Howard Savings Bank was history.

Was the Howard a victim of the economic environment or did the bank self-destruct? With over 1,000 bank failures in the 1979–92 period, certainly a lot of the bank's problems were related to the fall-out from Volcker's tight monetary policy. In many respects, the Fed policy could have bankrupted many more banks, many of whom had sizable clout in the money and capital markets. On the other hand, the board of directors of the Howard could have restrained the activities of Donald McCormick in the real estate markets. The board, in its objective wisdom, should have instructed the McCormick management to focus on the quality of new loans rather than their size. By hiring a supporting cast of cronies from outside the bank, McCormick lost sight of the expertise of his original staff (as in the case of the student loan problem). When he heeded the advice of an outside consultant, the end result was a blunder (dropping the PHEAA as servicer) which added $10.5 million to its nonperforming assets.

Murray Forbes was the only individual other than McCormick himself who had a broad power base within the Howard organization. When he retired from the board in 1984, there were no thoughts that the McCormick management would effectively bankrupt the bank. When

Forbes returned at the behest of Donald Peterson, the Mc-Cormick damage had already been done.

The collective guilt of all the managers of failed thrifts during the early 1990s was muted by the mere size of the number of failures. The financial history of the period will probably forever view these failures as the result of overwhelming economic forces.

Over lunch at the Exchange Inn in Jersey City, in the middle of the high interest period of the 1980s, Jack Saueracker (SVP and chief investment officer of the First Jersey National Bank) said that the levels attained on U.S. Treasury bonds and other high quality corporates and municipal bonds were the highest any of us would experience in our lifetime. Jack confidently spoke of the significant secular bull bond market which lay just ahead.

Shortly after the Howard Savings Bank was shut down, the easy money policy of Fed Chairman Greenspan eventually righted the mortgage market which might have brought the Howard out of its deep hole. With Bill Tuggle at the helm, we might all be better off.

☆ ☆ ☆

When the First Fidelity merged with the First Union Bancorporation in 1996, any semblance of a Howard connection was totally lost in the mega-merger. The last glimmer of the Howard, if any, will come when the First Union changes the name on all its branches to Wachovia. Increasingly, as the retail banking client seeks customized service, in this the computer era of the ATM machine, the personal touch of the Howard tellers at 768 Broad Street fades away.

When the Howard Savings Bank failed, it took a piece of New Jersey with it.

Many refused to accept the finality of the Howard's demise. Within the hallowed halls of the U.S. Federal Government, Republican politicians were concerned about the degree to which the numbers of bank failures would influence the November 1992 elections. Forever inventive, the

predominantly legally trained representatives circulated
the matter of the Chrysler bail-out in 1980.

In 1980, the Chrysler Corporation ranked as the third
largest United States manufacturer of automobiles. Ford
Motor Company and General Motors were the two leading producers. With Lee Iaccocca as its president and
CEO, Chrysler had introduced several new car models
during the most recent marketing period and sales proved
to be very disappointing. Even the more established
Chrysler lines were struggling along, as the Chrysler
products faced even stiffer competition from the Japanese
and other foreign manufacturers. Suddenly, Chrysler was
in deep financial trouble and faced the specter of default-
ing on its bond interest and subsequently filing for bankruptcy. Quickly, the window enabling Chrysler to finance
short-term dealer loans through the commercial paper
market was slammed shut. Chrysler seemed doomed.
Chrysler's days as a corporate entity were numbered, and
a death watch was put in place.

But Lee Iaccocca was no wimp, as evidenced by his
record as chief executive of the Ford Motor Company in
the 1960s. Twice, Lee Iaccocca rescusitated sales with the
introduction of the Mustang and the Thunderbird. Several ideas were in the hopper at Chrysler, and these would
take time to proceed from the drawing board to the show
room. Ever the bastion of confidence, Lee Iaccocca made a
special trip to Washington, D.C., to try to convince President Carter to in effect bail out the Chrysler Corporation
with federally guaranteed loans totaling $1.5 billion. Iac-
cocca was indeed convincing, and he secured the loans enabling Chrysler to obtain a three-year breather away
from the bankruptcy mavens.

The Chrysler bonds were divided into two issues both
of which featured 10% coupons and three-year call dates.
The initial maturities of the two issues were five and ten
years respectively. The bonds filled the void left by the
commercial paper market. The production lines were
humming and soon the LeBaron, which essentially re-
vived the convertible car to the United States market, was

rolling in new model sales. Spearheaded by the LeBaron's successes, Chrysler pulled back into the black. The Federal Government's involvement with private enterprise proved to be short-lived, as the Chrysler Corporation called the two issues at their early three-year call dates. Twelve years later, as the Howard Savings Bank floundered on the edge of bankruptcy, in the middle of the presidential campaign, there were efforts to revive the Chrysler precedent and hopefully save the beloved New Jersey bank.

The presidential election year of 1992 pitted incumbent Republican President George W. Bush against Democratic contender Bill Clinton, the former governor of Arkansas. Bush was counting on his popularity stemming from the United States' apparent success in the Persian Gulf War but feared problems arising from the deplorable state of the economy. The country was in a deep recession.

Clinton's popularity with the voters grew as his oratorical skills seemed to capture the independent block. He capitalized on the economic factors and also seemed to unite a lot of the special interest groups which Bush ignored. The fact that President Bush fell short of total victory in Iraq muted his triumph in the Persian Gulf, and may have been the main reason that Clinton defeated President Bush in his quest for a second term.

To the extent the state of New Jersey had political clout, it seemed to rest with the Republican Party, and so the viability of a Howard bail-out might have depended on a Bush victory. At a very critical time to the decision, FDIC Chairman William Taylor (a Bush appointee) died and he was replaced by a Democratic appointee. Suddenly, the discussion of a savings bank bailout shifted from New Jersey to the Democratic stronghold of Brooklyn (NY), which had delivered a solid voting majority for President-elect Bill Clinton.

Within a short period of time, the Dry Dock Savings Bank—headquartered in Brooklyn and knee-deep in real estate woes—received federal funds and was effectively bailed out by the new administration.

Thus ended the final attempt to save the Howard Savings Bank. In many respects, it was the victim of the times, political and economic. Coupled with their undisciplined actions in the real estate markets, their fate was sealed.

In certain respects, they dug their own grave.

Several stockholder suits were filed dating back to December 1989, when the Howard first revealed its anticipation of a $65 million loss for the fourth quarter of 1989. In general, the shareholder suits charged that the bank's senior management (the defendants) misled investors in 1989 with overly optimistic assessments of its earnings for the entire year. The defendants were also charged with setting loan loss reserves at too low of a level. Following the consolidation of eleven shareholder suits into one case, Donald McCormick, Leo Rogers, Joseph Wojak, and Andrew Aldi plus directors Donald Peterson and Saul Penster were named as defendants.

On October 23, 1993, the media reported that the defendants opted to accept a settlement of $7.75 million with the rationale that, while not admitting any wrong doing, they wanted to avoid any lengthy litigation and the higher legal fees associated with any extended investigations.

Chapter 9

September 11, 2001

September 11, 2001
Spring Lake, New Jersey

To the extent possible, this account of the events that occurred on September 11, 2001, combines the details of many reports broadly classified as the "media." In the absence of any survivors, we can only conjecture as to the specific activities within the flight cabin. The names of the hijackers have been withheld while the names of the crew and passengers are factual.

Early on the morning of September 11, 2001, the shrill sound of the alarm clock awakened Don and Jean Peterson from a sound sleep. Their plans included catching the 8:01 United Airline flight to San Francisco, securing a rent-a-car, and then driving roughly two hours to their final destination of Yosemite National Park where they would attend the annual family reunion.

The Petersons were veteran travelers. After Donald served briefly as the interim leader of the Howard Savings Bank during 1990, the Petersons started their work as Christian missionaries late in 1991. For their missionary exploits, the Petersons were constantly in the air. Most of the trips took them to the West Indies where they helped pregnant women with their laundry and counseled irresponsible fathers on drug addiction. The efficacy of prayer was essential to their beliefs.

Virtually nine years had passed since the closing of the Howard. As a long-time board member, Donald Peterson felt a deep sense of responsibility for the financial failure of the state's largest savings bank. Up until the fourth quarter of 1988, all reports seemed to indicate the bank was in good shape. His financial commitment to the Howard was reaping some handsome rewards with the stock trading at about $38 per share. But the negative earnings reports and loan losses came swift and hard.

The bright sun beaming down on Newark International Airport would give the United pilots tremendous visibility on the morning of September 11, 2001. The weather was just the beginning of a fabulous fall for the Northeast corridor of the United States. Bright sunny days, low humidity and mid-70s temperatures would prevail almost until the end of the year.

Arriving at the airport at 6:40 A.M., the Petersons were plenty early for their flight with a departure time of 8:01. After negotiating the security checkpoint, the Petersons arrived at Gate 34 at 7:01 A.M., exactly one hour before their flight time. Such minor acts of precision were a source of great satisfaction to the Petersons. But the Petersons were quite surprised by the number of passengers who were also early for their flight. They were informed over the local PA that the flight was fully booked and that there would be a 45-minute delay in the flight's departure time. A somewhat similar flight #93 was scheduled to leave about the same time, and upon checking availability, Peterson discovered that only 38 passengers were expected on the 200-capacity ten-year-old Boeing 757 and the flight was on time. He quickly booked his wife and himself on this flight. They were assigned seats 14a and 14b.

Awaiting the boarding call, the Petersons took convenient seats within the gated area for flight #93. They instinctively scanned the sparse crowd to see if they saw any familiar faces. As the flight time grew near, Don Peterson saw some dark-complexioned men approach the check-in desk. They wore light-colored long-sleeved shirts which were not tucked in at the waist. Peterson surmised they must be either Muslim, Indian, Iranian, or Arabian.

Forcing a manufactured smile, the United gate agent at the counter addressed the four foreigners, "Good morning, gentlemen."

A semblance of a groan emitted from the men. They did not speak, they just nodded to the clerk. They seemed to want to "lay low" and to be as inconspicuous as possible.

"May I see your tickets, passports, and identification?" asked the United agent.

One at a time, the solemn faced foreigners stepped forward to accommodate the agent's requests. As she checked the IDs of the Arab-appearing assemblage, she noticed that their tickets had been paid for with cash (about $750 each) just a few minutes before arriving at gate #17. Equally strange was the fact that none of the men had booked a return trip home. Nor had they any luggage—checked, carry-on or otherwise. With just the clothes on their backs, the four were headed for San Francisco, their ultimate destination unknown. All four looked like they were on a solemn mission.

Don Peterson and his wife Jean were somewhat intrigued by the weird behavior of these men, but as veteran fliers they were used to seeing all types of personalities in their travels. Airports were like melting pots, people were different, and that was that.

Don Peterson was glad to get away on a family vacation. At age 66, he needed to relax a bit. He was president and chief executive officer of the Continental Electric Corp., manufacturers of electric motors and generators. At the Newark-based firm, Peterson was an executive who favored the concept of hands-on management versus delegation of authority. He was not averse to visiting construction sites and literally getting his hands dirty. Since his graduation with an electrical engineering degree from MIT in 1957, his pervasive nature at Continental helped him work his way up the executive ladder and in 1975 he was selected president of the corporation. His exposure within the New Jersey business community led to his being appointed to the board of the Howard Savings Bank.

Although his working experience had been almost entirely in the manufacturing or industrial component of the economy, Peterson relished the opportunity as a Howard board member to expand his sphere of knowledge of the financial sector. At the time of his appointment in 1976, the Howard Bank was apparently sound. The bank seemed to run smoothly under the efficient management style of Murray Forbes. Once the bank went public, its stock was trading on a more-or-less "normal" level relative to its earnings per share. As a board member of the state's largest savings bank, Peterson expected to play little more than a passive role in monitoring a well-run institution. In his estimation, you couldn't find a stronger entity in the financial sector than the Howard Savings Bank.

The final passenger total for United Flight #93 Nonstop Newark to San Francisco was set at thirty-seven. Although carrying a relatively small passenger load, the gate agent and the staff began the boarding of the plane by the numbers.

"First-class passengers, disabled passengers, or those requiring assistance, and those traveling with small children can proceed with boarding," announced the hostess on the local public address servicing the gate #17 area.

As the passengers started to queue up for boarding, the Petersons noticed one first-class passenger in particular. He had to be at least 6′5″ tall, had a very athletic physique, and carried a briefcase with an engraved luggage tag resembling a business card. The card read,

Mark Bingham, President

Bingham Associates

"The Public Relations Company"

Mark was a former rugby player for the University of California (Berkeley) and at age 31 worked out regularly to keep himself in top condition. Mark quickly took his seat, #4D in first class. Unknown to everyone on the plane,

Mark was a prominent member of the gay community of San Francisco.

The remaining passengers were boarded by row numbers, with the rear of the plane going first. Holding tickets marked Row 14A and Row 14B, Donald and Jean Peterson boarded the plane on the second round of seat numbers called. Once he reached his designated seat, Peterson noted that the oddly behaving Arab contingent took their seats toward the front of the plane, just behind the first class section. Soon the modest list of passengers was fully seated and the door was closed.

Then unexpectedly the word came from the captain. "I regret the inconvenience, but we will be delayed for 15 minutes." Don Peterson frowned as he looked at his wife. The couple knew that if the captain immediately confessed 15 minutes, then the delay would probably be longer. The Peterson hunch was correct. Forty-five minutes passed before flight #93 was ready to pull back from Gate #17.

Loaded with enough fuel to carry it all the way to San Francisco and then some, the spacious Boeing 757 with all of thirty-seven passengers and seven crew members started its brief taxi toward the runway. Once on the taxi way, United Flight #93 was third to await take-off clearance from the airport control tower. All the passengers and crew members had their seat belts fastened.

Within minutes, the pilot received the signal and immediately broadcast over the public address system:

"Prepare for take-off." Seconds later, United Flight #93 was in the air and en route to San Francisco.

As soon as the flight attained a more-or-less horizontal flight position, the crew members set in motion preparations to serve breakfast. Once the carts containing breakfast allotments for each passenger had passed the rows where the Arabs were seated, the four strange looking men quickly moved in a concerted effort to take control of the airplane. The tallest of the Arab contingent raced through first class and thrust his right shoulder against the cockpit door. The strength of the locks on the cockpit door withstood the power of the muscular Arab's moves and he immediately implemented Plan B as he wrapped his arm around the neck of flight attendant Wanda Green. While brandishing a box cutter in his right hand, he threatened the young stewardess with her life if anyone on board did not cooperate. He quickly announced that the plane was being hijacked and that he was now in control of the flight.

Upon hearing the commotion in the cabin, First Officer LeRoy Homer unlocked the cockpit door to get a sense of the problem. The opportunistic Arab released the flight attendant and immediately pushed back the door and in one motion slashed the neck of the pilot with the box cutter. As the fatally wounded pilot fell to the floor, the Arab jumped into the vacated seat next to Captain Jason Dahl. He bluntly warned the captain he faced the same fate as his first officer unless he cooperated.

Meanwhile, in the cabin, the other Arabs each took one female passenger as a hostage and advised the remaining passengers to sit still. The other Arabs made it clear that any attempts to interfere with the hijacking would result in the death of either or both of the two hostages. By 9:15 A.M., the handful of evil Arabs had assumed control of Flight #93.

When the terrorist advantage had been achieved, their leader ordered the United pilot to change the direction of the plane and head toward Washington, D.C. He demanded the pilot reprogram the navigation system using the coordinates for the Camp David Complex. At the time, the plane was almost to Cleveland but took a sudden turn southward in compliance with the lead Arab's instructions.

The cabin was filled with fear. The passengers were immediately stunned and disadvantaged, as they had no leader, no weapons, and no strategy to combat the Arabs. The cabinets containing the breakfasts sealed off the second half of the plane. Impulsively, many of the less visible passengers—those located well to the rear of the breakfast cabinets—grabbed their cell phones and called home or their office with the details of the struggle. Also, a male passenger who had locked himself into the men's room alerted 911 that this was no hoax.

Those who connected with the outside world were quickly informed of the shocking news. A similar 757 Boeing Jet out of American Airlines had just crashed into the 110-story World Trade Center Tower number one. The WTC tower stood ablaze from the 90th floor to the top. The famous "Windows on the World Restaurant" was impacted, as it acted as the venue for innumerable business breakfast seminars.

As the passengers with cell phones whispered the news to the others, the reality became clear that this was not an isolated terrorist hijacking.

Rather, these innocent passengers and crew were part of a coordinated master plot of three, four, or more planes whose basic objective was to create as much human carnage in the United States as possible. Flight #93 had President George Bush as its dedicated target.

Because of their manpower disadvantage, the Arabs found it impossible to control the feedback of information to the passengers. Soon the fate of the second airliner hitting World Trade Center number two became public knowledge within the cabin. For certain, flight #93 was on a similar suicide mission to Washington, D.C., and one of President Bush's familiar retreats, i.e., Camp David.

Instinctively, Todd Beamer—one of the younger more athletic men on board—made a quick move in the direction of the cockpit. The only hope for survival was to forcefully wrest control of the plane from the Arabs. Once the WTC towers were hit, there was no room for negotiating with the Arab team on board flight #93. The hijacking team on flight #93 was not seeking release of their buddies held in a remote prison. With a suicide mission at its finger tips, "all or nothing" was the inalterable game plan of the hijackers.

Hoping to motivate the passengers into action, Beamer gave forth with the rallying cry, "Let's roll." Mark Bingham, who had spoken with his mother in San

Francisco and had verified the extent of the hostile operation, joined the group of passengers seeking to disarm the Arabs. The cabin soon became the scene of utter chaos.

As Donald Peterson moved to wrestle one of the Arabs, somehow it seemed that his entire lifespan passed before his very eyes in a matter of seconds. He had faced many challenges in his life, and had emerged somewhat successful from each one. The only experience about which he felt somewhat unfulfilled was his brief tenure as leader of the Howard Savings Bank. He had tried his best, reactivated former President Murray Forbes, but the problems of the Howard were immense and just too far gone. He appealed to the board of directors to bring in an experienced expert in banking. The board concurred and Bill Tuggle was named president. Peterson often wondered if his sudden interest in religion was a reaction to his inability to save the Howard.

Peterson quickly discounted the failure of the Howard Savings and focused on the hand-to-hand combat with the Arab nearest to row 14. Although his religion called for "turning the other cheek," Peterson instinctively became confrontational. Underestimating the strength and will of Peterson, the frustrated Arab let his guard down just an instant—probably distracted by the general level of confusion—and the elder Peterson dislodged the box cutter from his hand. Others in the immediate area moved in to tie up the hapless Arab.

As Beamer broke down the cockpit door, Bingham then made the move on the Arab leader. When Captain Dahl reached to grab his assailant, the Arab terrorist wrestled him from the pilot's chair, and he accidentally kicked the autopilot which kept the flight on line. During their struggle, one of the combatants kicked the autopilot disengage button on the yoke. Within seconds, the plane had spun from a horizontal to a vertical flight path. The plane was flying without its designated pilot crew, with one slain and the other sprawled unconscious on the cockpit floor. The Arab leader's accelerated training as a pilot did not include how to take a plane out of a nose-dive. As Beamer and Bingham were trying to figure out the vast array of instruments before them, as they tried to arouse the semi-conscious pilot for some instructions, the Boeing 758 plunged nose-first toward the Commonweath of Pennsylvania. They overheard the Arab leader mumble words into the radio speaker. He was talking in *Arabic* and he was saying "God is with us. We are all right."

The spontaneous actions of the thirty-seven passengers of United flight #93 prevented any further damage by prematurely snuffing out its suicide mission. They were among the instant patriots and national heroes of the fateful day of September 11, 2001. Indeed, the direct nose-dive to the ground saved the facilities and humans at Camp David from the fate that struck the WTC buildings and the Pentagon.

Don Peterson's perfectionist qualities had betrayed him. September 11, 2001, was not a good day to be a perfectionist. If only he and Jean had overslept. If only the limo had developed a flat tire en route to the airport. If only the couple had stayed with their original flight. He speculated why more of the passengers on his original flight hadn't made the shift. Was there an underworld of Arab support which, through clandestine networking, had steered potential Muslim fliers from making the shift? If, if, if!

As the ill-fated flight #93 sped toward the ground with its landing gear still encased inside the plane, Peterson led the passengers in prayer, perhaps hoping for some divine intervention.

It never came.

At approximately 10:15 A.M., isolated witnesses on the ground saw United Flight #93 crash straight down into the remote Pennsylvania countryside southeast of Pittsburgh. Donald Peterson, his wife Jean, Todd Beamer, and Mark Bingham, and thirty-three other passengers and crew perished almost instantly when the craft hit the ground. Fortunately, there were no victims on the ground in the area of the crash.

Once flight #93's participation in the overall master terror plan had been verified, the United States government weighed the possibility of shooting down the plane before it reached Camp David. The turn of events made this option unnecessary.

January 9, 2002
Cranbury, NJ

Liz Beamer gave birth to a daughter, Morgan Kay Beamer. According to the *Newark Star Ledger,* the baby was named in honor of her father Todd Morgan Beamer, "hailed as a hero for charging the hijackers on flight 93, which sent the plane crashing into a Pennsylvania field."

January 23, 2002
San Francisco, California

The Advocaste, the national gay and lesbian magazine, featured a front page picture of Mark Bingham and honored him as the "Person of the Year" for his heroic role aboard flight 93. An inspiring eulogy was offered by Arizona Republican Senator John McCain.

January 15, 2003

When the Provident Savings Bank issued its initial public offering on January 15, 2003, Sandler O'Neill & Partners was cited as being the investment bankers. Founded in 1988, the company's mission statement listed its exclusive interest in servicing banks, thrifts, insurance companies and REITs.

On September 11, 2001, the bulk of Sandler O'Neill's operation was located on the 104th floor of the World Trade Center II. When the building collapsed, at least 68 employees perished beneath the massive rubble.

The firm states that one of its business objectives is to help its clients face the various challenges within its related industry. Over a span of less than two years, Sandler O'Neill & Partners seems to have successfully responded to challenges of its own.

In most businesses, when tragedy strikes, management tries to convey a "business as usual" profile as it reorganizes to restore the level of business activity. Although the management was able to put the pieces back together, Sandler O'Neill's recovery was anything but another example of "business as usual."

Epilogue

In the wake of the Howard Savings Bank collapse, this editorial appeared in the *Newark Star Ledger* on October 11, 1992. Permission to reprint the editorial in its entirety has been granted by the *Newark Star Ledger* organization.

Howard-Powered Fall

"Thousands of New Jerseyans learned basic banking through the community-minded commitment of the Howard Savings Institution. The bank took special pains to invite the accounts of grammar school pupils. A deposit of as little as a nickel was welcome. Youngsters were taught how to fill out a deposit slip, had their own bank books, watched the balance grow each week and thrilled when interest boosted the total.

"Many of these young students never forgot the valuable Howard lesson of the benefits of regular, budgeted saving and compound interest. And many of them remained loyal Howard depositors through the years, supremely confident in the conservative banking practices of their institution.

"How difficult it must be for these Howard boosters to accept the shocking demise of what had been New Jersey's largest and most successful state-chartered bank—a 135-year history terminated by government action that perhaps had been delayed too long. More timely intervention might have saved money and stopped the shrinkage of assets at an earlier date.

"Perhaps state officials held off because they, too, shared in the veneration accorded this banking legend.

After all, the Howard had survived the Great Depression. Oldtimers can remember the run on the banks and the long lines that formed outside as depositors queued up to withdraw their savings. Howard employees walked up and down the lines, trying to reassure depositors that their money was safe and urging them to go home.

"The Howard was, indeed, safe in that dreary period when other banks around them were closing their doors forever, just prior to the bank holiday declared by President Roosevelt and the reopening under a new law that reassured depositors by insuring their accounts for the first time.

"Now, Howard has been taken over by a bigger, stronger bank—First Fidelity—because of a series of misadventures. It began with a departure from its conservative practices, and plunged the institution into financing a variety of real estate properties, some of which turned out to be risky business. These speculative gambits caused management problems on a costly scale and the combination eventually sank the unsinkable Howard.

"Lamentably, the Howard had deep community roots and a strong social conscience, so its passing from the scene will be a severe loss to many New Jerseyans. Many of them will continue to wonder what induced its management to chuck its sensible conservatism and go for illusory high stakes in a real estate rat race it was illequipped to win."

Demutualization:
A Bad Deal for almost All Parties
By Robert Turrill,
Consumer Loan Department
Howard Savings Bank 1975–92

Since we are not sure that "demutualization" is a real word, it seems appropriate that we define it as used in this writing. Demutualization is the process that a mutual institution (such as a savings bank, S&L, or insurance company) goes through in order to convert from a mutual form of ownership to stock form of ownership.

In the mutual form of ownership of a thrift institution (savings bank or S&L) the owners are the savings depositors. This is not an easy concept to grasp or accept for a few reasons. First the depositor base is a constantly changing one. And the new depositor pays nothing for his "ownership interest," and he receives no payment for his ownership interest while he is a depositor, nor when he closes his deposit account. Also, while he is a depositor, he has nothing as evidence of his ownership interest-there is no document such as a deed or certificate of ownership. In addition, the owners have no voice in the operation of the thrift. While the mutual thrifts do hold annual meetings, the owners are not permitted to attend, preventing them from expressing their opinions about the operation of the thrift. In addition, the board of directors (sometimes called "managers" or "trustees" are self perpetuating; meaning that they elect and reelect themselves.

So, within the limits of the law and banking regulations, the officers and directors of the thrift can do anything they want. This lack of owner influence may seem to be an unhealthy situation, but in this writers experience (over 25 years as an officer of two thrifts, the second being the Howard), the mutual thrift stands a better chance of remaining financially strong, and it is more likely to do things that will be good for the populace it serves. This has been the history of the mutual thrifts.

The mutual form of ownership is an old one. In the northeast and middle Atlantic states, there have been hundreds of thrift institutions created as mutuals, and many of them date back to the nineteenth century. The fact that these thrifts were able to survive for so many decades, weathering some very difficult economic times, is good evidence that the mutual form of ownership does work well. It works well because the thrifts' boards of directors, dating back to the original organizers, have been community leaders who have been dedicated to assuring that the thrifts business activities, pricings, etc., would be best for the organization *long term*. Little regard was given to profit performance for the current quarter or the next

All mutual thrifts have existed because the original organizers felt that the banking needs of the *people* in their communities were not being satisfied. They have been successful at what they set out to do. They have benefited the consumer, even to this day, by providing deposit accounts at competitive rates, and home mortgages and other consumer loans, also at competitive rates.

Over the years, the mutuals did not attempt to be anything other than retail banks, and this proved to be wise. Businesses fail financially at much greater rates than do consumers. Early on, the mutuals established another intelligent approach to their business, which continues to this day—that of a "prudent lender." And they did not just give lip service to that term. It was often mentioned internally, but it really was applied in the lending activities. Credit was not granted to noncreditworthy people. Value of collateral was verified, security interests were perfected, etc., etc.

And the thrifts have not felt any reason to be ashamed of the fact that they have adopted the status of "prudent lender." Often their materials distributed to the public, such as the Annual Report, will contain language something like, "We are in existence to satisfy the banking needs of the people in the areas where we maintain offices, and to better assure that we will always be there for you, we long ago adopted the status of "prudent lender."

As a career lender, the term "prudent lender" became a meaningful one to this writer. After 6 years in banking and finance, I joined New Haven Savings Bank (Connecticut), which is still a mutual at this writing. It was at NHSS that I first got to know the term "prudent lender" and it was a term expressed often enough during my 7½ years with them. In 1975, I joined the Howard, and during the seven years they were a mutual, "prudent lender" was used there also. But during the last 10 years of the bank's life, and I was with them until October 2,

1992, the last day, I never again heard the term "prudent lender." They had ceased to be one and they were honest about not pretending that they hadn't.

The conversion from mutual to stock form of ownership forces the bank to operate differently than it had before. No longer can its business plan focus upon activities that will be good for the bank long term. Stockholders have little interest in what management is doing for the long term good of the company. They want to know how earnings are going to be this quarter and the next.

So the bank may relax lending standards in order to garner higher loan yields, as the Howard did. Or it may try to generate other types of profits, by buying businesses it has little or no experience with, as the Howard also did. But while there was pressure to generate income, there also was an ego factor. It was fun to be able to mention to your friends at the Glen Ridge Country Club that you had recently acquired an insurance agency, a relocation company, or a Hilton Hotel.

The bank's conversion from mutual to stock form of ownership is detrimental to the community because it puts the bank at greater risk of failure or takeover by a larger bank. In either situation the community loses a competitor as to deposit and loan rates. The writer has attended depositor meetings held by three mutuals proposing to convert, and each time had expected to hear opposition voiced by the public. There was almost none.

With all the negatives to demutualization expressed here, the reader might reasonably ask, "Then why do mutuals convert?" The reason given by all the banks this writer has witnessed, were the same: to generate additional earnings using the capital raised by the stock sale. The writer's opinion of this reason, at least with respect to most cases, is "BULLFEATHERS!!!" The real reason for the conversion was the greed of the people who, upon conversion, would receive employment contracts and stock options. To those who disagree with me, I would ask, "How many proposals for conversion do you think would have been made by executive officers if their boards had first let it be known that if there be a conversion, no employment contracts or stock options would be granted?"

On many occasions this writer witnessed Don Mc-Cormick's performance to the Howard's Board, and he was very persuasive. Even so, I have been disappointed that the board did not respond by pointing out that the bank was still relatively well capitalized, and had gotten along quite nicely as a mutual for 136 years. The Howard wasn't broken, so why fix it? If this had been their response, I would not be participating in this obituary today, as the Howard would be alive and well, still providing the people of New Jersey with high-quality financial services.

Glossary

Listed below are definitions or explanations of terms used in the text of the book entitled "HOWARD POWERless." Chapter numerical designation by definition indicates where the glossary term is used or implied.

Asset-Liability Management In determining the "use of funds," a bank will assess the characteristics of an asset and try to create a liability which approximates the asset's maturity, coupon rate, and amount. For example, a bank lending out three-year money at 7% might issue three-year CDs as a source of funds. The bank's objective will be to maximize a "spread" between the two sides. (see Chapter 4)

Base Rate The rate paid by the Federal Government to bank lenders involved with the Department of Education student loan program. Has been at 7% level for many years and is supplemented by a quarterly add-on referred to as the "special allowance." (see Chapter 7A)

Bearer Security Securities whose owners are not registered in any name. They are negotiable as to endorsement and transferable by delivery. They carry numbered or dated dividend coupons. The likelihood of theft or outright losing securities has greatly reduced this form of issuing securities. (Chapter 4A)

Business Cycle The economy tends to exhibit cyclical patterns due largely to the volatile components of Gross Domestic Product. Business inventories are a critical "swing" factor in determining the phase of the business cycle. In times of expansion, a drive to build up business inventories can possibly lift the economy to a faster than expected growth rate. If final demand keeps pace with inventory buildup, then the expansion phase is sustained. If a slowdown in demand occurs, "involuntary accumulation" may take place, which eventually leads to "involuntary liquidation" and a slower economy. The other volatile components of GDP have a similar impact on the business cycle pattern. (General background)

Buy-Back Program When the corporation enters the open market with an order to buy its own common stock with the intention of reducing the amount of shares outstanding. Once reduced, the application of the same price/earnings ratio by market participants will result in a higher market price for the shares that remain outstanding. (Chapter 5)

Callable Allows a borrower to redeem a mortgage, loan, or bond prior to maturity. When the lender has the right to "call an issue," this is referred to as a "put." (Chapter 8)

Capital Note A form of long-term (generally 5 years or longer maturity) borrowing by a corporate entity where the purpose of the financing is to shore up the capital position of the borrower. (General background)

Cash Flow The reported net income of a corporation, plus amounts charged off for depreciation, depletion, amortization, and extraordinary charges to reserves. (General background)

Collateralized Mortgage Obligation (CMO) A fairly large security created from using the cash flows from interest and principal payments that result from the process of pooling many individual smaller mortgages. (Chapter 1)

Commercial Bank Designed primarily to finance production, distribution, and sale of goods as distinguished from the service of lending long-term or capital funds. Source of most funds are demand deposits which flow into short-term loans. Government regulation requires cash reserves against deposits, maximum interest rates on certain types of deposits, limits on loan size, and set minimal capital requirements. Ownership rests in the hands of common stockholders. (General background)

Commercial Loans   Principally loans made to business for the financing of inventory purchases and the movement of goods, as distinguished from personal loans or consumer credit loans. (General background)

Common Stock   Represents ownership in a corporation. Portion of the capital funds which represent the last claim upon assets and dividends in the event of a company's liquidation. Dividends on common stock may not be paid until interest on all bonds and dividends on preferred stock have been met. Common shareholders control the corporation, take the greatest risk, and over time should reap the largest rewards. (General background)

Compound Interest   Interest created by periodic addition of simple interest to principal, the new base thus established being the principal for the computation of additional interest. (Introduction)

Consumer Price Index: Consists of several components, the most heavily weighted being "rent." Measures the monthly change in the rate of inflation.

Consumer Credit   Credit extended by a bank to a borrower for the specific purpose of financing the purchase of a household appliance, alteration or improvement, a piece of equipment, or other personal needs. (Chapter 4)

Construction Loans   Funds extended on the security of real property for the purpose of constructing or improving a building. If a construction project takes three years to complete, a three-year construction loan is arranged which is paid off with the proceeds of permanent financing at the completion of all building. (Chapter 6)

Debenture   Throughout the twentieth century, these unsecured obligations representing the good faith of a corporation have been used as a vehicle for arranging debt financing. While utility companies favored mortgage backing for its bonds, high grade industrial issuers and the subsidiaries of ATT issued heavy volumes of debentures (most of which were rated AAA or AA). Mike Milken extended the debenture concept to the world of lower graded borrowers who used debentures to finance "leveraged buyouts" of their apparently undervalued common stock.

Demutualization   The process by which mutual savings banks convert from a depositor-owned institution to a shareholder-controlled bank. Implied pressures of reporting quarterly earnings reports, but also created the currency enabling the award of stock options and the like to executives and employees. (Chapter 1)

Discount Rate   A tool of Federal Reserve Bank monetary policy, the discount rate represents the rate at which members of the FRB system can borrow from the Fed. Viewed as a penalty rate. Increase in discount rate borrowings can be an indication of forthcoming economic weakness as banks reach to stretch out the expansion phase of the business cycle. (General background)

Disintermediation   The process by which bank depositors withdraw money to take advantage of higher rates available in the securities markets. Aggravated by ceilings on deposits (particularly "Reg Q") in times of rising rates, the Fed has continuously acted to gradually eliminate rate ceilings. (Chapter 1)

Diversification   Spreading investments among different companies in different fields. Avoiding a "concentration" of risk allocation to one sector of the economy. Policy of diversification is basically an admission that the uncertainties of all investments cannot be determined by prior analysis. (Chapter 1)

Dollar Diplomacy   An important part of the macro-economic picture is the value of the U.S. currency unit versus that of other major nations. The dollar tends to strengthen during periods of higher domestic interest rates as swing investors opt for the highest rates of return worldwide. When interest rates here fall, the marginal investor takes his money to another country's market. Often, the dollar is simply the residual investment resulting from the "flight to quality" or "flight to safety" syndrome exhibited in times of extreme economic uncertainty. (General background)

Equipment Trust Certificates   A type of security, generally issued by railroads and the airlines, as a means of financing the purchase of new equipment (i.e., locomotives or 747s). Title to the equipment is held by a trustee until the notes are paid off. Secured by a first claim on critical equipment (referred to as rolling stock), ETCs have an excellent credit history and defaults have been minimal. (Chapter 2)

Equity   Signifying ownership in a corporation. Used interchangeably with concept of common stock ownership. (General)

Federal Deposit Insurance Corporation   Established during FDR administration as a means of bolstering confidence in the nation's faltering banking system following the stock market crash of 1929. The FDIC insures every deposit up to $100,000. Some states offered insurance funds for their state chartered banks, which proved inadequate during the 1980s and caused runs on local banks in Ohio and Maryland. (Chapters 1 and 2)

Federal Funds   Cash reserves borrowed or lent between banks on an "overnight" basis. The Federal funds rate is the shortest rate that exists in the money market; i.e., one day. Fed monetary policy targets a rate for Federal funds as a means of implementing monetary policy. (Chapter 3)

Federal Reserve Bank Represents the Central Bank of the United States. Operations are delegated to twelve district banks across the nation. Main objectives are to maintain a stable price level within the economy (i.e., to fight inflation) and to foster a reasonable rate of long-term economic growth. Tools include discount rate policy, money market purchases and sales of securities, and changes in reserve requirements for member banks. (General)

Federal Reserve Chairmen There have been thirteen FRB chairmen who have served since the FRB system was established in 1913. The most recent appointees (Greenspan and Volcker) have been described in the media as being the "second most powerful" men in the United States.

Alan Greenspan, 8/11/87 to date (16 yrs.)

Paul Volcker, 8/6/79 to 8/11/87 (8 yrs.)

G. William Miller, 3/8/78 to 8/6/79 (under 2 yrs.)

Arthur Burns, 2/1/70 to 1/31/78 (8 yrs.)

William McChesney Martin, Jr., 4/2/51 to 1/31/1970 (20 yrs.)

Tom McCabe, 4/15/48 to 3/31/51 (almost 3 yrs.)

Marriner Eccles, 11/15/34 to 1/31/48 (over 13 yrs.)

Eugene Black, 5/19/33 to 8/15/34 (under 2 yrs.)

Eugene Meyer, 9/16/30 to 5/10/33 (2½ yrs.)

Roy Young, 10/4/27 to 8/31/30 (almost 3 yrs.)

Daniel Crissinger, 5/1/23 to 9/15/27 (over 4 yrs.)

W.P.G. Harding, 8/10/16 to 8/9/22 (6 yrs.)

Charles Hamlin, 8/15/14 to 8/9/16 (2 yrs.)

Federal Reserve Bank "Independence" Frequently an issue as the nation experiences a slow down in economic activity. Many presidents, especially those who face reelection, urge the Fed to lower interest rates as a means of stimulating the economy. The Fed portrays an image which places them above such economic pressure and should determine the course of monetary policy based on its assessment of the future of economic activity. (Chapter 8)

Fed Watcher A specialized economist whose main assignment is to figure out whether or not the Federal Reserve Bank is going to raise or lower rates in the near future. (Chapter 1)

Fixed-Income Market Includes any debt-bearing instrument, among them U.S. Government bonds, tax-exempt or municipal bonds, corporate bonds, financial futures, and money market funds. The overwhelming majority of these markets are "over-the-counter" while most of the volume in stocks runs through the major exchanges. (General)

G-5 (and subsequenetly G-7) The five major countries of the world represented by their national leaders. From the standpoint of economics, they frequently tried but often disagreed with one another about the policies of their respective central banks. The original G-5 consisted of the United States, Germany, Great Britain, France, and Germany. Later, the group was expanded to include Canada and Russia. (General)

Gold Buffs Recognized as a "store of value," gold is viewed as an investment alternative to stocks and bonds during times of rapidly increasing inflation. Expensive to finance, gold entails a negative cost of carry since it earns no interest or dividend. (General)

Green Shoe Provision When an underwriting of corporate securities is oversubscribed and essentially has more buyers than the number of shares being issued, the underwriters may reserve the right to issue, say, 10% more stock to satisfy the demand. Likewise, if an issue is selling slowly, the underwriter can shrink the size of the issue. The "over" or "under" allotment process is called using the "Green Shoe Provision." (Chapter 6)

Government National Mortgage Association (nicknamed "Ginnie Mae") An agency of the Department of Housing and Urban Development whose primary function is in the area of government approved special housing programs, by offering financing for low rent housing. (Chapter 1)

GNMA Participation Certificates Guaranteed by the full faith and credit of the United States, represent a pooling of the FHA or VA mortgages which are created around the same time, generally have similar coupon rates and states of origin, and are a regular diet for the mutual savings bank. (Chapter 1)

Housing Starts Has important "multiplier" impact on economy. Broken down into "existing home sales" and "new home sales."

Inflation Persistent increase in the general level of prices; i.e., devaluing the value of money. Due to excess demand (demand-pull inflation) combining with high costs (cost-push inflation) and resulting from excessive increases in the money supply (monetarism). "Too much money chasing too few goods." (Chapter 8)

Initial Public Offering (IPO) Issues of first public offerings of a security (usually common stock), an offering of previously authorized but unissued securities. Widely used by development stage companies when going public. There were $12 billion IPOs in 1980 and $128.5 billion in 1992. (Chapter 6)

Institutional House A brokerage firm that serves financial institutions (i.e., bank trust departments, mutual funds, foundations, and insurance companies) rather than individual investors. (Chapter 3)

Investment Banking Financing of the capital requirements of an enterprise rather than the current "working capital" requirements of a business. (Chapter 5)

Investment Securities   Investments purchased for a portfolio, as opposed to those for resale to customers. Those eligible for investments by banks include U.S. Treasury and government agency bonds, notes and bills, state and municipal bonds, and corporate bonds.

Refers to bonds in the top four rating classes (Baa-A-Aa-Aaa). (General)

Jobs Data Report (or "Employment Report")   A monthly report slated for every first Friday business day of the month. This report lists the growth or decline in the number of new jobs created within the economy, broken out into non-farm payrolls and other classes. The report also reports the unemployment rate for a given month. (General)

Junk Bond Issued by a corporation whose rating is below investment grade; i.e., Ba-BB rated and below by Moody's and S&P. (General)

Leading Economic Indicators   A list of indices which portend the direction of the economy. The items currently included in this index are: The Dow Jones Industrial Average, vendor performance, etc. (General)

Letter of Credit   Represents a guarantee by a bank of a specific contract. (General 8)

Leveraged Buy-Out (LBO)   Entrepreneurial firms such as Kolbert, Kravis, and Roberts (KKR) saw many undervalued equity plays in the early 1980s. The general public was more interested in double-digit bonds than it was in buying "uncertain" common stocks. Rather than buy a few shares of these companies, the KKRs of the world used debt financing (see *Debenture*) to buy all the stock of a company. Varying degrees of debentures were used (including some *mezzanine debenture financing)*. (General)

Lien   Claim on property to secure payment of a debt or the fulfillment of a contractual obligation. The law may allow the holder of the lien to enforce it by taking possession of the property. (General)

Liquidity   Amount of time required to convert an asset into cash or pay a liability. Refers to marketability. (Luscombe) Also reflects the ability of seller to move his security or product at a price at or near the last quotation. (General)

Long-Term Debt (Corporate)   A part of a corporation's capital structure which also includes common stock and paid-in surplus. Short-term debt such as commercial paper is carried as a current liability on a company's books. (General)

Machiavellian Plot   Niccolo Machiavelli (1469–1527) authored an early entry in the field of political science with his work entitled "The Prince," which called for a political leader to use any means possible to preserve the state, including cruelty, deception, and force if nothing else worked. The word "Machiavellian" has come to be identified with *cunning* and *unscrupulous*. (Source: *World Book Encyclopedia*) (Chapter 6)

Market Maker   Refers to the larger dealers on Wall Street as they buy and sell securities for their own account (as opposed to acting for others such as their clients or central banks). (Chapter 4)

Maturity   Represents the date on which the security is redeemed by the issuer. (General)

Monetary Policy   Central bank and central government policy to control the quantity of money in circulation, the interest rates, and the exchange rates. It now has the predominant role in the control of aggregate demand and therefore inflation. (General)

Municipal Bond   General category name for bonds issued by state and local governments and any political subdivisions thereof. The most unusual investment feature of these bonds is that the coupon income derived thereon is tax free from Federal income tax and also from the state income taxes levied by the state within issue. Tax exemption is somewhat efficiently reflected in the yields of these instruments, and most provide inadequate returns for savings banks which gain better tax benefits from maintaining their mortgage quota and from the preferred stock market. The Community Development Act has prompted some thrifts to buy municipals for reasons beyond their tax-exempt characteristics. (Chapter 1)

National Association of Purchasing Managers
Approximately 250 of the "purchasing managers" of the nation's largest industrial corporations are interviewed on a quarterly basis. They are surveyed as to whether they see the level of business activity in their company (a) expanding, (b) contracting, or (c) remaining the same. A reading of over 50% indicates an expanding economy; below 50% a declining economy. Many local groups (Milwaukee, Philadelphia, etc.) issue individual releases, which give a clue as to the overall direction of economic activity. (General)

Negative Convexity   Term used to describe lack of market performance by callable bonds in a bull market scenario. Generally speaking, a callable bond is limited in its upside potential by its call price and length of call protection. GNMA high coupon pass-throughs are callable at 100 at any time and are a good example of negative convexity. (Chapter 4)

Nonperforming Asset (NPA)   A loan or an investment which fails to make interest payments or a final maturity in a timely manner. (Chapter 6)

Passive Investment Portfolio   Implies that the portfolio of the mutual savings bank and the commercial bank exists strictly to provide liquidity in times of crisis or to invest the residual funds left uninvested by the mortgage or lending departments. Indicates a portfolio which does not "play" the interest rate cycle for marginal gains but essentially reflects a "buy and hold" philosophy. (Chapter 1)

PHEAA (Turrill) Abbreviation stands for Pennsylvania Higher Education Authority. PHEAA was not the normal student loan servicer; it had a customized data processing system which enabled it to readily fulfill the requirements of the student loan process. Many states sold their loans so that PHEAA could be their servicer. (Chapter 7a)

Preferred Stock A hybrid security, its dividend payments rank behind interest on debt but ahead of common stock dividends. Preferred stock dividends are declared quarterly. Failure to pay preferred stock dividends does not create an NPA or a bankrupt security, although the implications are negative for the issuer's overall credit profile. For the investor, preferreds offer higher yields and, in some cases, partial tax exemption. Better for investor if cumulative, watch for noncumulative feature. (General)

Qualifying Asset Applicable to Mutual Savings Banks, includes directly obtained residential mortgages and agency securities of the GNMA. Does not include first mortgage bonds issued by utility companies. As a rule of thumb, MSBs keep qualifying assets at 65% of their total in order to attain certain very favorable tax advantages. (Chapter 1)

Real Estate Loans Loans secured by real estate, regardless of the purpose. (General)

Real Estate Development Loans Made with projects entailing significant size and which take two to three years to complete. May involve one building or multiple structures, access roads, and a broad spectrum of smaller projects within the larger complex. (Chapter 1)

Regulation "Q" The regulation of the Federal Reserve Bank which set interest rate ceilings on certificates of deposit issued by its member banks. At various times in U.S. financial history, "Reg Q" has worked havoc on the banking system when market rates exceeded administered rates by the banks and led to substantial disintermediation. Reg Q ceilings were mostly eliminated or phased out by the entry of the Volcker administration in 1979. (Chapter 1)

Reserve Requirements A proportion of a bank's deposits which are kept on deposit at the bank's central bank. The percentage is set by the central bank and is used as a tool of monetary policy. Amounts held in reserve accounts are usually insufficient to cover a run on the bank in times of dire economic stress. (General)

Residential Mortgage A loan extended for which real estate is given as collateral. The collateral is usually a single-owner occupied home or a small number of dwelling units. Unlike most other debt instruments, borrower traditionally pays back principal and interest on a monthly basis, based on a thirty-year schedule. Banking institutions now offer a variety of adjustable rate mortgage rates. (Chapter 1)

Retail Banking or Brokerage Banking services offered to the general public, including commercial enterprises, consumers, and small businesses. (General)

Risk-Based Capital Represents anything other than cash or U.S. Government securities. Thus a sale of corporate bonds and a purchase of U.S. Treasuries fortifies a bank's risk-based capital ratio. (Chapter 6)

Securities & Exchange Commission (SEC) Created in 1934, the SEC ensures the provision of full fair disclosure of all material facts concerning securities offered for public investment, initiates litigation for fraud cases when detected, and provides for the registration of securities offered for public investment. (Chapter 6)

Securitization Pooling and repackaging of similar loans into marketable securities that can be sold to investors. Distinguished from whole loans and whole loan participation. Provides process for improving the liquidity of assets and capital to asset ratios while increasing earnings. (Chapter 1)

Sinking Fund Provision A program whereby a corporate issuer pays down its bonded indebtedness through a schedule of prepayments. In the case of the Howard's $30 million ten-year issue, the bank paid off portions of the issue in years 6, 7, 8, and 9 and a balloon of $18 million in the final year. (Chapter 4)

Special Allowance The amount added onto the base rate in a student loan which brings the overall rate more in line with other market rates. The original formula was the ninety-one-day U.S. Treasury bill index (bond equivalent basis) minus 3.85 basis points. (Chapter 7a)

Spread Generally speaking, the difference between the yield or rate of return available on a fixed income investment versus a comparable U.S. Treasury note or bond due in the same maturity spectrum. Most corporate bonds are quoted strictly in "spread" rather than at specific dollar prices. If the quoted spread is too "tight," the investment in question is regarded as having less than sufficient value compared to the U.S. Treasury curve. If the corporate is depicted as being "wide" to the curve, it represents better than normal value. (Chapter 6)

Stock Option Arrangement for compensating top management, in addition to salary, with the opportunity to buy a certain amount of company stock, often under the market price. Controversy arises over accounting for the cost of options. Coca-Cola recently decided to take stock options (as additions to base salaries) as expenses in the year granted. (Chapter 6)

Tax Shelter Investment at risk to obtain something of value, with the expectation that it will produce income that will reduce or defer taxes and that its ultimate disposition will result in the realization of a gain. Often started as limited partnerships. Abusive when transactions are without any economic purpose other than generation of tax benefits. (Chapter 6)

Thrift Institution Generally refers to a mutual savings bank, a savings and loan association, and possibly a credit union. (General)

Trade Deficit (or Surplus) Total exports minus total imports. Up until recently, has been a major drag on the U.S. economy. Entirely based on current account figures. (Balance of payments includes moves in capital accounts from country to country.) (General)

Treasury Bills The U.S. Treasury auctions ninety-one-day and one-hundred-eighty-day bills on a weekly basis as a means of funding its short-term requirements. The Treasury supplements these financings with a monthly offering of one-year bills. The rates established at these actions can be used as indices for other short-term instruments where the rate is constantly adjusted on a spread basis. (Chapter 7)

Treasury Stock Company's own stock which has been fully paid for by stockholders, legally issued, reacquired by the corporation, and held by the corporation for future issuance. A "parking spot" for shares acquired in a buy-back program. May be reissued to accommodate options programs. (Chapter 5)

Tweaking Accounting practice whereby corporate treasurer makes minor adjustments to earnings in order for them to show up in the current quarter or possibly to delay earnings to a seasonally less productive quarter. (Chapter 5)

Yield Rate of return received from one's investment in a specific security or property. (Chapter 6)

Yield Curve Graphic relationship between yields and maturities of comparable rated securities. (General) Possible shapes of the yield curve:

- Normal Yield Curve: Yields show a gradual increase in yield as you move out on the curve.
- Flat Yield Curve: All maturities along the curve show the same yield.

- Negative Yield Curve: When long maturities yield substantially less than shorter paper.

Yield Spread   Difference in yields on varying stocks or bonds. (General)

Yield to Maturity   Percentage rate of return on an investment when it's retained until maturity. Concept contains "heroic assumption" that investor will continuously reinvest income streams at the same rate of return, i.e., the rate of the yield to maturity itself. (General)

Zero Coupon Bonds   First appeared on large scale in 1981; sell at discounts to reflect accumulated interest payments plus a rate of return on those payments. Popular method of locking in high interest rates. Disadvantage: accrual or amortizing of discount requires holder to pay taxes on income not received. (Chapter 1)